MORE THAN
BIRDS

MORE
THAN BIRDS

Adventurous Lives of
North American Naturalists

Val Shushkewich

DUNDURN
TORONTO

Editor: Jennifer McKnight
Design: Jennifer Scott
Printer: Webcom

Library and Archives Canada Cataloguing in Publication

Shushkewich, Val, 1950-
    More than birds : adventurous lives of North American naturalists / Val Shushkewich.

Includes bibliographical references.
Issued also in electronic format.
ISBN 978-1-4597-0558-6

1. Naturalists--North America--Biography. 2. Natural history--North America--History. I. Title.

QH26.S58 2012   508.7092'2   C2012-903236-0

1   2   3   4   5   16   15   14   13   12

  Conseil des Arts
du Canada Canada Council
for the Arts   Canada  ONTARIO ARTS COUNCIL
CONSEIL DES ARTS DE L'ONTARIO

We acknowledge the support of the **Canada Council for the Arts** and the **Ontario Arts Council** for our publishing program. We also acknowledge the financial support of the **Government of Canada** through the **Canada Book Fund** and **Livres Canada Books**, and the **Government of Ontario** through the **Ontario Book Publishing Tax Credit** and the **Ontario Media Development Corporation.**

Care has been taken to trace the ownership of copyright material used in this book. The author and the publisher welcome any information enabling them to rectify any references or credits in subsequent editions.

J. Kirk Howard, President

Printed and bound in Canada.

COVER IMAGES:
Top left: Cordelia Stanwood, courtesy of the Stanwood Homestead Museum and Stanwood Wildlife Sanctuary.
Top middle: Roger Tory Peterson (L) and Robert Bateman, courtesy of Birgit Freybe Bateman.
Top right: Robert Ridgway, courtesy of the Smithsonian Institution Archives, image #SIA2008-4347.
Middle images: Composite image by Jennifer Scott
    Background: © Perter Zelei/iStockphoto
    Bird: © ilbusca/iStockphoto
    Plants: © Olga Axyutina/iStockphoto
Bottom left: John James Audubon, painting by John Syme, 1826.
Bottom middle: Percy Taverner (L) and Allan Brooks, courtesy of the Canadian Museum of Nature, Neg. No. 56275.
Bottom right: Kenn Kaufman, courtesy of Kimberly Kaufman.

Visit us at
Dundurn.com | Definingcanada.ca | @dundurnpress | Facebook.com/dundurnpress

Dundurn
3 Church Street, Suite 500
Toronto, Ontario, Canada
M5E 1M2

Gazelle Book Services Limited
White Cross Mills
High Town, Lancaster, England
LA1 4XS

Dundurn
2250 Military Road
Tonawanda, NY
U.S.A. 14150

To the memory of my parents,
George and Irene Cuffe,
who gave me a love of nature.

Contents

Acknowledgements

The author would especially like to thank Barry Penhale of Dundurn Press (formerly with Natural Heritage) for encouraging her with this book and a previous book, *The Real Winnie: A One-of-a-Kind Bear*. She is extremely appreciative of his believing in her writing, and for the valuable advice he has given her, as well as for his overall guidance. A special thanks is also given to Jane Gibson for her editorial support on both books.

The author would also like to acknowledge the interest and friendship of Claudia Angle of the Smithsonian Institution National Museum of Natural History, and to thank her for sharing information about the North American bird specimens and exhibits.

Introduction

The twenty-two naturalists in this book exhibit selflessness in their pursuit of knowledge. They are driven by an inner passion, and are not motivated by money or fame. They love their work and persist in it, often enduring hardships and sometimes the skepticism and criticism of others who cannot appreciate what they are accomplishing.

This book shows some of the connections between one generation of naturalists and the next. In reading about the life of one of these individuals, the names of some of the others very often appear. These people are eager to share their knowledge and often go out of their way to make contact with each other. In some cases an aging naturalist and one just starting out become good friends. They do not resent the accomplishments of others, perhaps because they are so self-confident in their own abilities and achievements. The greatest men and women in science are often also the most modest; perhaps because they have found that the more you discover about the natural world, the more you realize how little you really know about it.

More Than Birds: Adventurous Lives of North American Naturalists shows a progression and course of development in nature studies, with later advances building upon earlier work. It shows how bird studies have evolved and changed direction over time. The book does not attempt to include all of those individuals who were players in this intriguing story of development, but selects some of the most notable men and women involved.

In the early years, the whole of North America was a great unknown, and there was an emphasis on documenting the species and conditions of this vast new world. The eighteenth and nineteenth centuries were a remarkable time for natural history in North America. There was a great deal of drive and activity among the many naturalists who were in the process of describing and cataloguing the species that exist on the continent. There was considerable cooperation among them as they needed to work together in collecting, exchanging, organizing, and studying the huge influx of new specimens. It was a period of rapid advancement in nature study and knowledge. In some ways this period is a very romantic one, with naturalists describing wilderness areas where huge numbers of various species thrived. The early naturalists saw Eskimo Curlews, Carolina Parakeets, and Passenger Pigeons in abundance. At the time that the nineteenth-century naturalists were collecting specimens, these species were plentiful. Now, due to over-hunting and human-made changes in the landscape, the Eskimo Curlew is down to just a handful (and may be extinct), and the Carolina Parakeet and Passenger Pigeon no longer exist. It is thought-provoking to read about these thriving wilderness areas and realize how greatly man has altered the landscape, making it more sterile and inhospitable to the diversity of life. It attests to the rate at which man is accelerating the pace of species extinction.

At the time when the earliest of these naturalists were in the field and before the use of binoculars, it was common practice to kill specimens, which were then preserved and later examined and studied. This was a way to identify and describe species. However, these early naturalists did not believe in the massacre of large numbers of fauna for sport or profit. They commented on the huge numbers of individuals of various species that were found in North America, but they also warned that in spite of these large numbers, the population could be drastically reduced or even extinguished in a relatively few years if practices of killing vast numbers were continued. Because these naturalists respected birds and other animals so much, they wanted to ensure their survival, and they dreaded the thought of their extinction.

As the nineteenth century drew to a close, there was increasing concern about conserving living natural resources and about creating nature preserves where wildlife and the natural environment would be protected. The focus changed from collecting and describing physical characteristics of birds and other animals to studying their life histories in order to try to understand their needs. This goal, as well as educating the public about its responsibility to care for the natural world and its living resources, is the current objective of natural history studies.

Each of the chapters can be considered separately or the book can be taken as a whole, with the common thread of the passion these individuals have for studying nature, and the connections between them. The book focuses on the involvement of these people in advancing bird studies, although many of them have diverse interests in natural history. All of them are exceptional observers of the natural world and notice things that most people remain unaware of. They are all also excellent communicators and describers of what they have observed. They are great success stories and show what good people can achieve when they pursue their passion.

CHRONOLOGY

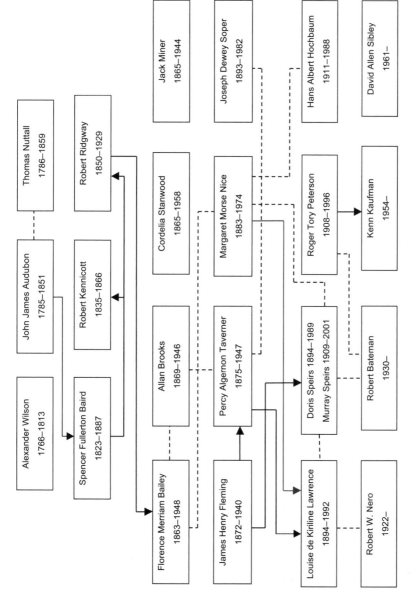

Alexander Wilson 1766–1813

John James Audubon 1785–1851

Thomas Nuttall 1786–1859

Spencer Fullerton Baird 1823–1887

Robert Kennicott 1835–1866

Robert Ridgway 1850–1929

Florence Merriam Bailey 1863–1948

Allan Brooks 1869–1946

Cordelia Stanwood 1865–1958

Jack Miner 1865–1944

James Henry Fleming 1872–1940

Percy Algernon Taverner 1875–1947

Margaret Morse Nice 1883–1974

Joseph Dewey Soper 1893–1982

Louise de Kiriline Lawrence 1894–1992

Doris Speirs 1894–1989
Murray Speirs 1909–2001

Roger Tory Peterson 1908–1996

Hans Albert Hochbaum 1911–1988

Robert W. Nero 1922–

Robert Bateman 1930–

Kenn Kaufman 1954–

David Allen Sibley 1961–

Major Influence ⎯⎯⎯▶   Mutual Influence - - - - - -

Biographies of the Twenty-Two Naturalists

PART ONE: EARLY NORTH-AMERICAN NATURALISTS

Chapter One: Alexander Wilson (1766–1813) was born in Renfrewshire, Scotland, but came to North America at age twenty-eight. He is considered the "Father of American Ornithology" and his book, *American Ornithology*, set the standard for ornithologists to follow. His thorough and accurate field work made previous books obsolete and his drawings were correct renderings of the birds.

Chapter Two: John James Audubon (1785–1851) single-mindedly overcame enormous obstacles and criticism to pursue a lifelong fascination with the birds, and the successful production of his great work, *The Birds of America*. Born in Saint Dominique (now called Haiti), his father was a sea captain and French naval officer who had acquired estates in France, Saint Dominique, and Pennsylvania. With the support of his wife, Lucy, and his two sons, John Woodhouse and Victor Gifford, Audubon finally succeeded in completing the monumental work *The Birds of America*, followed by the *Ornithological Biography* in 1839.

Chapter Three: Thomas Nuttall (1786–1859) was born and died in England, but spent most of his professional life in North America. A man of science and a great adventurer, he was one of the greatest field naturalists to ever travel across the American West. Nuttall's contributions in ornithology were acknowledged when the first ornithological association was formed in America in 1873. Centered at Harvard University, where

Nuttall taught, its publication, *Bulletin of the Nuttall Ornithological Club*, later became the well-known ornithological journal *The Auk*.

PART TWO: THE SMITHSONIAN COLLECTIONS AND CLASSIFICATION

Chapter Four: Spencer Fullerton Baird (1823–1887), a native of Pennsylvania, was the man most responsible for the scientific advancement of ornithology in the mid-1800s in North America. A great naturalist in his own right, he encouraged and arranged for the placement of many young naturalists on early government expeditions that were exploring and mapping the continent. He was most responsible for the great bird and other collections which are housed in the National Museum of Natural History of the Smithsonian Institution in Washington, D.C.

Chapter Five: Robert Kennicott (1835–1866) was brought up on the prairies of Cook County, about eighteen miles northwest of Chicago. An enterprising, self-taught naturalist, at age twenty-one he helped establish the Chicago Academy of Sciences and founded a natural history museum at Northwestern University. In 1857 Spencer Baird asked him to come to work at the Smithsonian Institution, and then sent Kennicott on an expedition to acquire information on the little-known flora and fauna of Russian America (now Alaska), the territories controlled by the Hudson's Bay Company (now northern Canada), and the Arctic.

Chapter Six: Robert Ridgway (1850–1929) was the curator of the Smithsonian Institution's bird collections for forty-nine years and made great advances in the systemization and classification of North American birds. When Ridgway found it was difficult to consistently describe the colours of birds, he invented a system of colour nomenclature, which is still used extensively today in ornithology as well as in industries that use colours in their work.

PART THREE: FOR THE LOVE OF BIRDS

Chapter Seven: Florence Merriam Bailey (1863-1948) was an extremely talented nature writer who could write in both an informative as well as an entertaining way about the lives of the birds. She became a serious ornithological writer who wrote up her varied field experiences into articles, books, manuals, and government publications, which were read and used by the general public as well as ornithologists. She was the first woman associate member of the American Ornithologists' Union in 1885, its first woman fellow in 1929, and the first woman recipient of its prestigious William Brewster Medal in 1931.

Chapter Eight: Allan Cyril Brooks (1869-1946) spent his entire life observing nature, recording it in his memory, drawing it, writing about it, and painting it. His self-taught knowledge about all aspects of natural history and his ability to accurately portray what he had seen led to his becoming one of the foremost realistic bird painters of the early twentieth century. Allan Brooks illustrated many ornithological works, including William Leon Dawson's *The Birds of Washington* and *Birds of California* and Percy Algernon Taverner's *Birds of Western Canada* and *Birds of Canada*. His illustrations also appeared on calendars and cards issued by the National Association of Audubon Societies to the general public.

Chapter Nine: Cordelia Stanwood (1865-1958) did not become an ornithologist until she was in her early forties. During the last fifty years of her life she was devoted to the study of birds and became known as Ellsworth, Maine's "Famous Birdwoman." She published twenty bird life histories in the periodicals *Journal of the Maine Ornithological Society*, *The Auk*, *Bird Lore*, *Nature Magazine*, and *Wilson Bulletin*, and she was probably the first woman bird photographer. Her specialty was nests and fledglings.

Chapter Ten: Jack Miner (1865-1944) was the true inventor of modern conservation practices, and he is popularly known in North America as the "Father of Conservation." Following his death, and to honour him for his pioneering work in wildlife conservation, in 1947 the Canadian Government created the National Wildlife Week, to be observed annually during the week of April 10, Jack Miner's birthdate.

PART FOUR: ORNITHOLOGY AS A SCIENCE AND
THE NEED FOR PROTECTION

Chapter Eleven: James Henry Fleming (1872–1940) spent his entire life collecting information about birds, and his knowledge of collectors, collections, expeditions, ornithologists, and their work was tremendous. Fleming was not a private collector as such, and he shared his immense store of knowledge and material with other ornithologists. Over his lifetime he acquired the world's largest and most comprehensive private ornithological collection, and at the end of his life he gave all of his work, collections, library, and miscellaneous objects relating to birds, with no restricting conditions, to the Royal Ontario Museum of Zoology in Toronto.

Chapter Twelve: Percy Algernon Taverner (1875–1947) was Canada's first professional ornithologist and he built up the natural history collection at the Museum of Geological Survey of Canada (which later became the National Museum of Canada, then the National Museum of Natural Sciences, and is now the Canadian Museum of Nature). Taverner produced the comprehensive works *Birds of Eastern Canada, Birds of Western Canada,* and *Birds of Canada.* He had a major hand in bird conservation and was instrumental in getting Point Pelee established as a national park, and Bird Rocks in the Gulf of St. Lawrence and Percé Rock and Bonaventure Island off the Gaspé Peninsula in Quebec declared as bird sanctuaries.

Chapter Thirteen: Margaret Morse Nice (1883–1974) was instrumental in changing the focus of much of the study of ornithology to one of careful observation, recording of even the smallest details, and attempting to understand the behaviours of other species. She conducted detailed field work over a period of eight years on the lives of Song Sparrows and completed major works on the population and behaviour studies of the Song Sparrow and other passerines. Her publication in 1937 of *Studies in the Life History of the Song Sparrow I: A Population Study of the Song Sparrow* and in 1943 of *Studies in the Life History of the Song Sparrow II* were pioneering works in the field of ethology, the branch of zoology that studies the behaviour of animals with emphasis on the behavioral patterns occurring in their natural habitats.

Chapter Fourteen: Joseph Dewey Soper (1893–1982). The principal enduring theme throughout Soper's life was the exploration and description of natural history, and he recorded his discoveries in prolific writings, some of which were factual and scientific in nature, and some of which were written in a more narrative vein about what it is like to experience living in the Arctic. Soper spent nearly eight years in the early part of his career in Arctic exploration, and a lifetime studying its natural history. In 1957 the Government of Canada established the Dewey Soper Bird Sanctuary on Baffin Island, where Soper had emphasized there was a major migratory and breeding bird habitat.

PART FIVE: THIRST FOR KNOWLEDGE

Chapter Fifteen: Louise de Kiriline Lawrence (1894–1992) was born in Sweden into an aristocratic family and went with her first husband to Russia at the time of the Russian Revolution. Following his death, she came to Canada in 1927, where she began a new life and eventually settled near North Bay, Ontario, where she became a behavioural ornithologist and a great nature writer. Her nature book *The Lovely and the Wild* won the John Burroughs Medal for distinguished writing in natural history in 1969 when Louise was seventy-five years old, and her last book, *To Whom the Wilderness Speaks*, was published in 1980 when she was eighty-six years old.

Chapter Sixteen: Doris H. Speirs (1894–1989) and J. Murray Speirs (1909–2001) were a husband and wife team of ornithologists who together conducted detailed studies of Evening Grosbeaks, American Robins, Black-capped Chickadees, and Lincoln's Sparrows. Murray Speirs was a leading ornithologist in Ontario for over sixty-five years. He published the two large volumes of *Birds of Ontario* in 1985, and became known as the "Quiet Giant" of Ontario ornithology. Both Doris and Murray Speirs encouraged and had a large influence on other ornithologists, naturalists, and bird artists.

Chapter Seventeen: Roger Tory Peterson (1908–1996) revolutionized the science and art of recognizing and learning about birds. His *A*

Field Guide to the Birds was the first to simplify and clarify the identifying characteristics of similar species. Roger Tory Peterson's life was totally dedicated to birds, and the output and influence from his extensive work in the fields of art, photography, writing, education, and conservation is a well-known legacy.

Chapter Eighteen: Hans Albert Hochbaum (1911–1988) first came to Delta Waterfowl Research Station at Delta Marsh on Lake Manitoba in 1938 and later became its research director, a position he held until his retirement in 1970. Hochbaum spent a lifetime studying waterfowl and describing their actions in books and drawings. His book *The Canvasback on a Prairie Marsh* won him the William Brewster Memorial Award in 1945 as well as the 1944 Literary Award of The Wildlife Society, and his book *Travels and Traditions of Waterfowl* won him a second Literary Award in 1956.

PART SIX: CONSERVATION AND PRESERVATION OF SPECIES

Chapter Nineteen: In Robert W. Nero (1922–) there is a unique blending of scientific field study of unsurpassed excellence, with the eloquent and poetic expression of what this study means. His extensive field studies of the life histories of the Great Gray Owl and the Red-winged Blackbird were published as *The Great Gray Owl: Phantom of the Northern Forest* (1980) and *Redwings* (1984) by the Smithsonian Institution. Nero's enthusiasm and passion for natural history studies is infectious and is passed on to everyone he encounters personally, as well as through his writing and poetry.

Chapter Twenty: Robert Bateman (1930–) has united his extensive knowledge and understanding of the natural world with his equally encompassing knowledge of art and painting to become one of the world's foremost wildlife artists. Born in Toronto, he now lives on Salt Spring Island between the British Columbia mainland and Vancouver Island. Bateman has received twelve honourary doctorate degrees, and in 2010 the Society of Animal Artists gave him their Lifetime Achievement Award. He is affiliated with and a member of numerous naturalist and conservation groups.

Chapter Twenty-One: Kenn Kaufman (1954–) is one of the world's best-known experts on the lives of birds and has made a special study of nearly all of the North American birds. He shares his knowledge about birds and is a regular contribution to *Audubon*, *Birding*, and *Birder's World*. He also writes a regular full-length column called "After the Spark" in *Bird Watcher's Digest*, and has written many books, including *Lives of North American Birds*, *Peterson Field Guide to Advanced Birding*, the *Kaufman Field Guides*, and *Kingbird Highway*. In 1992 Kaufman received the Ludlow Griscom Distinguished Birder Award, and in 2008 he received the Roger Tory Peterson Award from the American Birding Association.

Chapter Twenty-Two: David Allen Sibley (1961–) is acknowledged as one of North America's most well-known bird illustrators. He has published some of the bestselling nature field books of all time, including *The Sibley Guide to Birds*, *The Sibley Guide to Bird Life and Behavior*, and *The Sibley Guide to Trees*. Sibley has a deep concern for habitat preservation and environmental health and has become an ardent advocate for the welfare of the natural environment and birds.

PART ONE

Early North-American Naturalists

Chapter One

Alexander Wilson
(1766–1813)

"I confess that I was always an enthusiast in my admiration of the rural scenery of Nature; but, since your example and encouragement have set me to attempt to imitate her productions, I see new beauties in every bird, plant or flower I contemplate."

— Letter from Alexander Wilson to William Bartram, March 31, 1804, in *American Ornithology* by Alexander Wilson, with a sketch of the author's life by George Ord.

It is amazing that Alexander Wilson, who was almost entirely self-taught, was able to achieve so much in such a short span of time. The period from when he first met William Bartram and began his serious study of depicting the images and natural history of the birds of North America until the completion of his tour to solicit subscriptions for the first volume of *American Ornithology* was a period of less than seven years. What makes his accomplishment even more astounding is that during that time he also had to earn a living, first as a teacher and then as an assistant editor, and therefore could not devote all of his time and attention to the study of birds.

Alexander Wilson was born in the Seedhills of Paisley in Renfrewshire, Scotland, in 1766. He attended the Paisley grammar school, where he learned to read and write. At thirteen years of age he became apprenticed to his brother-in-law to learn the art of weaving. Even at that time he was writing poetry and yearning for an outdoor life. He continued weaving as his only available means of earning a living until 1789, when he joined his brother-in-law in a tour of eastern Scotland as a peddler. When he returned, Wilson, who was a great admirer of Robert Burns, continued writing verses. In 1790 he published a volume of his poetry that was not a success, and in 1792 he went back to weaving, but was again unhappy and poor. He continued publishing occasional poems in the local papers and sometimes wrote sarcastic verses on civil authorities. Those verses brought charges of libel against him, and he was fined and punished for his writings.[1]

Following this episode, Wilson made up his mind to leave his native country and travel to North America, which offered greater freedom of expression. He and his nephew sailed on a ship from Belfast on May 23, 1794, reaching the mouth of Delaware Bay in July. Wilson had just turned twenty-eight. The two weavers found no openings for men of their trade in Philadelphia.

Portrait of Alexander Wilson by Rembrandt Peale.

Wilson, who was always of a rather delicate constitution and unsuited for hard labour, found a position as a country school master at a school a short distance north of Philadelphia. He proceeded to teach himself algebra and trigonometry so as to be able to teach these subjects. He found that only by being a stern disciplinarian was he able to be an effective teacher to his pupils. He became attached to the students, but found he needed to take regular walks into the countryside to remain in good condition and health for that type of work. He was also over-worked and underpaid. Lonely, disheartened, and despondent, Wilson consoled himself by writing poetry. In February 1802, he relocated to a school at Gray's Ferry, just outside the city of Philadelphia. This proved a very fortuitous move, as it led to a new purpose for his life.

At Gray's Ferry, Wilson lived down the street from the famous naturalist William Bartram, who operated the Bartram Botanical Gardens. Wilson and Bartram soon became good friends who shared a common interest in natural history. Bartram was then sixty-one years old, and he became a mentor to Wilson, allowing him free access to his extensive library. It was Bartram who directed Wilson to the study of ornithology. At that time, the first requirement in the study of anything in natural history was to make a drawing of the object you were describing. Thus Wilson began to study and learn how to draw birds. He worked at night by candlelight after his teaching obligations were done, trying to produce satisfactory pictures of the birds he wished to describe. His acquaintance and friend, Alexander Lawson, a well-known Philadelphia engraver, gave him instruction, and Miss Nancy Bartram, the niece of the famous naturalist, also helped him with his drawings. Although Wilson never attained a great artistic ability, through dogged perseverance he was finally able to produce faithful-to-life bird portraits, in a style superior to any work published in North America up to that time.

In March 1804, Wilson wrote to Bartram:

> I send for your amusement a few attempts at some of our indigenous birds, hoping that your good nature will excuse their deficiencies, while you point them out to me. I am

Plate in Alexander Wilson's American Ornithology, *featuring a Belted Kingfisher.*

Reproduced from *Alexander Wilson: Naturalist and Pioneer* by Robert Cantwell, J.B. Lippincott Company Publishers, 1961.

Plate in Alexander Wilson's American Ornithology, *featuring a Snowy Owl.*

Reproduced from *Alexander Wilson: Naturalist and Pioneer* by Robert Cantwell, J.B. Lippincott Company Publishers, 1961.

almost ashamed to send you these drawings, but I know your generous disposition will induce you to encourage one in whom you perceive a sincere and eager wish to do well.... Be pleased to mark on the drawings, with a pencil, the name of each bird, as, except three or four, I do not know them. I shall be extremely obliged to you for every hint that will assist me in this agreeable amusement.[2]

At about the same time Wilson also wrote to the engraver Lawson, telling him:

I am most earnestly bent on pursuing my plan of making a collection of all the birds in this part of North America. Now I don't want you to throw cold water, as Shakespeare says, on this notion, Quixotic as it may

appear. I have been so long accustomed to the building
of airy castles and brain windmills, that it has become
one of my earthly comforts, a sort of a rough bone that
amuses me when sated with the dull drudgery of life.[3]

In October 1804, Wilson took a trip to visit his nephew at Ovid, and the
two of them continued to Niagara Falls, which Wilson found very impressive. On this trip, he watched for birds with the eye of an ornithologist. He
later went on more such journeys in various parts of North America.

In his *American Ornithology*, Wilson recorded what he had witnessed
in nature on his various trips. He found inaccuracies in the current writings on North American ornithology, and was critical of those which
either did not make sense to him, or contradicted what he had observed.
He wrote to Bartram on April 29, 1807:

From the opportunities I have lately had, of examining
into the works of Americans who have treated of this part
of our natural history, I am satisfied that none of them
have bestowed such minute attention on the subject as
you yourself have done. Indeed they have done little
more than copied your nomenclature and observations,
and referred to your authority. To have you, therefore, to
consult with in the course of this great publication I consider a most happy and even auspicious circumstance;
and I hope you will, on all occasions, be a rigid censor,
and kind monitor, whenever you find me deviating from
the beauties of nature, or the truth of description.[4]

Upon his return from Niagara Falls, Wilson had sent a letter and
drawings of two birds that he had secured on his journey, along with an
introduction from Bartram, to President Jefferson. The president sent
back an appreciative letter and commented on the drawing of the Canada
Jay. In 1806, Wilson again wrote to Jefferson, applying for a position on
the expedition then being outfitted by the government to explore the

sources of the Arkansas River. However, no attention was given to his application. In his letter he stated his intention to publish:

> Having been engaged, these several years, in collecting materials and finishing drawings from Nature, with the design of publishing a new Ornithology of the United States of America, so deficient are the works of Catesby, Edwards, and other Europeans, I have traversed the greater part of our northern and eastern districts; and have collected many birds undescribed by these natural-ists. Upwards of one hundred drawings are completed, and two plates in folio already engraved.[5]

Wilson was occupied in a great deal of reading and studying of the scientific literature at that time, and in 1806 he succeeded in securing a position as assistant editor of Rees's *New Encyclopedia*, then being pub-lished by Bradford and Company of Philadelphia. The position gave him a salary of $900 a year and freed him from the duties of his school, but unfortunately his work involved long days of confinement in the heart of the city, which he detested. However, Wilson was no doubt aided in his plans to publish by his association with Bradford and Company, the company which eventually issued his work.

In the fall of 1808, carrying with him a sample copy of volume one, Wilson set out to canvas the country in order to acquire the 250 sub-scribers who were considered necessary before the publication run could begin, given that the subscription price was $120 (approximately $2,120 today). Because of the large offering sum for the series of volumes, Wilson was obliged to seek out wealthy potential patrons in the towns he visited, as well as those interested in natural history. Wilson made two trips for the dual purposes of soliciting subscribers and collecting information on all the North-American birds. In September 1808, he journeyed through the eastern states, through Boston to Maine, and back through Vermont, obtaining forty-one subscribers. Soon after returning from this trip, he set off on horseback with the objective of obtaining more subscribers and studying the birds of the Carolinas. Between those two trips, Wilson had visited all the towns within one hundred miles of the Atlantic, from Maine to Georgia.

In March 1809, he wrote to Bartram from Savannah, Georgia:

> This has been the most arduous, expensive, and fatiguing expedition I ever undertook. I have, however, gained my point in procuring two hundred and fifty subscribers, in all, for my *Ornithology*; and a great mass of information respecting the birds that winter in the southern states, and some that never visit the middle states; and this information I have derived personally, and can therefore the more certainly depend upon it. I have also found several new birds, of which I can find no account in Linnaeus.... As far north as Wilmington, in North Carolina, I met with the Ivory-billed Woodpecker.... The common people confound the *P. principalis* and *P. pileatus* together.[6]

Wilson returned to Philadelphia to labour on the completion of the volumes. The second volume was published in January 1810. It contained nine new species that Wilson had discovered in Pennsylvania: the Marsh Wren, Solitary Vireo, Bay-breasted Warbler, Cerulean Warbler, Mourning Warbler, American Tree Sparrow, Field Sparrow, Song Sparrow, and Pine Siskin.[7]

In January 1810, Wilson set out on the longest expedition he was to make. From Pittsburgh he travelled alone in a small skiff, which he had named *The Ornithologist*, over seven hundred miles down the Ohio River to Louisville. There he sold his skiff and went on foot to Lexington. As he walked to Lexington, he observed Passenger Pigeons that flew above him in the millions, hour after hour, darkening the sky for as far as he could see.[8]

At Lexington, he bought a horse and rode to Nashville. From Nashville, he wrote to Lawson that he had been advised not to travel south through the Choctaw territory:

I was advised by many not to attempt it alone; that the Indians were dangerous, the swamps and rivers almost impassable without assistance, and a thousand other hobgoblins were conjured up to dissuade me from going alone. But I weighed all these matters in my own mind; and attributing a great deal of this to vulgar fears and exaggerated reports, I equipped myself for the attempt. I rode an excellent horse, on which I could depend; I had a loaded pistol in each pocket, a loaded fowling-piece belted across my shoulder, a pound of gunpowder in my flask, and five pounds of shot in my belt. I bought some biscuit and dried beef, and on Friday morning, May 4th, I left Nashville.[9]

Wilson met no hostile Natives on the way, but he did endure a violent storm and soakings in deep creeks. He and his horse had to get through horrid swamps. After seventeen days and suffering much from dysentery, he reached Natchez and travelled down the Mississippi to New Orleans, where he was able to recover at the home of a hospitable planter. Once he had regained his strength, he travelled among the plantations and gained many new subscribers. Over the course of his journey, Wilson had discovered many new birds, including the Mississippi Kite, Magnolia Warbler, Kentucky Warbler, Tennessee Warbler, and Nashville Warbler.[10] All things considered, Wilson was well satisfied with his trip.

During 1811 and 1812, Wilson lived almost continuously at Bartram's while writing *American Ornithology*. The work advanced rapidly and he finished the third through sixth volumes during this period. Deciding he had somewhat neglected the water birds, Wilson often travelled to the New Jersey coast, and particularly to Cape May and Great Egg Harbour, where in the spring the coming onshore of vast numbers of Horseshoe Crabs during their annual mating ritual attracts huge numbers of migrating shorebirds.

In 1813, Wilson was pushing himself to complete the volumes. In May, he spent four weeks at Cape May with his ornithologist friend George Ord, and then returned to his labours. It was difficult to retain good colourists for his work, and in 1813 all his colourists left, at which time he was obliged to take on this part of the production as well. In mid-August,

Wilson became ill with dysentery. Worn down from extremely hard toil, he succumbed after ten days. He was forty-seven years old. George Ord saw to the posthumous publishing from Wilson's notes and drawings of the final volumes eight and nine of *American Ornithology* in 1814.

At the time of his death, Wilson was just beginning to gain recognition as the "Father of American Ornithology." In 1812 he was elected a member of the American Society of Artists, and in 1813 a member of the American Philosophical Society and the recently formed Academy of Natural Sciences.

Wilson's *American Ornithology* set the standard for ornithologists to follow. His thorough and accurate field work made previous books obsolete. His drawings were correct renderings of the birds. His text was of such high quality that naturalists from Audubon and Nuttall to Arthur Cleveland Bent drew from it. Bent quoted Wilson in nearly all of his *Life Histories of North American Birds*, a comprehensive study of the existing knowledge about birds, which was published in a twenty-one volume series from 1919 to 1968.[11]

Wilson produced an incredible amount of work in a short time, in spite of the fact that he often did everything himself — from observing, collecting, recording, drawing, and colouring plates to selling subscriptions. In his *American Ornithology* he described 320 birds of 278 species, fifty-six of which had not previously been described. He spent all the money he had on this work, and was eventually forced to resign his position editing the *New Encyclopedia*, so full were the demands of his own publication. At the time the second volume was ready for press, he wrote to Bartram: "I assure you my dear friend that this undertaking has involved me in many difficulties and expenses which I never dreamed of and I have never yet received one cent from it. I am therefore a volunteer in the cause of Natural History impelled by nobler views than those of money."[12]

In the preface to the fifth volume, Wilson stated: "The publication of an original work of this kind in this country has been attended with difficulties, great, and it must be confessed, sometimes discouraging to the author whose only reward hitherto has been the favorable opinion of his fellow citizens and the pleasure of the pursuit."[13] With his *American Ornithology*, Wilson firmly established the beginning of the science of ornithology in North America.

Chapter Two

John James Audubon

(1785–1851)

*"And of his work we can truly say that no paintings have inspired
more men to follow on the path he trod, and no text on bird life
has been read with more consuming interest."*

— Witmer Stone, "John James Audubon, Ornithologist,
1780–1851," in *Leading Men of Science*.

The name of John James Audubon is synonymous today with birds and
conservation. The life of the man himself is sometimes romanticized
into that of a folk hero. In reality, Audubon was a person who single-
mindedly overcame enormous obstacles and criticism to pursue a lifelong
fascination with birds and the successful production of his great work, *The
Birds of America*. In character, he was generous and faithful. He cared greatly
for his wife and family. He was a humanitarian and always looked for the
best in people. In those instances where he found he had misplaced his good
faith in others, he chose to forgive and forget, and proceeded to succeed on
his own terms due to his hard efforts. In short, he was an honourable man.

The circumstances surrounding Audubon's birth and early childhood
are somewhat obscured. It appears he was born as Jean Rabin on Saint
Dominique (now called Haiti). His father was a sea captain and French
naval officer, and had acquired estates in France, Saint Dominique, and
Pennsylvania. Audubon's mother died shortly after he was born, and
sometime later he was brought to France by his father to be raised by his
father's new wife.

Portrait of John James Audubon by John Syme in 1826.

The situation in France following the 1789 French Revolution was tumultuous. After Louis XVI was guillotined in January of 1793, thousands of loyalist peasants rose up against the revolutionaries. Civil war and chaos reigned in Nantes, where the Audubon family lived.

Audubon's early schooling was somewhat limited. He had no interest in mathematics, but enjoyed drawing, geography, fencing, and music. He was inclined to go about the countryside with other boys, searching for birds' nests, fishing, and shooting. He liked to draw, especially birds.

In 1803, when Audubon was about seventeen years of age, his father sent him away from France, where Napoleon was conscripting young recruits into his forces, to go to America to look after the Pennsylvania estate at Mill Grove. There, surrounded by nature, Audubon fished, shot, and rode on horseback to his heart's content. He also studied the birds around the estate and made drawings of them. During that period, Audubon invented a method whereby he could position his birds in various three-dimensional poses, so as to be able to bring them to life while still drawing them accurately in two dimensions. His method was to use a grid board set on edge, with steel wires pointing towards the artist, and the specimen impaled on the wires. This arrangement put the grid behind the specimen and made the bird seem to float in space in whatever position Audubon had arranged it.[1]

At Mill Grove, Audubon spent much time with Lucy Bakewell, whose father owned the adjoining property. Audubon returned to France to obtain his father's permission to marry Lucy, but his father thought that Audubon should be established in some kind of business so as to be able to support a wife. While in France, Audubon drew more birds. Again there was an imminent threat of his being drawn into Napoleon's navy. Audubon's father and the father of Ferdinand Rozier helped their two sons draft a partnership agreement, which was signed at Nantes on March 23, 1806. This agreement stated that the two sons would go to America and investigate possible businesses in which they might engage. The two fathers also arranged false passports for their sons, with Audubon having a passport stating he was born at New Orleans, and Rozier having a Dutch passport. The two young men travelled to New York and on to Mill Grove.

For a time, Audubon worked in New York City learning the retail business at a store owned by Lucy's uncle. He had ample time to explore the nature around the city, and he drew a large number of ducks while there. After he had worked less than a year at the store, he and Rozier decided to sell Mill Grove as soon as they could do so profitably, and establish their own shop in Louisville, Kentucky. Taking out a loan from Lucy's uncle, they purchased merchandise and sent it ahead to Louisville.

In 1807, President Jefferson ordered all American ports be closed to export shipping and put severe restrictions on imports in order to punish both England and France for actions they had taken against American vessels. This embargo also effectively cut off correspondence between the United States and Europe. On April 8, 1808, Audubon, aged twenty-three, with or without his father's consent, married Lucy Bakewell, aged twenty-one, at Lucy's father's home.

Audubon, Lucy, and Rozier then set out for Louisville, where they established a general store. While Rozier tended to the affairs of the store,

Audubon hunted and fished to provide their meals. He also pursued his drawing, painting his specimens at life size. Audubon's and Lucy's first-born son, Victor Gifford, arrived on June 12, 1809. At the Audubon and Rozier store in Louisville, Audubon met Alexander Wilson, who came in one day in 1810 to sell a subscription to his *American Ornithology*. Audubon at first was tempted to subscribe, but his partner advised against it. The cost was $120, which was a lot of money, and their business was not doing that well.

Subsequently, Audubon and Rozier decided to move their business 125 miles downriver, from Louisville to Henderson, a less competitive place. Audubon continued to paint birds, including an Ivory-billed Woodpecker, Scarlet Tanager, White Pelican, and Sandhill Crane. He also kept detailed field notes on his excursions.

Rozier was not happy in Henderson because no one there spoke French and he spoke little English. He wanted to relocate to Ste. Geneviève, below St. Louis on the Mississippi River. Audubon complied, but left Lucy and Victor safely behind in Henderson until he could be sure of the new place. On their way to Ste. Geneviève, Audubon and Rozier were caught when the Mississippi River froze, and they were forced to wait six weeks until the ice broke up. Their camp was close to that of a group of about fifty Shawnee Indian families. On Christmas day in 1810, Audubon was awakened early by the sounds coming from the Shawnee encampment as they were preparing for a hunt, and he requested permission to join them. On a large lake nearby hundreds of Trumpeter Swans gathered every morning. On this hunt Audubon witnessed the killing of more than fifty of these beautiful birds, whose feathers "were intended for the ladies in Europe."[2]

On arrival at Ste. Geneviève, the partners decided to go their separate ways. Rozier found the French town to his liking, while Audubon missed his wife and son at Henderson. Audubon bought Rozier out and headed back to Henderson. Between 1815 and 1820 he worked successfully as a merchant. Audubon's and Lucy's second son, John Woodhouse, was born on November 30, 1812. During that period Audubon also met with a disaster to his drawings. One time when he was going to Philadelphia on business, he had put many of his original drawings in a wooden box

Painting Trumpeter Swan (Cygnus Buccinator) *by John James Audubon.*

From John James Audubon's *The Birds of America*, 1838.

and left them in charge of a friend. On his return, several months later, he pathetically recounts what happened to them: "A pair of Norway rats had taken possession of the whole, and reared a young family among gnawed bits of paper, which but a month previous, represented nearly one thousand inhabitants of the air!"[3] This loss was a great shock to him, but after some time Audubon rallied and decided that now he would make even better drawings than before.

During the period of easy credit and general business expansion following the War of 1812, Audubon built a sawmill and opened two branch retail stores. That period of general economic growth was followed in 1819 by an economic crisis, which dragged on into a major depression. Many businesses went bankrupt, including Audubon's, and he had to pay everything he owned to his creditors, save the clothes on his back, his drawings, and his gun. Leaving Lucy and their sons in Henderson with friends, he set out walking to Louisville to look for work. This was probably the lowest point in his life. He says it was: "the only time in my life when the Wild Turkeys that so often crossed my path, and the thousands of lesser birds that enlivened the woods and the prairies, all looked like enemies, and I turned my eyes from them, as if I could have wished that they had never existed."[4]

At this time, Audubon fell back on one of his talents as an artist — that of drawing facial portraits of people in black chalk. Audubon was very good at this and he worked quickly. There were no cameras then, and people were eager to have portraits of themselves and their loved ones. After initially asking a low price for his work, he was soon able to charge more as word spread of his talent. With Lucy's encouragement, he began to work on the enlargement of his portfolio of bird drawings with the idea of producing and selling them. With this purpose in mind, in January 1821, he left for New Orleans, engaging Joseph Mason as an assistant to draw the scenery background for his pictures. Audubon paid their living expenses by painting portraits and giving lessons in drawing, music, and French. In December 1821, Lucy, then thirty-five years old, Victor, twelve, and John, nine, joined him in New Orleans. During the winter of 1822, Audubon worked very hard to meet his goal of drawing a bird a day. He was always looking to improve his bird drawings and make them more life-like. In 1821 he had started under-painting multiple coats of watercolours before applying pastels. Then, on reviewing his earlier drawings, he had decided to re-do them, thus adding even more to his workload. He wrote: "I have few acquaintances, my wife and my sons are more congenial to me than all others in the world, and we have no desire to force ourselves into a society where every day I receive fewer bows."[5]

Audubon's generous nature, even in the face of personal loss and adverse circumstances, was revealed. One day he encountered an old friend from Louisville, an elderly professional flutist, who was down on his luck, wandering in the market in rags, broke and hungry. Even although Audubon was struggling to keep his own family fed, he invited the man into his home as a guest for two months.[6]

Lucy began working as a teacher to help support the family. With Lucy's encouragement, Audubon went to Philadelphia to obtain work and to get support for the publishing of his portfolio of drawings. However, on April 15, 1824, he wrote: "Those interested in Wilson's book on the American birds advised me not to publish, and not only cold water, but ice, was poured upon my undertaking."[7]

In Philadelphia Audubon met Charles Lucien Bonaparte, an avid ornithologist, and the nephew of Napoleon Bonaparte. Bonaparte introduced

Audubon and his drawings to the Philadelphia engraver, Alexander Lawson, who ridiculed them as being "ill drawn, not true to nature, and anatomically incorrect."[8] Fortunately, Audubon did not take Lawson's criticisms to heart.

Audubon did meet some men who were interested in his work, including Edward Harris, a wealthy young gentleman farmer. When Audubon was about to leave Philadelphia, Harris seemed interested in purchasing some of Audubon's drawings and Audubon offered to sell him a picture of the Falls of the Ohio at a very low price. Harris declined the offer, but as he was leaving, he squeezed a hundred dollar bill into Audubon's hand, saying "Mr. Audubon, accept this from me; men like you ought not to want for money."[9]

Audubon also travelled to New York, where he sought out interest in his drawings. Then he returned to Beech Woods, where Lucy was teaching. There he taught music, French, drawing, and cotillion dancing. By May 1826, between the two of them, they had saved enough to send Audubon and his bird paintings to Europe to solicit interest there in having them published.

After a slow start in Liverpool, Audubon began to succeed, and suddenly a great interest in his paintings and in himself, as representing the "American Woodsman," began to grow. Audubon was asked to arrange a selection of his drawings for display at the Royal Institution. This was very well received and he was encouraged to begin charging admission. His new friends in Liverpool gave him letters of introduction, and he wrote to Lucy: "I am cherished by the most notable people in and around Liverpool, and have obtained letters of introduction to Baron Humboldt, Sir Walter Scott, Sir Humphry Davy, Sir Thomas Lawrence."[10]

From Liverpool, Audubon went to Edinburgh, where he showed his work to William Lizars, the best engraver in the city. Lizars, upon looking into Audubon's portfolio exclaimed: "My God, I never saw anything like these before!"[11] Lizars began engraving the plates. In order to raise money to keep the expensive project going, Audubon kept on collecting admissions to his exhibitions of drawings, selling subscriptions, and producing nature paintings in oil, which he sold on the side. His very successful exhibition of drawings at the Edinburgh Royal Institution closed on December 23, 1826. By March 1827, Audubon was collecting letters of introduction from his friends and preparing to leave Edinburgh for London, intending to make stops along the way to sell needed subscriptions to *The Birds of America*, for which he had now issued a prospectus. In March he was elected as a fellow of the Royal Society of Edinburgh, which he felt was a great honour.

Upon his arrival in London, Audubon received word from Lizars that the engraver's colourists had left him and he could no longer produce the plates. Searching for a new engraver, Audubon eventually found Robert Havell and his son, who agreed to do the plates for a lesser amount than Lizars had been charging. From that time on, Audubon worked with an unrelenting intensity to finish *The Birds of America*. Whether it was travelling in order to collect and draw the birds he was missing, or writing up his voluminous notes into the *Ornithological Biography*, he worked doggedly, took little time off to rest, and pushed himself constantly towards completing the monumental task he had set for himself as his life's work. Audubon employed William MacGillivray, the Scottish ornithologist, to edit and add to the notes for the *Ornithological Biography*.

Returning to America in the spring of 1829, Audubon spent a year collecting and painting birds he had not already procured. Then, in the spring of 1830, he again sailed to England, this time accompanied by Lucy. While absent in America, he had been elected a fellow of the Royal Society of London, and on May 6 he took his seat in the great hall. From 1830 on Audubon officially brought his wife and two sons into the business.

Audubon returned to America twice more during the publication of his work in order to procure additional material, one visit lasting from August 1831 to April 1834, and the other from July 1836 to the following summer. In October 1832 Audubon sent his son, Victor Audubon, to England to superintend the publication of the work during his father's absence.

Back in North America, on one of his excursions to add more birds, he was in Charleston along with a young taxidermist assistant and a landscape painter named George Lehman, who was engaged to draw the backgrounds for his bird paintings. While in Charleston, Audubon met John Bachman, a serious amateur ornithologist, who was absolutely thrilled to meet him. Audubon wrote to Lucy: "Mr. Bachman would have us all to stay at his house. He would have us to make free there as if we were at our encampment at the headwaters of some unknown rivers."[12] Audubon and Bachman became good friends, as did their two families, and in later years Audubon and his family were welcomed back into the Bachman household. Both of Audubon's sons married Bachman's daughters. Unhappily, both of Audubon's daughters-in-law died very young of tuberculosis.

In the summer of 1833, Audubon set out for Labrador with his son John Woodhouse and four other young men who had been invited to join the expedition. Audubon was growing older and he left the exploratory and collecting work to the younger men, while he stayed on board the ship *Ripley*, constantly drawing and writing up his notes.

In his writings, Audubon warned about the unbridled destruction of birds and other animals by man and admonished that it could not go on indefinitely without causing the disappearance of the species. He commented on this when he discussed the massacres he had witnessed of the Passenger Pigeon and of the buffalo. But perhaps his strongest warning was after he witnessed the damage the eggers were inflicting on the nesting seabirds of Labrador. On June 23, 1833, he wrote:

> We heard today that a party of four men from Halifax, last spring, took in two months four hundred thousand eggs, which they sold in Halifax at twenty five cents a dozen. Last year upwards of twenty sail of vessels were engaged in this business; and by this one may form some idea of the number of birds annually destroyed in this way.... The eggers destroy all the eggs that are sat upon, to force the birds to lay fresh eggs, and by robbing them regularly compel them to lay until nature is exhausted, and so but few young ones are raised. These wonderful nurseries must be finally destroyed, and in less than half a century, unless some kind government interposes to put a stop to all this shameful destruction.... These people gather all the eider-down they can find, yet, so inconsiderate are they, that they kill every bird that comes in their way. The puffins and some other birds they massacre in vast

numbers for the sale of their feathers. The eggs of gulls, guillemots, and ducks are searched for with care also.... This war of extermination cannot last many years more.[13]

In 1839 Audubon completed *The Birds of America* and the *Ornithological Biography*. *The Birds of America* consists of four volumes in a set. They are elephant folio size — more than three feet long and two or more feet wide. The birds, of which there are 1,055 specimens in 435 plates, are all life size — even the great eagles.[14] The work is worthy of the highest praise. It was accomplished because of the unswerving determination, energy, and perseverance of a very gifted and talented man, with the unfailing encouragement and support of his devoted wife. "Few enterprises involving such labor and expense have been carried through against such odds."[15]

Audubon wrote upon finishing this work: "now, good reader, the task is accomplished. In health and in sickness, in adversity and prosperity, in summer and winter, amidst the cheers of friends and the scowls of foes, I have depicted the Birds of America, and studied their habits as they roamed at large in their peculiar haunts."[16]

Audubon proceeded to produce a reduced set of Octavo volumes which were copies of the original publication, with the figures reduced and lithographed. He did this with the help of his sons, John Woodhouse reducing the figures using a camera-lucida, and Victor Gifford looking after the printing and publishing. These volumes appeared from 1840 to 1844. This edition had 1,100 subscribers and finally earned the Audubon family a profit of about $36,000 (about $840,000 today). Audubon called the Octavo edition his saviour, as it supported the growing families for years.[17]

In 1842, Audubon and his extended family built a house, called "Minniesland," on fourteen acres of land fronting the Hudson River. Audubon's last years were spent there with his sons (both of whom had remarried) and grandchildren, surrounded by the nature he loved. His eyesight began to fail him, such that he was no longer able to see middle distances correctly and could no longer focus on the canvas.

Chapter Three

Thomas Nuttall

(1786-1859)

"To converse, as it were, with nature, to admire the wisdom and beauty of creation, has ever been, and I hope ever will be, to me a favorite pursuit."

— Thomas Nuttall, in the preface to his book
The North American Sylva, 1871.

Although Thomas Nuttall was born and died in England, he spent most of his professional life in North America. He was one of the greatest field naturalists ever to travel across the American West. He was a man of science who was also a great adventurer. Although Nuttall's principal passion was botany, he was also interested in geology, mineralogy, and ornithology, and he wrote the first book on the ornithology of North America that was sized and priced for purchase by the ordinary person. In the preface to his book on the trees of the United States and Canada, he wrote what amounted to a brief autobiography of his life in North America:

> Thirty-four years ago, I left England.... In the ship *Halcyon* I arrived at the shores of the New World and entered the Capes of the Delaware.... The forests apparently unbroken, in their primeval solitude and repose spread themselves on either side. The extending vista of dark Pines gave an air of deep sadness to the wilderness....

Painted portrait of Thomas Nuttall.

Scenes like these have little attraction for ordinary life. But to the naturalist it is far otherwise; privations to him are cheaply purchased if he may roam over the wild domain of primeval nature.... How often have I realized the poet's buoyant hopes amid these solitary rambles through interminable forests! For thousands of miles my chief converse has been in the wilderness with the spontaneous productions of nature; and the study of these objects and their contemplation has been to me a source of constant delight.[1]

Thomas Nuttall was born in Long Preston in western Yorkshire in 1786. He completed an apprenticeship in the printing business in Liverpool from 1800 to 1807. During that time something sparked his interest in natural history and he became determined to pursue his passion in North America. Arriving in Philadelphia in 1808, he took a job in printing and continued studying plants. Shortly after his arrival, he enquired about finding a book on botany and was referred to the standard reference book at the time, *Elements of Botany* by Benjamin Smith

Barton. Unable to find a copy to purchase, he boldly looked Barton up and went to see him. Barton was Professor of *Materia medica*, natural history, and botany at the University of Pennsylvania, as well as being a practicing physician. At the time, Barton was in need of a new assistant who would go out in the field and find him new specimens. In Nuttall he found a young man who, although academically untrained, had an impressive self-taught knowledge of botany, and who was intelligent and enthusiastic about natural history.

Barton asked Nuttall to undertake an extensive collecting trip to the great plains of the West over a period of two years. It seems that Barton had ambitions to secure a name for himself by writing a book on the flora and fauna of a large part of North America, and was using Nuttall to help him achieve that goal. Previously, William Clark, of the Lewis and Clark expedition of 1803 to 1806, had asked Barton to take Lewis's notes on plants and animals and write them up. Barton had agreed to do it, saying it should take only a short time, and then proceeded to do nothing, thereby hindering Lewis and Clark's receiving the scientific credit due to them for many of their natural history discoveries.

As part of Nuttall's undertaking for Barton, Barton had him sign a long, formal contract whereby Nuttall was to keep a daily journal of observations for Barton's exclusive use, and to give all his collections to no one else except Barton. Nuttall was to collect "animals, vegetables, minerals, Indian curiosities, etc." a portion of which he might retain, but strictly for himself lest "they might otherwise fall into the hands of persons who would use them to my [Barton's] disadvantage."[2]

Nuttall proceeded to Detroit, where he happened upon the surveyor of the new Territory of Michigan, who was going to Mackinac Island to survey the holdings of the settlers. The surveying party started from Detroit in July 1810 in birch bark canoes, and Nuttall accompanied them. As Nuttall travelled through Lake Huron, "the wild cries of the loons echoing over the great northern waters carried to him the conviction that Nature reigned undisturbed in these remote regions, for their weird, echoing calls, instead of disturbing solitude, only deepen and confirm it."[3] The party arrived at Michilimackinac on August 12. There Nuttall met up with an expedition that was planning to follow the Lewis and Clark route from St. Louis to the mouth of the Columbia River. Nuttall was invited to join the brigade, which was about to depart for St. Louis and then ascend the Missouri River in the spring.

The members of the travelling party generally found Nuttall's behavior very odd, although it was really only that of a dedicated naturalist. They described him thus: "Whenever Nuttall's boat touched shore he hurriedly alighted to pursue his plant collecting interests, losing himself in the vegetation. This habit occasioned exchanges of witticisms among the French Canadien voyageurs, who began to doubt the sanity of a person who dug up 'weeds' with such excitement and devotion."[4] The voyageurs called Nuttall "*le fou*," or "the fool."

Nuttall stayed in St. Louis until mid-March. He spent many hours wandering about the countryside noting the terrain, the birds and their migrations, and the plants. The most exotic birds he saw were Carolina Parakeets. He described them darting in screaming flocks through dense forests on the river banks, feeding on fruits of the sycamore.[5] Travelling from St. Louis up the Missouri River, the party entered potentially hostile Native country. At that time the men needed to reassure themselves that their firearms were in good order, and they discovered that Nuttall's gun had been put to strange uses. One version of the story is that the muzzle was plugged with earth because it had been used as a trowel, pick, and shovel to release the roots of plants from the soil. Another version is that knowing that the guns would be kept safe and dry, he had used the cylinder of the gun as a safe place to store packets of seeds he had collected. Nuttall clearly had a single-minded devotion to nature.

When it became apparent that there was going to be a war between Great Britain and the United States (the War of 1812), Nuttall decided to sail from New Orleans back to Liverpool. Before sailing, he sent Barton his herbarium specimens, seeds, and notes of his journey. Nuttall had by then realized that the terms of Barton's contract were excessively one-sided and that Barton had taken advantage of the young naturalist's desire to explore and collect the flora and fauna of uncharted western lands. Yet, except for slight alterations in Barton's totally unrealistic itinerary, Nuttall had kept his part of the contract. However, Barton still became incensed that Nuttall had not returned to Philadelphia to describe and name his plant collections (and probably also those of the Lewis and Clark Expedition). It seems that Barton had neither the field nor scientific knowledge to be able to do this himself. William Barton's death in December 1816 freed Nuttall from the contract and its numerous prohibitions.

Nuttall spent the years of 1812–15 in England. In London he published his *Catalogue of New and Interesting Plants Collected in Upper Louisiana and Principally of the River Missouri, North America*. Nuttall attracted attention because of his field collections and his knowledge of North American flora, and his *Catalogue* became a standard reference to the flora of the American west. He was elected a member of the Linnaean Society of London. When he returned to Philadelphia in 1815, Nuttall began to be recognized as an authority on botany. He earned a living by collecting and selling specimens and seeds to botanical gardens, private collectors, and botanists. In 1817 Nuttall received local recognition as a naturalist through election to the Academy of Natural Sciences of Philadelphia, and to the American Philosophical Society.

Nuttall was the first field botanist to both collect and describe his own specimens from the west. He spent long days on his systematic treatment of the North American flora. He did the work at the Academy of Natural Sciences, as he had no library of his own and no adequate space to spread out specimens for comparison. He often worked through the night, taking short naps at the Academy. On July 14, 1818, at a meeting of the Academy, he presented a copy of his classic work on the taxonomy of North American plants, *Genera of North American Plants and a Catalogue of the Species through 1817*. There was no publisher, and Nuttall financed the printing. Tradition has it that Nuttall set much of the type himself. One of Nuttall's innovations was to publish his *Genera* in English, rather than Latin, thus making it useful to amateur collectors as well as academics. The *Genera* was not particularly well received in America. Given the extreme ambitions of some botanists at this time in competing to be the first to describe new species of plants, many of the early reviews in America were not complimentary. However, his *Genera* was a great success in Europe, which over time led to its subsequent acceptance in North America.

At age thirty-two, Nuttall was no longer as naïve about his fellow botanists. He also did not have the same romantic ideas about exploring in North America. But he still had the same passion and drive to make discoveries in the wilderness. In 1818 he set out on his own to explore the southwest. He travelled on the Ohio River to the Mississippi River to Fort Smith. Travelling by himself, as a civilian without any government sponsorship, it was unusual for the commander of the garrison at Fort Smith to have allowed him to travel into the Native country beyond the Fort, but Nuttall managed to win the officer over, and he was allowed to go exploring. In general, the Natives of the area did not know what to make of him, and Nuttall admitted he was fortunate to have been able, as a lone white man, to travel amongst them unharmed.

On his collecting trips from the Fort, Nuttall collected about a hundred new herbs. In May 1819, he was invited to accompany a party of seven soldiers and two Cherokees, who were setting out for the Red River. He wrote:

> In my solitary, but amusing rambles over these delightful prairies, I now, for the first time in my life, notwithstanding my long residence and peregrinations in North America, hearkened to the inimitable notes of the Mockingbird. After amusing itself in ludicrous imitations of other birds, perched on the topmost bough of a spreading elm, it at length broke forth into a strain of melody the most wild, varied, and pathetic, that ever I had heard from any thing less than human. In the midst of these enchanting strains, which gradually increased to loudness, it oftentimes flew upwards from the topmost twig, continuing its note as if overpowered by the sublimest ecstasy.[6]

Nuttall's main objective was to reach the Rocky Mountains. With this purpose, he joined an experienced trapper who was heading out from the fort. However, Nuttall became dangerously ill with a recurring malarial fever, and they were forced to turn back. Nuttall was becoming disillusioned by his experiences with pilfering and potentially dangerous Natives and with recurrent bouts of sickness. He realized that he could not sufficiently look after himself in the wilds of the west. However, his collecting activities had been a great success. Besides specimens for his own use, he had brought back miscellaneous zoological material, including fossil shells, insects, and fish, which he gave to other scientists to study and publish papers on.

Nuttall returned to Philadelphia in 1820, attended meetings of the Academy of Natural Sciences and the American Philosophical Society, and promptly became thoroughly involved in their activities. He and Thomas Say, another passionate naturalist whose principal interest was in the insects, edited and printed the Academy of Natural Science's scientific journal. By the end of May, Nuttall received permission to use the Hall of the Academy of Natural Sciences for a course of lectures on botany. These proved hugely successful, and he continued them the following spring.[7]

Nuttall's patrons encouraged him to write an account of his Arkansas trip. He had kept a full daily record during his travels. He laboured for a year and a half to write *A Journal of Travels into the Arkansas Territory during the year 1819, with occasional Observations on the Manners of the Aborigines*. In the preface he stated:

> For nearly ten years I have travelled throughout America, principally with a view of becoming acquainted with some favourite branches of its natural history. I have had no other end in view than personal gratification, and in this I have not been deceived, for innocent amusement can never leave room for regret.... To communicate to others a portion of the same amusement and gratification has been the only object of my botanical publications; the most remote idea of personal emolument arising from them, from every circumstance connected with them, could not have been admitted into calculation. I had a right, however, reasonably to expect from Americans a degree of candour, at least equal to that which my labours had met with in Europe. But I have found, what,

indeed, I might have reason to expect from human nature, often, instead of gratitude, detraction and envy. With such, I stoop not to altercate; my endeavours, however imperfect, having been directed to the public good; and I regret not the period I have spent in roaming over the delightful fields of Flora, in studying all her mysteries and enigmas, if I have, in any instance, been useful to her cause, or opened to the idle wanderer one fruitful field for useful reflection.[8]

In 1823, Nuttall accepted an appointment as Curator of the Botanic Garden in Cambridge, and Instructor in Natural History and Botany at Harvard College. His salary as Curator was a meagre $500 a year, and from Harvard College he received $100 for each course he gave in natural history. During his decade at Harvard, Nuttall was considered an inspiring lecturer. He published on various topics in natural history. His salary was eventually doubled and he was awarded an honourary Master of Arts degree. However, he was never appointed a professor at Harvard. Besides the excuse by Harvard College of a lack of funds to pay a professor's salary, there was also the fact that while Nuttall was recognized as a brilliant botanist and scientist, he had no formal academic training and no degrees.

The textbooks used at Harvard were generally written or edited by the professors who gave the courses, and published by the university bookstore. In 1826 Nuttall began to work on his own textbook, *An Introduction to Systematic and Physiological Botany*. This textbook was on sale for $1.33 in the spring of 1827, and a second enlarged edition came out in 1830.

The year that Nuttall arranged to write his botanical textbook, William Hilliard of the university bookstore took into partnership James Brown, who later founded the Boston publishing company Little, Brown. Brown, probably knowing that Nuttall was somewhat bored by the routine of his academic duties, suggested to him the publication of a handbook on North-American birds, to be modestly printed and priced for the use of the average person. No such field guide to the birds of North America then existed. Nuttall decided to take Brown up on the idea.

Starting in early 1829 when he had a long stay in Philadelphia, Nuttall studied the fine collection of skins and mounted birds, including Alexander Wilson's specimens, which were at the Peale Museum. He took measurements of them and drew up concise descriptions. Field observations were supplemented by intensive reading in the works of Wilson, Charles Lucien Bonaparte, the first volume of Audubon's *Ornithological Biography*, and ornithological works by various Europeans. He also consulted the observations written by travellers in the Americas. The two resultant volumes on the birds are well-rounded compilations of the then-known facts for each species, with Nuttall's own observations and his symbolic representations of the various calls and songs of the birds. For the first volume on the land birds, Nuttall watched birds over two breeding seasons. At that time birds were abundant everywhere "in the most populous and noisy streets of Boston [the Red-eyed Vireo] is commonly heard from the tall Elms."[9] Cambridge's Botanic Garden attracted many nesting pairs and heavy spring populations could be observed in the surrounding countryside, with its open land, marshes, and woods.

Nuttall's *A Manual of the Ornithology of the United States and Canada, I, Land Birds* was received with great appreciation in 1832. Before *Land Birds* was issued, Nuttall was already afield in pursuit of ducks, sea, and shore birds for his second volume on the water birds. He could be found at various times of the day and night in the marsh or on the beach. He writes: "On the 6th of October (1831) having spent the night in a lodge, on the borders of Fresh Pond, employed for decoying and shooting ducks, I heard, about sunrise, the Yellow-breasted Rails begin to stir among the reeds that thickly skirt this retired border of the lake."[10]

In the summer of 1833, John James Audubon had gone to the Labrador coast to observe and collect birds for his elephant folio. On his return, he sent information to Nuttall about such northern birds as kittiwakes, jaegers, petrels, eiders, Harlequin Ducks, Gannets, and guillemots. Nuttall was extremely grateful and sent a very kind thank you letter to Audubon.[11] In each instance, Nuttall acknowledged the source of his information in a footnote in his book.

The knowledge presented in the books Nuttall wrote on ornithology remained current long after their initial publication. Three popular

PL.XIX

Plate from Thomas Nuttall's A Popular Handbook of the Birds of the United States and Canada: *1. Gadwall Duck, 2. Scaup Duck, 3. American Golden-eye, 4. Harlequin Duck, 5. Surf Duck.*

editions of it were printed in 1891, 1896, and 1903, only slightly revised. Nuttall's contributions in ornithology were acknowledged when the first ornithological association was formed in America in 1873. It was centred at Harvard University and was called the Nuttall Ornithological Club. In 1876, it started a publication *Bulletin of the Nuttall Ornithological Club*, which later became the well-known ornithological journal, *The Auk*.

Nuttall's final years in Cambridge were busy, with numerous leaves of absence to go exploring, preparation of the *Ornithology*, public lectures, and his regular duties in the Botanic Garden and classroom. In 1834 Nuttall received an offer to accompany Nathaniel Wyeth on a trip across the Rockies. It had always been his dream to travel across the Rocky Mountains, and even at age forty-eight he could not resist a chance to make new discoveries in unknown areas. With mixed feelings, Nuttall resigned from Harvard on March 20, 1834.

Nuttall had written to Wyeth that he had invited a second scientist to join the party, by the name of John Kirk Townsend, a twenty-four-year-old ornithologist who had been elected to the Academy of Natural Sciences in September 1833. The party followed what was to become the Oregon Trail, and after a very difficult journey they arrived at Fort Vancouver on September 16, 1834. Nuttall and Townsend had seen much in the way of new flora and fauna, and they both kept detailed journals. In the fall, the two naturalists decided to go to the Sandwich Islands, now the state of Hawaii, in order to observe and collect Pacific flora and fauna. After a month's sea journey, they arrived off "Diamond Hill, Ouau" (Oahu). There they were received and treated well by the native Hawaiians. In March 1835, they set sail for the return journey to the Columbia River. There they separated, as Townsend wanted to stay longer and Nuttall decided to return via Cape Horn. Nuttall sailed to Santa Barbara and San Diego, where he waited for the ship *Alert* to depart.

While Nuttall was strolling along a beach near San Diego collecting shells, he was recognized by one of his former students from Harvard, who had become a sailor for a time. Richard Henry Dana wrote a book about his experience on sailing ships called *Two Years Before the Mast*. In his book, Dana described meeting his former professor:

> This ... was no one else than a gentleman whom I had known in my smoother days, and the last person I should have expected to see on the coast of California — Professor Nuttall, of Cambridge. I had left him quietly seated in the chair of Botany and Ornithology in Harvard University, and the next I saw of him, he was strolling about San Diego beach, in a sailor's pea-jacket, with a wide straw hat, and bare-footed, with his trousers rolled up to his knees, picking up stones and shells. The second mate ... told me that they had an old gentleman on board who knew me.... He could not recollect his name, but said he was a "sort of an oldish man, with

white hair, and spent all his time in the bush, and along
the beach, picking up flowers and shells and such truck,
and had a dozen boxes and barrels full of them."[12]

It took the *Alert* four long months to sail around Cape Horn and
enter Boston Harbor on September 20, 1836. At that time, John James
Audubon had serendipitously back in America, after having spent two
years in England. He learned that Nuttall and Townsend had forwarded
to the Academy of Natural Sciences about a hundred skins of new western species of birds. Audubon needed species from the western prairies,
plains, mountains, and far west in order to complete his work. Although
the academy allowed Audubon to examine the skins thoroughly, they
would not allow him to buy them in order to paint them, as they thought
some of their members might be interested in publishing the new species,
if the collectors did not wish to do so themselves.

Audubon went to meet Nuttall shortly after the *Alert* had arrived.
Audubon wrote: "In he came, Lucy, the same Thomas Nuttall, and in a
few minutes we discussed a considerable portion of his travels, adventures,
and happy return to this land of happiness. He promised to obtain duplicates of all the species he had brought for the Academy at Philadelphia ...
and we parted as we have before, friends, bent on the promotion of the
science we study."[13] Audubon was extremely grateful to Nuttall and he
wrote in his *Ornithological Biography*: "Mr. Nuttall generously gave me of
his ornithological treasures all that was new, and inscribed in my journal
the observations which he had made respecting the habits and distribution of all the new and rare species which were unknown to me. All this
information ... while it proves his zeal for the furtherance of science, it
manifests the generosity of his noble nature."[14]

Committed to the task of publishing the tremendous numbers of his
new plant species, Nuttall spent his last few years in America describing
her flora. He managed to publish papers fairly quickly because he had
a good system. He first studied his plants thoroughly and slowly, being
cautious in coming to conclusions — what at first could look like a new
species might be a known one in an early stage of development. Nuttall
prepared small labels for each species, with the name, a technical analysis,

and the general locale where he had found it. When he was preparing to compile a paper, he could assemble the slips in their proper order and write up the data on the slips. Then he added any further notes based on the observations recorded in his field journals.

Nuttall was always enthusiastic towards young people who indicated an interest in natural history. In 1838 he met William Gambel, who essentially became his apprentice. Over the next three years, Nuttall took him along on collecting trips, taught him how to prepare specimens, and shared with him his varied knowledge on botany, ornithology, and mineralogy.

In 1841, at the age of nineteen, Gambel set out for the west as a collector for Nuttall. He joined a party on the Santa Fe Trail, continuing on to California. Eventually he gained employment under several naval officers with whom he sailed along the California coast, continuing to collect as he went. Gambel did not return to Philadelphia until July 1845. Among his many discoveries were two new species, Gambel's Quail (*Callipepla gamelii*) and the Mountain Chickadee (*Parus gambeli*). Nuttall also named a new subspecies of White-crowned Sparrow (*Zonotrichia leucophrys gambelii*) after him. During these years, Nuttall worried about Gambel's safety and financial security.

After having spent thirty-four years exploring, describing, and teaching about the flora and fauna of his adopted country, on December 29, 1841, a very reluctant Nuttall was forced to leave America. When his uncle in England died childless in 1841, he had left the estate to his nephew, with the stipulation that Nuttall not remain outside of England for more than three months in any calendar year. Nuttall had no choice but to return to England, as he had little other means of support; he was financially unable to renounce his inheritance. During the time he was at Harvard, he had taken almost yearly leaves of absence of three or more months to go to unfamiliar areas to observe and collect. These travels had consumed a large part of his salary. When the opportunity had arisen to reach the Rockies and Oregon, he had given up his salary for unforeseeable expenses. Then, while studying and describing his western collections, as well as preparing the supplement to Michaux's *Sylva of North America*, he had used his savings for living expenses.

In 1846 in England, Nuttall received Gambel's collection of about 350 species of plants and became engaged in preparing technical descriptions of selected specimens and preparing a report. Nuttall added to Gambel's collection those of his own unpublished western specimens that were related to Gambel's. In the end, about 40 percent of the hundred plants included in Nuttall's report were his own, although he titled the paper "Descriptions of Plants Collected by William Gambel, M.D., in the Rocky Mountains and Upper California."[15] Nuttall returned briefly to the United States in October 1847, and in February 1848 he read the paper on Gambel's plants to the Academy of Natural Sciences. After visiting old friends in Cambridge and Boston, he left North America again in March 1848, thereby complying with the conditions of his uncle's will that he not spend more than three months in a calendar year absent from the estate.

When Gambel returned to Philadelphia from the west, he published a series of papers peaking with his list of 176 species of birds, several described for the first time, that he had seen on his western trip. Much of this information was incorporated into John Cassin's book on the birds of the Pacific Coast. John Cassin was the first serious bird taxonomist in the United States and had been made honourary curator of the Philadelphia Academy of Natural Sciences in 1842. Gambel became assistant curator of the Academy, and then left the Academy over conflicts with his supervisor, John Cassin.

Gambel had also studied medicine after his return from the West and had received his medical degree. He decided to begin a medical career in California where the Gold Rush was on, and in 1849 joined a group of settlers heading across the country. Unfortunately, at one stage he decided to go with a slower-moving party whose pace afforded him more time for field collecting. This party reached Nevada at the end of a very dry fall, after losing most of their cattle and horses along the way. They started to climb the east edge of the Sierra after the first snows. (This was not the famous Donner Party who had crossed the Sierra Nevada Mountains in 1846 to 1847.) Only a few members of the party, including Gambel, made it across the mountains. Reaching Rose's Bar on the Yuba River, Gambel was helping a group of sick gold miners when he caught typhoid fever and died on December 13, 1849. Although his life had spanned only twenty-eight years, he had accomplished much as a Western explorer, naturalist, and ornithologist during this time.

In 1850, Nuttall was devastated when he received the news of William Gambel's premature death in California. Nuttall never felt at home back at the estate at Nutgrove in England, and for a while he actually became ill, he was so homesick for what had become his home in North America. He now devoted most of his time to horticulture and the greenhouse. He passed away on September 10, 1859. His diverse contributions and advancements in many fields of the natural history of North America, and especially in botany, are truly unparalleled. He was an explorer and a scholar who published extensively on the new species he found. Nuttall is considered one of the greatest North American natural history scientists. In her *Botanical Exploration of the Trans-Mississippi West, 1790–1850*, Susan McKelvey made a detached assessment of Nuttall's contributions:

"If I estimate the importance of the collectors included here on the three counts of scientific qualifications, breadth of knowledge of the living plant derived from actual field experience, and publication of personal discoveries, I find that Nuttall rates high on each count and stands virtually alone as the possessor of all three desiderata."[16]

PART TWO

The Smithsonian Collections and Classification

Chapter Four

Spencer Fullerton Baird
(1823-1887)

"I tell you truly, Professor, you may think us a quiet set in the way of letting you hear from us by letter but I am sure that not one day has passed since we have been out in the field but what your name has been brought up in some way or other.... With noble true friends like you I feel as brave as a lion and shall never fail to succeed and the light of your precepts and example shines in upon my mind brighter as the days go by."

— Letter written to Spencer Fullerton Baird from
Henry Elliott, Cheyenne, Wyoming, October 28, 1870.

Spencer Fullerton Baird was probably the man most responsible for the scientific advancement of ornithology in the mid-1800s in North America. A great naturalist in his own right, he encouraged and arranged for the placement of many young naturalists on the early government expeditions that were exploring and mapping the continent. He was most responsible for the great bird and other collections that are housed in the National Museum of Natural History of the Smithsonian Institution in Washington, D. C.

Baird was devoted to natural history collecting and identification. His great enthusiasm and indefatigable energy in these areas were passed on to others, who in their turn accomplished amazing feats in species collection and identification, often under the most difficult circumstances.

Because he befriended these young naturalists and put great efforts into provisioning and training them, they were happy to face extreme hardships and risks in order to collect for him and make observations about the natural world as it then existed. In Baird's first twenty-eight years at the Smithsonian Institution, over 400,000 specimens were redistributed to other museums and individuals, and the Institution's general holdings still increased from around 6,000 to several hundred thousand specimens. By the time of his death in 1887, there were over 2.5 million items in the Smithsonian.[1] This growth was largely due to Baird's tireless efforts in growing the collection and acquiring scientific knowledge that is useful to both the public and future generations of scientists.

Spencer Baird was born in Reading, Pennsylvania. He grew up and was educated in Carlisle, Cumberland County. As a boy he roamed far and wide around the Cumberland Valley area, either on his own or in the company of his older brother, William. The surroundings consisted of meadows, marshes, streams, ponds, wooded hills, and limestone bluffs. Birds, turtles, fishes, and snakes (mostly harmless ones) were in great abundance. Even at an early age, Baird was methodical about keeping lists of things that he considered of interest, such as lists of "songs that I sing," accounts of money received and expended, and lists of books borrowed, lent, and read by him. "An amusing page of statistics is a statement of the ages of the various members of the family, including uncles and aunts, one or two of which, among the ladies, he notes that he was unable to obtain."[2]

At the age of thirteen, Baird entered Dickinson College, where he studied for four years. During that period, he and his brother William undertook the collection of a complete series of the birds of Cumberland County. Specimens from this collection still form part of the collection at the Smithsonian. When he was seventeen, Baird and his brother obtained a flycatcher that they could not identify. Characteristic of his relentless enthusiasm for obtaining the truth about natural history, Baird gathered enough courage to write to John James Audubon, who in 1840 was acknowledged as the most eminent ornithologist in North America, enclosing a description and measurements of the bird. Audubon replied promptly and graciously to this letter, as the following extract shows:

On my return from Charleston, S.C. yesterday, I found your kind favor of the 4th instant in which you have the goodness to inform me that you have discovered a new species of flycatcher, and which, if the bird corresponds to your description, is, indeed, likely to prove itself hitherto undescribed, for, although you speak of yourself as being a youth, your style and the descriptions you have sent me prove to me that an old head may from time to time be found on young shoulders!... Being on the eve of publishing the *Quadrupeds* of our Country, I have thought that you might have it in your power to procure several of the smaller species for me, and thereby assist me considerably. Please to write me again soon, as I must resume my travels in 8 or 10 days.[3]

This flycatcher and a new second one were subsequently described in a paper published in 1843 by the two Baird brothers.[4] The two new birds were the Yellow-bellied Flycatcher and the Least Flycatcher.

This initial correspondence between Audubon, the naturalist who was nearing the end of his life adventures, and the youthful Baird, who was about to start his career, began a regular exchange of letters over a period of more than seven years. In 1841, Baird went to New York to study medicine. Once in New York, he immediately went to visit Audubon at his house, where he was cordially received. Audubon even offered to teach him to paint and draw after his own peculiar manner, on condition that Baird tell no one his secrets. Baird wrote to his brother William on December 20, 1841: "Being so much at Mr. Audubon's I have an opportunity of seeing a great many North American Quadrupeds. He has made a most beautiful drawing of our Squirrel, it being put in a group with a Gray and a Black variety; Cat Squirrel. It is in the attitude of leaping from one bough of a hickory to another and you expect every minute to see it in the air."[5]

In 1845, Baird was elected an honourary professor of natural history and curator of the cabinet of Dickinson College in Carlisle, Pennsylvania. There was no salary attached to this position. In 1846, his honourary professorship became an actual one with a small starting salary of $400 the first year, which the college promised to increase the next year, providing their earnings were adequate. Also in 1846, Spencer Fullerton Baird married Mary Helen Churchill.

In 1843, Baird had met James Dwight Dana, a prominent geologist. At that time Baird had given much of his time to assisting Dana on his collection of Crustacea at the Patent Office Museum. In 1847, Dana wrote to Baird suggesting that he apply for the position of curator at the Smithsonian Institution. Baird promptly proceeded to write to Professor Joseph Henry, the secretary of the Institution, and asked Audubon, Dana, and others to write letters of reference for him. It seems that Dana's advice had been a little premature, as Professor Henry wrote back saying that the Board of Regents would probably not be appointing a curator until the building was ready to house natural history specimens, which could take five years. However, Baird persevered and continued to keep up correspondence with Joseph Henry concerning his interest in the Smithsonian. On July 5, 1850, Baird's appointment as assistant secretary of the Smithsonian Institution was confirmed. He was about to embark upon his life's work — to build a great national museum of natural history that would be of use to the public and future scientists.

The Smithsonian Institution is one of the world's greatest museums and research centers. Its beginnings were in October 1826, when James Smithson, a British gentleman scientist, wrote in his will that if his nephew were to die without leaving a child, the whole of his property was to be given to the United States of America, to found at Washington, under the name of the Smithsonian Institution, an establishment "for the increase and diffusion of useful knowledge among men."[6] James Smithson's estate was worth about half a million dollars, a huge sum at the time. Smithson's nephew died childless in 1835 and the property came due to the United States and was paid into the Treasury in 1838. For the next eight years, Congress debated what to do with the money. They finally passed a bill providing for an institution that would create a museum, art gallery, chemical laboratory, and library. No branch of knowledge was to be excluded and the institution was to initiate projects to increase knowledge, but not use up more of its own resources than what was necessary to ensure the success of these projects.

The Smithsonian Institution.

Courtesy of the author.

The first secretary of the Smithsonian Institution was Professor Joseph Henry of Princeton University, a renowned physicist. Spencer Baird very happily served as assistant secretary under Professor Henry from 1850 until Henry's death in 1878, at which time Baird succeeded him as secretary of the Smithsonian.

The great life work of Spencer Baird in building the National Museum of Natural History from nothing to the foundation of what it is today is a record of extraordinary toil, all aimed towards the advancement of the natural sciences. Although he was a modest and soft-spoken man, Baird was passionate about the natural sciences and he was more than willing to share any of the knowledge he had acquired. He was not shy to ask people to do things for him, and was able to inspire many people who believed in him and in what he was trying to accomplish. Baird realized the need for a complete zoological exploration of North America so that a full accounting of all species could be made. As a means of doing this, he managed to place naturalists on many

Spencer Fullerton Baird.

Smithsonian Institution Archives,
Image #SIA2007-0021.

of the government-sponsored expeditions, including various boundary and geological surveys and the Pacific Railroad Surveys, which were to find the most practical and economical route for a railroad from the Mississippi River to the Pacific Ocean.

Baird personally made sure that all the field collectors were as well equipped as possible. The Smithsonian issued a pamphlet of "Directions for Collecting, Preserving and Transporting Specimens of Natural History." This was an instructional manual which listed and described all items necessary for field collectors; described how to skin and dry birds, mammals, reptiles and fish; how to preserve items in liquids; how to prepare skeletons; how to press plants; and how to pack nests and eggs.

Baird was able to oversee all the collectors because he had great organizational abilities and an astounding memory. He was also a great correspondent, and once the men were in the field he wrote letters of personal encouragement, emphasizing the importance of the work they were doing and how pleased he was with the results. The diligence and thought that Baird employed in his association with the collectors is described by his daughter, Lucy Hunter Baird:

> My father was interested primarily, of course, in seeing that among the explorers sent out by any Government Survey or Expedition, there should be as many com-petent collectors as possible, and he gave his earnest supervision to the preparation of collecting outfits, and also to preparing instructions for the collectors.... No bride ever devoted more thought and attention to her trousseau than did my father to the fitting out of each of these explorers, and he watched the progress of each missionary with anxious personal interest. The reward of his labors came in the enormous collections sent in, sometimes more than could easily be handled with the force then available in the Museum. The route of each expedition was studied by my father, and it used to be a source of amusement among his friends to note the exact geographical knowledge which he gained by investigation and correspondence. It seemed sometimes as if he knew as much of the ground as if he had traversed it himself.[7]

The Baird family home was always open to all visiting men of science. Spencer Baird, his wife, and daughter also hosted any young naturalists who were staying in rooms at the Smithsonian while they worked there. Almost every Sunday evening, these young scientists were welcomed to dine and participate in enlightening discussions at the Baird home. Baird carefully recorded all visitors in his *Journal* and this record shows that over a period of five years there were only six days when there were no guests of the house. Christmas dinner always included all the unmarried Smithsonian students who were in the city.[8]

Baird constantly asked the collectors to "Collect the COMMONEST species." A frequent mistake was to ignore the familiar species around them because these species were so common and taken for granted, and instead to focus on an unusual species in the area. However, Baird

Young naturalists drawing birds displayed in the bird gallery at the Smithsonian Institution's National Museum of Natural History.

Courtesy of the author.

recognized that a common species in one area is often rare or absent in another area, while a rare species may be common in a different area.

In addition to looking after the many field collectors, Baird had an enormous number of ongoing duties as assistant secretary of the Smithsonian. His correspondence, as well as meeting with visitors to the Smithsonian, took up a considerable amount of his time. He also was called upon to undertake setting up a system of Smithsonian International Exchanges. This was an arrangement with foreign governments by which boxes of pamphlets and books sent by scientific men or institutions as a gift to colleagues or societies on both sides of the Atlantic, under the letterhead of the Smithsonian, were passed through custom houses without being opened. This distribution of work was done without charge by the

Smithsonian, and for some years the transatlantic steamship companies carried the freight for a very low rate. In the earlier years when there were few regular employees, Baird (with the assistance of any friends who were willing to volunteer their time to help) personally prepared hundreds of packages for export to learned societies, in return receiving packs of papers and journals.

Baird also did much writing and editorial work on the zoological reports for the government surveys. With the assistance of John Cassin and George Lawrence, he wrote volume nine on the birds for the Pacific Railroad Reports, which appeared in 1858 and was re-issued in 1860 as the *Birds of North America*. Baird wrote much of this ornithological classic in short periods of about fifteen minutes each, when he could get away from his other duties. In 1874, with the assistance of Thomas Brewer, Robert Ridgway, and Elliott Coues, he completed the three-volume *A History of North American Birds* on the land birds, which was followed by *The Water Birds of North America* in 1884.

Over time Baird devoted less time to birds and more to fish. He had always been a generalized zoologist. When the U.S. Fish Commission was created by Congress in 1871, Baird was appointed commissioner. He chose Wood's Hole on the coast of Massachusetts for its headquarters. As commissioner he worked hard to improve the east coast fish stocks and also directed marine research. This role was in addition to his position at the Smithsonian.

During his lifetime, Baird received worldwide acknowledgement for his great scientific endeavors. In 1850, he was honoured by Dickinson College with a doctorate degree in physics, and in 1875, a doctorate of laws from Columbia University. In 1878 he received the silver medal of the Acclimatization Society of Melbourne, and in 1879, the gold medal of the Society of Acclimatization of France. In 1880, the *vester Ehrenpriez* of the International Fischerei Ausstellung at Berlin was given him by the emperor of Germany. From the king of Norway and Sweden, he received the decoration of Knight of the Royal Norwegian Order of St. Olaf in 1875.

Baird was one of the early members of the National Academy of Sciences, and a member of its council. He was one of the early secretaries of the American Association for the Advancement of Science. Foreign societies honoured him as well, and he was a member of the Linnaean Society of London, the Zoological Society, honourary member of the Linnaean Society of New South Wales, and a member of all the leading French, German, and Italian scientific bodies.[9]

In spite of the honours bestowed upon him, Baird remained an extremely modest and unaffected man, whose main interest remained the work. After a lifetime of service to science, Spencer Fullerton Baird died on August 19, 1887, at age sixty-four at Wood's Hole, Massachusetts.

Chapter Five

Robert Kennicott
(1835-1866)

"Ruled by all-wise laws, every animal fills its appointed place exactly, existing not alone for itself, but forming a necessary part of the vast system of Nature. One class of animals keeps in check certain plants; others prevent the too great increase of these; while those having few enemies are not prolific. Man interferes unwisely, and the order is broken."

— Robert Kennicott, in *The Quadrupeds of Illinois, Injurious and Beneficial to the Farmer*, 1856.

R obert Kennicott was extremely enthusiastic, energetic, and tireless when it came to activities that involved natural history. He also was very mature at a young age. He had little formal education, but trained himself in natural history, making rapid progress. He had great ideas as well as detailed plans for executing them. For example, when he was only twenty-one he helped establish the Chicago Academy of Sciences, and at age twenty-two he established a natural history museum at Northwestern University.

Robert Kennicott's father had a large influence on developing his son's innate interest in natural history. John Kennicott was interested in botany, although he earned a living as a physician. In 1836, shortly after Robert's birth, John moved his family to the Midwest and founded a homestead on the prairies of Cook County, about eighteen miles northwest of Chicago.

His property spanned 250 acres and came to be called "The Grove." Robert Kennicott suffered from poor health during most of his youth, and as a result he had very little formal schooling and was taught at home by a tutor. In an effort to improve his stamina, he was encouraged to spend time outdoors. Growing up, his primary natural history interests involved mammals and snakes. Indeed, he was extremely interested in snakes and in determining which ones were poisonous and which were not. Robert was also interested in the life habits of all the different species of squirrels, mice, and other small mammals. He began making large collections of all types of natural history specimens. At the age of sixteen he went to Cleveland to study during the winter under Jared Kirtland, a friend of his father's, who taught him the fundamentals of entomology, followed by lessons in the fine art of bird skinning and how to properly preserve different types of natural history collections.

Kirtland encouraged Robert to correspond with other American naturalists, most of whom worked in museums in the East. In 1853 Kennicott began a correspondence with Spencer Baird, and began to send all kinds of specimens to Baird in Washington. Baird was delighted with the specimens, "several of which were new to science."[1]

In 1854 Kennicott began to publish a series of articles in the *Prairie Farmer*, an influential agricultural newspaper. While written with farmers in mind, the articles were based on careful, accurate observations, and were also useful to scientists. Kennicott showed a true love and respect for all animals. When writing about the Snow Bunting, he noted that these hardy little birds seemed to thrive "in the most savage weather."[2] Expressing delight at their appearance, he often scattered grain for them.

In a paper published in three parts from 1856 to 1858, Kennicott wrote detailed life histories of many of the known Illinois mammals. "The Quadrupeds of Illinois, Injurious and Beneficial to the Farmer" was the longest and most comprehensive of his papers. In early 1857, the board of trustees of Northwestern University at Evanston asked him to create a natural history museum. Kennicott accepted, and later that year he also helped found the Chicago Academy of Sciences. In 1857, Baird asked him to come to the Smithsonian Institution to help organize the reptile and amphibian section, and Kennicott spent the winters of 1857 to 1859 in Washington doing this.

*The Megatherium Club.
Standing L–R: Robert
Kennicott and Henry
Ulke; seated L–R:
William Stimpson and
Henry Bryant.*

These times in Washington were happy ones for Kennicott. He became an intimate friend of Professor and Mrs. Baird and their child Lucy. He also made friends with the other young naturalists at the Smithsonian, including William Stimpson, who was an expert on marine invertebrates.

Stimpson had rented a house near the Smithsonian and took in scientific-minded boarders. In 1857 several of these fun-loving naturalists, including Kennicott, formed the Megatherium Club, named for the recently discovered remains of an extinct sloth. Club members spent their days at the Smithsonian in the rigorous and demanding work of describing and classifying species. At the end of the week, they temporarily abandoned their studies, had a good time, and then recuperated on Sundays by taking long walks in the woods — "the true Church," according to Stimpson. These good times often did not last long, as most of the naturalists left Washington periodically to work in the field. The Club thus met sporadically over a period from 1857 to 1866. Its members were among the most dedicated naturalists North America has ever seen. Their philosophy was summed up by Stimpson thus: "What more noble pursuit for immortal souls? Riches? War and Butchery? Political chicanery? Superstition? Pleasure? What we seek is the TRUTH!"[3]

At the time, Spencer Baird was very aware that there was a paucity of information available on the flora and fauna of Russian America (now Alaska), the territories controlled by the Hudson's Bay Company (now northern Canada), and the Arctic. Georg Steller had made a few collections in the eighteenth century, and John Richardson had made observations on John Franklin's Arctic explorations, but there was very little natural history material and few observations on the boreal north. To Baird, this region offered the greatest possibilities for collecting and discovering new facts and species.

Spencer Baird picked Robert Kennicott as the person to send to the boreal north to acquire information on the flora and fauna of the region. He probably had no idea at the time how enterprising Kennicott would become in this endeavour. Kennicott's infectious enthusiasm, and coaching of new recruits to collect and record, added immensely to the Smithsonian's northern collections. By inspiring agents at all the Hudson's Bay Company posts in the area to get involved in the collection and recording process, he was able to stimulate what led to a huge increase in knowledge of the region's natural history which was far greater than any one man could have accomplished collecting on his own.

By 1859 Baird had sufficient funding in place to send Kennicott to the far north. He insisted that the Smithsonian receive examples of all the species collected, and Kennicott insisted on the same arrangement for the Chicago Academy of Sciences. Other specimens were divided among the sponsors of the trip on a pro-rata basis according to the amount of their investments.[4] One of the main aims of Kennicott's venture was to find the unknown breeding grounds of many of the familiar birds that migrated north each spring. The priority therefore was to obtain eggs and to identify the parents. Kennicott arrived at Fort William on Lake Superior in May and started out for Lake Winnipeg in the company of Canadian voyageurs. Describing this mode of travel, he wrote:

*Robert Kennicott in his
field clothes.*

Smithsonian Institution Archives,
Image #SIA2011-0145.

The three canoes were each about thirty-six feet long, four
in width, and two and a half deep in the middle; the bow
and stern taper to a compressed point and are suddenly
elevated a foot or two. The outer shell is formed entirely
of birch bark, placed with the fibers transversely in the
same position as it grew upon the tree, but with the inside
outward.... One of these canoes, after some use, weighs,
when empty, about three hundred pounds, and it will
carry nearly three thousand pounds, besides the crew....
The proper crew of such a canoe is eight men, a bowsman,
steersman, and six middlemen.... Our manner of travelling was to me very novel and interesting. At three or four
o'clock in the morning we were aroused by lusty shouts
of *levé! levé!* from the guides, when all hands were quickly
engaged in launching the canoes and loading them, and
often we were paddling briskly off within ten or fifteen

minutes of the first awakening....We stopped for about an hour to cook breakfast at from eight to ten o'clock. Dinner was generally eaten without stopping to cook.... We camped at night at about eight or nine o'clock, when the first care of the voyageurs was to unload the canoe and take it ashore, when it was turned up on edge in such a position as to shelter the crew who slept under it.[5]

In June, Kennicott met with Governor Simpson at Norway House. Simpson promised him every assistance from the Hudson's Bay Company personnel who controlled the area, and allowed him to travel freely in the area for a period of two years, with the option to extend it longer. In July, Kennicott met chief trader Bernard Rogan Ross, and they travelled to Fort Simpson on the Mackenzie River. Kennicott realized that on his own he would be able to gather only a very limited collection, so he decided to travel from post to post to obtain the help of the Company's factors and traders through personal contact and encouragement. In November 1859, Kennicott wrote to Baird: "I hope you'll get specimens of various kinds next summer from nearly every post in the District. Mr. Ross has written to every one and I supplied pamphlets of instructions and a little alcohol to each and arsenic to some, besides giving some lessons in the fall on bird skinning."[6]

Kennicott wrote about the severe winter: "Mr. McFarlane, the officer now in charge of Ft. Good Hope ... says he went during the winter to the Esquimaux at the mouth of the Anderson. He took a thermometer, one I had given him, mercury *constantly frozen* for 22 days of his voyage! Yet he says they only got frozen *one* day that they were short of provisions and obliged to push on with a heavy wind in their faces."[7]

In the spring, Kennicott decided to spend the collecting season at Fort Resolution on the south shore of Great Slave Lake. An entry in his journal reads: "Saw a number of *Dendroica aestiva* [Yellow Warbler], and an *Empidonax* [Flycatcher]. Shot *Numenius borealis* [Eskimo Curlew]. The base of the bill is not yellowish in life, but brownish flesh colour."[8] In August, he went further north, down the Mackenzie River almost to the Beaufort Sea. Then he travelled west over the Richardson Mountains to the Porcupine River, and thence down to Fort Yukon, at the junction of the Porcupine and Yukon Rivers, arriving in late September.

Kennicott had made an excellent decision in choosing to collect on the Yukon Flats. In June 1861, he worked for eighteen hours a day collecting egg specimens. When the short egg-laying season was over, he spent days writing notes and labels and blowing eggs. The great influence and impression that Kennicott exerted on the collecting efforts of the Hudson's Bay Company employees is revealed in a letter he wrote to Baird:

> Lockhart and I have now something over a bushel of eggs of *Aythya affinis* [Lesser Scaup], *Aythya marila* [Greater Scaup], *Aythya valisineria* [Canvasback], *Anas americana* [American Wigeon] and *Anas acuta* [Northern Pintail] to say nothing of one next of *Bucephala albeola* [Bufflehead], one of *Anas crecca carolinensis* [Green-winged Teal], one of *Anas clypeata* [Northern Shoveler] and a solitary egg of *Melanetta velvetina* [White-winged Scoter].... Antoine Hoole the interpreter of the post is as I have said a very keen hunter and takes kindly to the collecting, in which I have gotten him thoroughly interested.... I consider his work and interest with the Indians a matter of prime importance to arctic zoological operations. I have bribed him with many very acceptable presents and shall give him some of the things sent from The Grove for my own use. That *accordion* you sent he has been very anxious to get, as he will.... I hear good reports from the gentlemen in other quarters especially Mr. Ross, and Clarke seems to be *going into it* on the zoology. I hope you have written to them all. Do you not know that you have a persuasive way with you that enables you to make everybody do just as you like, as far as any external influence can have effect?... The operations in zoology here are getting quite in earnest and we can now turn the crank and keep the "wheels" you mention going from the Smithsonian, with its long arms under your control.[9]

In early spring of 1862, Kennicott received word that his father was critically ill. He also received news of the start of the Civil War. Although he had planned on spending another year in the North, he instead journeyed south to Chicago. Once at home, he was persuaded not to enlist in the war, and instead went to work at the Smithsonian again. In the first half of 1863, most of the members of the Megatherium Club were residing in the Smithsonian Castle. The leaders of the Club, Stimpson and Kennicott, were reunited and quickly rigged up a trap door between their rooms, on rainy days leading footraces through the Castle's Great Hall.[10]

For more than ten years after Kennicott's return, collections continued to pour into the Smithsonian from the Hudson's Bay Company collectors in the North, until those who had been inspired by Kennicott retired from active service.[11] One of the most important observations arising from those collections was that many of the California birds, never seen in the eastern part of the continent, go there to breed.[12]

The Smithsonian had agreed to allow Kennicott's share of the Canadian collections to be set up at the Chicago Academy of Sciences and generously promised to also supply the new museum with their duplicates from every department of natural history.[13] In 1864, Kennicott was elected Curator of the Chicago Academy and was busy arranging for the packing, transporting, and arranging of these specimens. Unfortunately, most of them were destroyed in the Great Chicago Fire of 1871. Kennicott was also working on the Smithsonian's proposed "Report on Arctic Zoology." Then his career again took an abrupt turn in direction.

In 1863, the first Atlantic cable between North America and Europe had failed, and the Western Union Telegraph Company was looking at carrying a telegraph line along the Western coast of America and across Bering Strait through Siberia to Europe. Because of Kennicott's unique experiences in the vast Hudson Bay northern territories, he was recommended as the chief naturalist on what was called the Western Union Telegraph Expedition. Kennicott was made the director of the Scientific Corps. The role of the several naturalists under Kennicott was to explore and report on the natural history of Russian America (now Alaska). The field notes, specimens, and other reports that this party of naturalists sent back to Baird played a part in persuading the United States Congress to purchase Alaska from Russia in 1867.

When Kennicott's scientific party arrived at San Francisco, they found that the success of the entire expedition was becoming compromised due to the endless disputes over the next course of action. The expedition leaders, surveyors, wire stringers, and scientists all argued over what should be done. In spite of Kennicott's greater experience, his suggestions were hostilely put down. There was a critically long delay in starting out, given the short summer season in the north.[14]

In August, Kennicott's team was at Sitka, and it was not until mid-September that they finally arrived on the shores of Norton Sound in northwest Alaska where their provisions and equipment were off-loaded. While part of the team under William Dall went to work on the Siberian side before returning to San Francisco for the winter, Kennicott took a group up the west side of the Yukon River to the Russian fort at Nulato, where they were forced to wait for the spring thaw before they could move on. Kennicott wanted to complete the scientific exploration of the northwest extremity of the continent between Fort Yukon, at the junction of the Yukon and Porcupine Rivers, and Nulato, the most eastern Russian post on the Yukon River.

During the winter at Nulato, Kennicott was discouraged and worn down by the dissension in the expedition. He always worried about failing, which is probably what drove him to be so successful. It had been Kennicott's recommendation to use the Hudson Bay route for the telegraph line, as William Dall later wrote:

> The route was ill chosen for the proposed line. Had it been over the well-trodden paths from St. Paul, Minnesota, through the Hudson Bay Territory to Fort Yukon, and then down the Yukon, there is reason to believe that the line might have been built at a less cost than the amount wasted on the west coast, in the mountainous region and dense forests of British Columbia. The Hudson Bay route was recommended by Mr. Kennicott, but other counsels prevailed.... The line which was put up in

British Columbia, with the exception of the very small portion in use, is said on good authority to be already out of repair and quite useless.[15]

Just before the ice broke up at Nulato, on May 12, a Russian named Tarentoff was caught offshore between ice-cakes in a birch-bark canoe and was sinking. Kennicott went to his aid and rescued him. After the Russian had changed his clothes, he came expressing his gratitude to Kennicott, who answered, "Do not thank me, Tarentoff; thank God."[16] That night, Kennicott could not sleep. He rose early and went for a walk on the beach near the fort, working on taking the angles of the mountains in the vicinity for a proposed map of the area. There, he died suddenly of a heart attack or from some other natural cause. He was thirty years old.

William Dall determined to follow through with Kennicott's plans to explore Russian North America (Alaska). On the one-year anniversary of Kennicott's death, Dall had a cross erected at Nulato. On the tablet was written:

IN MEMORY OF
ROBERT KENNICOTT,
NATURALIST,
Who died near this place,
May 13th, 1866, aged thirty.[17]

Chapter Six

Robert Ridgway
(1850–1929)

"*The personal charm of Robert Ridgway will ever be recognized as one of his finest attributes. It is an attribute that we all can afford to cultivate.*"

— From Dayton Stoner, "Ninety Minutes with Robert Ridgway," in *The Wilson Bulletin*, 1934.

Robert Ridgway was one of North America's greatest ornithologists. He was the curator of the Smithsonian Institution's bird collections for forty-nine years and made great advances in the systematization and classification of North-American birds. He made several field trips to obtain specimens for the Smithsonian Institution collections, including a two-year trip to California and Utah undertaken when he was only seventeen years old. He also made three arduous and dangerous expeditions to Florida, where he obtained the Carolina Parakeet and the famous Ivory-billed Woodpecker, as well as making several trips to Costa Rica for the bird collections. He published voluminous works on birds, as well as five to six hundred papers in professional journals.

Ridgway was one of the key founders of the American Ornithologists' Union. He was also an excellent true-to-life artist. When he found it was difficult to consistently describe the colours of birds, he invented a system of colour nomenclature that is still used extensively today in ornithology, as well as in industries which use colours in their work.

Robert Ridgway.

Smithsonian Institution Archives,
Image #SIA2008-4347.

Because of his natural inclination towards nature study and his extreme industry, he rose to become one of the great men of ornithology.

Robert Ridgway was born in 1850 in Mount Carmel, in southeastern Illinois. He was the eldest of ten children. All his life Ridgway felt an attachment to the area where he was born. Robert's father and an uncle had established a growing pharmaceutical business in Mount Carmel. However, the business eventually failed due to a combination of unforeseen events, including a fire, and later a tornado, which partially destroyed their building.

Robert developed an interest in birds and plants at a very young age. As early as three or four years old, he was drawing accurate bird forms. This interest in the natural world was partially inspired by his parents. He wrote about his boyhood experiences: "Almost the only recreation of my father was hunting, or on Sundays, when he never hunted, taking walks into the country, especially through the woods, on both of which occasions I usually accompanied him. It was thus that the foundation of my nature love was laid, for my father was exceptionally well informed on the subject of wild birds."[1] Prior to ten years of age, Robert was collecting and drawing birds, nests and eggs, leaves of trees, and other natural objects. His drawings were true-to-life and remarkably good for someone so young. He creatively mixed his own watercolours in his father's drugstore, showing an early interest in how various colours combine to produce other different colours.

Robert's mother was firm with her children, but she also made sacrifices for them, as when Robert recalls:

> I can never forget an instance of self-sacrifice on her part in order to please me. We were visiting in Olney, and one day I accompanied her on a shopping tour. We entered a store where books were sold in addition to the regular line of goods. My eye caught the title of a sumptuous leather-bound, gilt-lettered volume which I asked the proprietor to let me examine. It was a thick royal octavo of 680 pages, very profusely illustrated, of which the first 354 pages were devoted to birds. The embossed cover-title was: *The Animal Kingdom Illustrated....* I was so fascinated with it that I timidly expressed a wish to own it, not at all expecting the possibility of such a thing, as the price seemed to me prohibitive (somewhere between eight and twelve dollars); but Mother with sympathetic understanding opened her slim purse and handed over the price, and thus the coveted book became mine, but I am very sure at the sacrifice of practically all her "spending money." This book with some of the front pages gone and many of the woodcuts disfigured by my efforts to colour them is still one of my prized possessions.[2]

In 1864 an event occurred that set Ridgway on his lifetime career. He and two friends had observed a bird that they could not identify on their excursions in the woods. Ridgway was discussing this with the other boys at their home when the boys' mother suggested that Robert should write to the commissioner of patents in Washington, and she gave him an envelope with the commissioner's address on it. Ridgway wrote a letter describing the bird and its habits, and enclosed a coloured drawing he had made of both the male and female birds perched on a tall weed, the seed of which he had seen them eating. This letter found its way into the hands of Spencer Baird of the Smithsonian Institution, who replied promptly, saying it was a Purple Finch. Thereafter, whenever Ridgway found a bird he could not identify, he would make a coloured drawing of it and enclose it with a letter to Baird.

Within three years of starting this correspondence, Ridgway received a letter asking him if he was available to come to the Smithsonian to become outfitted for a position of zoologist on the Fortieth Parallel Survey Expedition. At that time, Ridgway was seventeen years old. After resolving some initial hesitation on the part of his parents, Ridgway went to Washington, where he spent two weeks getting acquainted with western birds and learning how to make a good bird skin. Then he travelled to New York where he met the party he would be with for the next two years. They travelled to San Francisco via Panama, and proceeded by river steamer to Sacramento, where they established their first camp. From there, the expedition journeyed on horseback to Salt Lake City and as far eastward as the Uinta Mountains of Utah. Frequent stops of two weeks to three months were made along the way so as to allow the topographers and geologists to explore the country. During these stops, Ridgway collected natural history specimens. The trip was not always an easy one for Ridgway. He describes his worst experience:

> On arriving at the Humboldt Marshes, where we remained for a week, I was down with malarial fever and so weak that no collecting could be done. It was the most uncomfortable camp in all my experience; the water used for drinking and cooking was so charged with sulphur that it smelt like ancient eggs, the air was redolent of the stench of rotting tules, and at night we suffered the torment of millions of blood-thirsty mosquitoes.[3]

Ridgway almost got himself killed while climbing the "Pyramid" in Pyramid Lake, Nevada, in search of a Peregrine Falcon nest. The Pyramid is an immense triangular rock rising about 400 feet above the surface of Pyramid Lake. Its three sides are virtually sheer precipices for half their height. After making it to the top, Ridgway and his climbing companion were only able to make it down again because the man who had rowed them out to the rock gestured to them from the boat as to which way they should take down.

At the conclusion of the Fortieth Parallel Survey Expedition, Ridgway returned to the Smithsonian. Spencer Baird was not able at that time to offer him a full-time appointment, and Ridgway was put to work writing the technical descriptions and providing some of the drawings for the treatise on North American birds which Baird and Thomas Brewer were in the process of compiling. Ridgway performed this task so satisfactorily that his name was added as the third author of *A History of North American Birds*.

Shortly after arriving at the Smithsonian, Ridgway had received a very tempting offer inviting him to become an ornithologist at the American Museum of Natural History in New York. The annual salary of $1,500, to be gradually increased, was more than double the $600 that he was making at the Smithsonian with no guarantee of advancement. However, after talking it over with Baird, Ridgway turned the offer down.

While a young man working at the Smithsonian Institution, Ridgway had an office next to the top of one of the towers. In order to reach his office, he often took the eighty-seven steps two at a time. In the early seventies, Ridgway saw Julia Evelyn Perkins walking in the main hall of the Smithsonian building. She was the daughter of one of the engravers engaged to cut the wood blocks to print the illustrations for *A History of North American Birds*. Ridgway was smitten with her. He arranged to meet the young lady, and after a courtship they were married on October 12, 1875. Ridgway's marriage was a very happy one. He commented:

> It does not always happen that the wife of a naturalist or other 'scientist' is in full sympathy with her husband's occupation.... In this respect, I have been exceedingly fortunate, for from first to last Mrs. Ridgway was more

Robert Ridgway in his office at the Smithsonian Institution.

Smithsonian Institution Archives, Image #SIA2010-1672.

interested in my work than in anything else, the only part of it which she did not approve being the collecting of specimens, and this disapproval was the result of her extreme tenderness of heart toward all living creatures, birds especially.[4]

The Ridgways had one son, Audubon Whelock Ridgway, who was born on May 15, 1877. Their son developed interests in birds, drawing, and photography. In 1900, when Ridgway was asked if he could recommend someone for assistant to the Curator of Birds in the Chicago Field Museum, he nominated Audubon on his merits. Audubon went to Chicago and was doing a good job. However, while out skating, he became overheated and then chilled, caught pneumonia, and died on February 22, 1901. This was a devastating blow to both parents, and especially so to Mrs. Ridgway, who never fully recovered from it.

Robert Ridgway was one of the principal founders of the American Ornithologists' Union in 1883. He played a key role on the AOU committee on classification and nomenclature of North and Middle American birds. Ridgway held various titles during his forty-nine year tenure at the Smithsonian, but by 1886, he was curator of birds, a title he held until his death. In 1887, he produced *A Manual of North American Birds*. Just as the book was about to go to press, Spencer Baird died and Ridgway quickly added a grateful tribute to his greatly admired adviser.

Ridgway was exact in his work and he realized very early that there was a need to establish a uniform series of named colours and to standardize colour names, so that there would be no uncertainty as to what was meant by the colours written in descriptions. In 1886 he produced *Nomenclature of Colors for Naturalists and Compendium of Useful Knowledge for Ornithologists*. This work contained 186 named colours and was greatly appreciated and immediately used by naturalists, especially ornithologists, who were able for the first time to definitely call out the various shades in their descriptions. However, Ridgway was still dissatisfied with the limited number and unscientific arrangement of the colours presented. He continued to study colour on a more scientific basis sporadically over the next twenty-five years. In his extremely detailed work *Color Standards and Nomenclature*, published in 1912, he presented a scientific breakdown of 1,115 colours. The book has fifty-three plates showing 1,115 named colours in small rectangles. The plates are accompanied by tables giving the precise proportions of each mixture for each colour. The enormous difficulties in producing this work are revealed in a letter written by Ridgway in 1913:

I think there is no danger that the edition will soon be exhausted, for necessarily, there is a limited demand for works of this sort. Five thousand sets of the plates are being prepared, but only 1,000 will be bound as a first edition.... When the 5,000 copies are disposed of, the work can be reproduced only by doing it all over again, because it is all *hand work*; that is to say, each separate colour was mixed in one "batch" (enough for the 5,000 copies), then large sheets of paper were evenly coated *by hand* with this one mixture, and these sheets afterward cut into the small pieces which represent the colours on the plates. In this way, only, can absolute uniformity of different copies be guaranteed, for the possibility of variation is thus wholly eliminated. No mechanical methods (at least none known at the present time) would answer the purpose, and chromo-lithography would not do because the oil or varnish used in the composition of printing inks would cause eventual change of colour through oxidation of the vehicle.[5]

This work was accepted as a standard by the scientific, artistic, and industrial world, since it was the only one among the books in its field that rested on a firm foundation of scientific principles. Ridgway was surprised to see that when the book came out, naturalists had bought fewer than one out of every five copies sold. Most copies were bought by representatives of various trades, as well as some government departments including the Bureau of Standards, the National Museum, and the Bureau of Plant Industry at the Department of Agriculture. Ridgway commented that "What surprised me most, however, was an order for 10 copies (!) from one firm of civil engineers after having already bought one copy."[6]

In 1894 Dr. G. Brown Goode, the assistant secretary of the Smithsonian Institution in charge of the National Museum, had instructed Ridgway to make it his top priority to publish "the results of the ornithological work of the Government, as represented in the collection of the Smithsonian Institution."[7] This was a monumental assignment. In 1901 Volume I appeared of *The Birds of North and Middle America: A Descriptive Catalogue of the Higher Groups, Genera, Species, and Subspecies known to Occur in North America, from the Arctic Lands to the Isthmus of Panama, the West Indies and other Islands of the Caribbean Sea, and the Galapagos Archipelago.*

In 1916, the Ridgways moved to the slower pace of Olney, Illinois, where eventually they bought two properties. One was an area of eighteen acres in the country, which Ridgway named "Bird Haven." The other was a home in the outskirts of Olney that he called "Larchmount." In this relative seclusion, he continued to write steadily, producing the eighth volume of *Birds of North and Middle America* in 1919. Ridgway was able to finish the first ten volumes before his death. The remaining two volumes were completed by Alexander Wetmore. As a break from his writing, Ridgway developed the trees and shrubs in the garden at Larchmount and maintained the grounds at Bird Haven. Mrs. Ridgway passed away in May 1927, and Robert Ridgway died in March 1929, at the age of seventy-nine.

Robert Ridgway's many works are major contributions to the advancement of systematic ornithology. As a man, Ridgway was friendly, but retiring. He avoided the limelight, preferring to work quietly in the background. In 1920 he was awarded the Daniel Giraud Elliot Medal of the National Academy of Sciences, and in 1921 he received the William Brewster Memorial Award. He was elected a member of the National Academy of Sciences in 1926. He was also the recipient of the Walker Grand Prize of the Boston Society of Natural History in the amount of $1,000, granted to him in 1913 for his work on *Birds of North and Middle America.*

PART THREE

For the Love of Birds

Chapter Seven

Florence Merriam Bailey
(1863-1948)

"Far more than all the statistics is the sanity and serenity of spirit that comes when we step aside from the turmoil of the world to hold quiet converse with Nature."

— Florence Merriam Bailey in the Introduction to an
1899 version of *Birds Through an Opera-Glass*.

Florence Merriam Bailey was tireless in pursuing those things that were important to her lifelong interest in birds. When she became aware that the birds she loved were being slaughtered at a horrific rate so that women could wear the feathers and even the whole birds atop their stylish hats, she took action to educate and inform as many people as she could about the interesting lives of the birds. She felt that if people knew more about the living birds as fascinating creatures, they would stop wearing these hats, and the atrocities that were being committed in the name of fashion would stop.

Florence Merriam Bailey was an extremely talented nature writer. She could write in both an informative as well as an entertaining way about the lives of the birds. She became a serious ornithological writer who wrote up her many varied field experiences into articles, books, manuals, and government publications. These were read and used by the general public, as well as ornithologists. She received the honour of being the first woman associate member of the American Ornithologists' Union in 1885, its first woman fellow in 1929, and the first woman recipient of its prestigious William Brewster Memorial Award in 1931.

Florence Merriam Bailey.

From *The Condor*, 1904.

Florence Merriam was born in 1863 in Locust Grove, New York, near the Adirondack Mountains. Both her father and her older brother were interested in and knowledgeable about the wildlife surrounding their home. While her brother, C. Hart Merriam, was more interested in collecting specimens, she became interested in observing the lives of the birds she saw, and she came to adore them as living creatures: "Whenever she went into the woods, she tucked some seeds in the pocket of her dress, and often a chickadee or other woods bird would come close enough to feed without being frightened away. She soon learned the benefits of being quiet so she could watch the birds in their home grounds."[1]

Florence and her older brother Hart were always very close. Hart's interest in natural history developed into a lifelong career. Although he completed medical training in 1879 and practiced as a doctor for five years, at age twenty-six he gave up the practice of medicine and moved to Washington, D.C., to head a newly created division of the U.S.

Department of Agriculture, which later separated to become the U.S. Biological Survey.

In 1882, at age nineteen, Florence went to Northampton, Massachusetts, to attend Smith College. There she spent as much time as possible outdoors to improve her health. She was suffering at the time from the effects of tuberculosis and tended to tire easily. At Smith she continued studying the birds she saw. During the fall of 1885, her final year at the college, she was assigned to write an article for the college science association. She wrote to Hart:

> After casting about in my mind for the one thing in my incapacitating ignorance that was less staggering than the others, and for which I had a present interest, I thought of — now, don't laugh, just wait till I explain — birds. Of course I know as well as you do how absolute my real ignorance of the subject is, but you see the girls here know less about it than I do, and I thought that by reading up I might write an article that would serve to interest or at least call their attention to the common birds we have here, and at the same time give them a few points on general habits, etc. that they have failed to notice.[2]

In her article, Merriam included a comment on the destruction of birds for the millinery trade. Her article was so well-written that it was subsequently reprinted in two local newspapers.

Florence was appalled to hear all the girls at Smith College talking about the hats with birds on them that they wanted to buy, and she determined to make them aware of how interesting living birds were. At that time, George Bird Grinnell, the editor of the outdoor journal *Forest and Stream* (later *Field and Stream*) started the Audubon Society for the Protection of Birds. The goal of this society was to educate the general public about birds. Florence and her birding friend, Fannie Hardy, determined to create a similar bird group at Smith College. They cut out articles on bird destruction from newspapers, including graphic descriptions. Egrets and herons were being massacred on their breeding grounds for their breeding plumes. Although the following description is from a somewhat earlier year, it is typical:

> A few miles north of Waldo, in the flat pine region, our party came one day upon a little swamp where we had been told herons breed in numbers. Upon approaching the place the screams of young birds reached our ears. The cause of this soon became apparent by the buzzing of green-flies and the heaps of dead herons festering in the sun, with the back of each bird raw and bleeding.... Young herons had been left by scores in the nests to perish from exposure and starvation.[3]

That year only a dozen breeding herons were left near the outlying Florida keys, where sailors had reported there had been thousands only six years before.[4]

The Smith College Audubon Society was formed on March 17, 1886. Florence and Fannie also led nature walks around the campus. Florence wrote to John Burroughs, the famous nature writer, inviting him to come to Smith, and she was thrilled when he agreed to come in the first week of May. When she spread the word about his visit, forty or fifty girls signed up for his nature walks. Florence wrote:

> It was early in the spring for birds, and our numbers were enough to have frightened back to the South the few that had ventured North; but the strong influence of Mr. Burrough's personality and quiet enthusiasm gave just the inspiration that was needed. We all caught the contagion of the woods.... With gossamers and raised umbrellas we would gather about him under the trees, while he stood leaning against a stump, utterly indifferent to the rain, absorbed in incidents from the life of some goldfinch or sparrow, interpreting the chipping of the swift as it darted about overhead, or answering the questions put to him, with the simplicity and kindliness of a beneficent sage.[5]

Within three months, almost a hundred girls, one-third of the total enrollment, had become members of the Smith College Audubon Society.

In 1886, Florence returned to Homewood, where she helped her parents and did social work. She had determined to make writing her life's work. She wrote to Hart: "To ease the burden of the world, and help others to the truer higher living ... this is my aim and to leave the world better for my having lived, and I feel that I can fulfill it better through my pen than in any other way."[6]

In 1889, at the age of twenty-six, Florence put together the articles on common birds that she had previously written for *Audubon*, as well as new ones, and published them all as her first book, *Birds Through an Opera Glass*. In it, she gave her "Hints to Observers":

> When you begin to study the birds in the fields and woods, to guard against scaring the wary, you should make yourself as much as possible a part of the landscape. Most birds are not afraid of man as a figure, but as an aggressive object. The observance of a few simple rules will help you to be unobtrusive.
>
> *First.* Avoid light or bright-colored clothing.
>
> *Second.* Walk slowly and noiselessly.
>
> *Third.* Avoid all quick, jerky motions.
>
> *Fourth.* Avoid all talking, or speak only in an undertone.
>
> *Fifth.* If the bird was singing, but stops on your approach, stand still a moment and encourage him by answering his call. If he gets interested he will often let you creep up within opera-glass distance.
>
> *Sixth.* Make a practice of stopping often and standing perfectly still. In that way you hear voices that would be lost if you were walking, and the birds come to the spot without noticing you when they would fly away in advance if they were to see or hear you coming toward them.
>
> *Seventh.* Conceal yourself by leaning against a tree, or pulling a branch down in front of you.[7]

Florence did not write under a pen name as was usual at the time. She wrote: "Like other ladies, the little feathered brides have to bear their husbands' names, however inappropriate. What injustice! Here an innocent creature with an olive-green back and yellowish breast has to go about all her days known as the Black-throated Blue Warbler, just because that happens to describe the dress of her spouse!"[8]

Florence was increasingly suffering from the effects of tuberculosis and she determined to leave the cold, damp weather behind and go to Utah and later California, where the drier, sunnier climate would prove beneficial. Fortunately, after repeated trips to sunny climates, her tuberculosis was cured by 1895. In Southern California, she stayed for a time with an uncle at Twin Oaks, which is the post office for the scattered ranch houses in a small valley at the foot of one of the Coastal Ranges. It is thirty-four miles north of San Diego, and twelve miles from the Pacific Ocean.

Florence's field notes from Twin Oaks formed the basis for her book *A-Birding on a Bronco*. All spring she was able to ride her horse Billy around the ranch, stopping and resting for hours at key spots to observe the birds and their activities. For several days she watched a pair of tiny Bushtits building their hanging nest. She observed them continuously taking nesting material inside. One morning, the nest fell to the ground and the birds moved to another spot to try all over again. After some time Florence took the old nest home and pulled it to pieces. She found that:

> the wall was from half an inch to an inch thick, made of fine gray moss and oak blossoms. There was a thick wadding of feathers inside. I counted three hundred, and there were a great many more! The amount of hard labor this stood for amazed me. No wonder the nest pulled down, with a whole featherbed inside! Why had they put it in? I asked some children, and one said, "To keep the eggs warm, I guess;" while the other suggested, "So the eggs wouldn't break."[9]

Upon her return from the west, Florence moved to Washington, D.C., to live with Hart, his wife, and their two young daughters. Besides the opportunity to be close to her brother and his work, she was attracted by the scientific activities in Washington. She went to work with the American Ornithologists' Union Committee on the Protection of North American Birds, as birds were still being slaughtered in great numbers for the millinery trade. Continuing with her education efforts, Florence helped to found the Audubon Society of the District of Columbia in 1897.

The following summer, she took part in one of her brother's expeditions to study the flora and fauna of Mount Shasta. Vernon Bailey, a friend of her brother's, and then the chief field naturalist for the survey, was also in the party. Florence's paper on the Clark's Nutcrackers and other birds that she had watched during the expedition was read at the American Ornithologists' Union annual meeting in November, and then was published in *Bird-Lore*. On December 16, 1899, Florence married Vernon Bailey, and they moved to an apartment in Washington prior to building a house there.

The Biological Survey sent Vernon into the field to help farmers resolve problems with small mammals. He was provided with a specific itinerary to follow. Whenever she could, Florence went with him to study the birds and gather field notes from which to write articles and books. They soon made several trips to the Southwest together. When Florence returned to Washington, she became occupied in researching and writing the *Handbook of Birds of the Western United States*. In order to compile all the data for this major work, she spent many days over the winter writing. She also spent months studying the bird skins in the "cramped but delightful old bird gallery of the Smithsonian, receiving generous help from Mr. Ridgway."[10]

With her book on the western birds, Florence combined the best scientific knowledge and field experience of the time into one field guide. This book remained a standard reference for fifty years and went through many printings. It was informative as well as enjoyable reading, and incorporated Florence's talented writing style. For example, in describing the Hermit Thrush, she said its nest was "in bushes or low trees, 3 to 10 feet from the ground; partly made with moss," and its food consisted of "flies, ants, weevils, and other insects and berries." About its voice, she said, "As you travel through the spire-pointed fir forests of the western mountains,

Florence Merriam Bailey conducting field research in the Guadalupe Mountains, New Mexico.

Courtesy American Heritage Center, University of Wyoming.

you know the thrush as a voice, a bell-like sublimated voice, which, like the tolling of the Angelus, arrests toil and earthly thought."[11]

In the summer field season of 1903, Vernon was to make a detailed biological survey of the Territory of New Mexico. Florence joined him to add to his survey with her own studies of New Mexico birds. This survey trip was a very strenuous and demanding one, as Vernon and Florence were constantly on the move. However, Florence's health was by now fully repaired, and she enjoyed her husband's companionship and exploring the nature of the Southwest, which she loved.

Their summer field trip in 1907 was to southern California. Along the Pacific coast, Florence described the feeding behavior of the Marbled Godwit:

> As a wave rolled up, combed over and broke, the white
> foam would chase them in, and as they ran before it,
> if it came on too fast, they would pick themselves up,

open their wings till the cinnamon showed, and scoot
in like excited children. But the instant the water began
to recede they would right about face and trot back with
it.... As they went their long bills — in the low afternoon
sun strikingly coral red except for the black tip — were
shoved ahead of them, feeling along through the wet
sand, the light glinting from them; and if anything good
was discovered deeper, the hunters would stop to really
probe, sometimes plunging the bill in up to the hilt, on
rare occasions when the tidbit proved out of reach, actually crowding their heads down into the sand.[12]

For the next three summers Florence stayed in Washington, where
she reorganized the Audubon Society's bird classes, arranging three sec-
tions: one for lectures, and two more for beginner and advanced studies
of bird skins. The classes were widely advertised and attracted both teachers and members of the general public. For years afterwards, Florence
either taught these classes or directed the work. By 1902 there were five
classes and fifty or sixty members, and by 1913 it took a dozen or more
teachers to accommodate the membership of between one and two hundred. "Mrs. Bailey must be given the principal credit for the popularity
and success of this rather remarkable activity which continued for more
than a quarter of a century."[13]

When Vernon had a new field assignment to complete a biological
survey of North Dakota, an area of increasing importance to farmers,
Florence decided to accompany him. She wrote: "the *Northern Pacific*
carried us out across the dead level of the old bed of Lake Agassiz and
then up over the North Dakota coteau whose gentle moraine swells were
left by the ice sheet. The bigness of the great open prairies slowly sinks
into your consciousness as hour after hour you look out upon grain
fields interrupted only at long intervals by a farm house, or a way station made conspicuous by tall grain elevators."[14] Three years later she
returned to North Dakota for further field study and wrote that after the
train left behind "the beautiful spruce and tamarack swamps of northern Minnesota, the sign *Manitoba Junction* stirred my blood. How good

it would have been to follow the straight northward pointing rails that seemed headed for the top of our world!"[15]

In 1914 the Baileys went west to coastal Oregon, and in 1917 they went to Glacier National Park. Vernon was to study and write about the mammals, and Florence the birds, to be published in a new government publication. For two months they roamed the glaciers and around the lakes of the park, spending one month of it on a pack trip to the Canadian borderlands of Alberta and British Columbia. The Baileys published the guidebook for park visitors *Wild Animals of Glacier National Park* in 1918.

In 1923, they were in the lower peninsula of Michigan to help the county agent with humane live traps. This was an ongoing major interest of Vernon's, as he realized the need for methods to live-trap animals so they could be moved to a habitat where they were less threatening to farmers and ranchers. He was very proud of his work in developing the VerBail Trap, a humane trap which did not harm the animal. Vernon invented a beaver trap for the biological survey, which became widely used in restocking operations, and also the so-called foot-hold trap. This consists of a "chain, released by a spring [that] catches and holds without breaking the leg of the animal caught in it."[16]

Florence's *Birds of New Mexico* was published in 1928. Most of the original plates were done by Major Allan Brooks, the bird artist and friend of Louis Agassiz Fuertes who had done many of the illustrations in Florence's earlier books. The American Ornithologists' Union presented Florence with its coveted William Brewster Memorial Award for her work on *Birds of New Mexico*. In 1933 the University of New Mexico presented her with an honourary LL.D. degree.

In 1933, Vernon retired from the U.S. Biological Survey after forty-six years of service. Florence and Vernon continued to make some cross-country trips, one with Florence's niece acting as chauffeur. In 1942 Hart died in California, and two months later Vernon passed away. Florence continued to live at her home in Washington, D.C., until her death in 1948.

Chapter Eight

Allan Cyril Brooks
(1869–1946)

"Competent, modest and proficient in all his endeavors, Allan Brooks succeeded in embodying and perpetuating the maxims of that wise and gifted protagonist of the truth and beauty of animal life, Joseph Wolf. The slogan of both was, 'We see distinctly only what we know thoroughly.'"

– Harry Harris in "An Appreciation of Allan Brooks, Zoological Artist: 1869-1946" in *The Condor*, Vol. 48, No. 4, July-August 1946

Allan Brooks was a born naturalist. He was studying birds as soon as he could walk. He spent his entire life observing nature, recording it in his memory, drawing it, and writing about it. He remained a freelance naturalist, turning down several offers of museum positions, including those of the Provincial Museum of British Columbia in Victoria in 1916, the Museum of Vertebrate Zoology in Berkeley, California, in 1920, the State of Georgia Museum in 1923, the American Museum of Natural History in 1923, and Cleveland Museum joint expedition in 1923.[1] He preferred to be free to take on commissions from museums and naturalist organizations, first in specimen collecting, and then in illustration and painting.

To satisfy these commissions, Brooks made many field trips throughout his life. His self-taught knowledge about all aspects of natural history, and his ability to accurately portray what he had seen, led to his becoming one of the foremost realistic bird painters of the early twentieth century.

Allan Brooks in the field with his binoculars in 1938.

Courtesy of the Art Gallery of
Ontario, Research Library & Archives.

Allan Brooks in his studio at Okanagan Landing, circa 1939.

Greater Vernon Museum & Archives Photo No. 18329.

Allan Brooks illustrated many ornithological works, including William Butts Merson's *The Passenger Pigeon*, William Leon Dawson's *The Birds of Washington* and *Birds of California*, Edward Howe Forbush's *Birds of Massachusetts*, John Charles Phillips's *Natural History of Ducks*, and Percy Algernon Taverner's *Birds of Western Canada* and *Birds of Canada*. Many of his bird illustrations were published in *The Auk, The Condor, The Wilson Bulletin,* and *National Geographic Magazine* over a period of fifty years. Many of his larger paintings were sold to museums and private collectors.

Brooks's illustrations also appeared on calendars, cards issued by the National Association of Audubon Societies, and "covers on Keystone school exercise books [that] all familiarized Canadian children and adults not only with North American birds and mammals, but also with the work of this eminent zoological illustrator."[2]

Allan Brooks was born in 1869 in northern India, where his father was working as a civil engineer with the East Indian Railways. His father was also an amateur ornithologist who collected in India for the British Museum in London. As soon as he could walk, Allan was allowed to handle skins from his father's collection. In 1873, Allan was sent home to Northumberland, England, where he was raised by aunts. He attended

Painting of a Yellow-rumped Warbler by Allan Brooks.

Courtesy of *50birds.com*.

Painting of Northern Shovelers by Allan Brooks.

Courtesy of *50birds.com*.

school for the next eight years and enjoyed walking around the moors, usually alone, exploring the nature there. He associated with naturalists and learned the art of egg-blowing, and gathered information about botany, especially the trees.[3]

In 1881, Allan's father returned to England and then decided to take up farming in Canada. When the family's ship arrived in Quebec, Allan's mother was in poor health, and she soon passed away. She was only forty-four. His father bought a 200-acre farm near Milton, Ontario.

There in Milton, Allan was able to correctly identify all the birds in the area after a period of five years, save for one misidentification of an immature Cape May Warbler.[4] Allan had access to his father's full kit of brushes and watercolours, and he painted birds day and night until every species in his collection was reproduced in colour.[5] In 1885, Allan visited Thomas McIlwraith in Hamilton, Ontario, where he learned how to prepare a well-made bird skin.

When Allan was eighteen, the family moved to British Columbia to farm at Chilliwack on the Lower Fraser River. In 1890 the Brooks's home

Painting of a Red-necked Grebe by Allan Brooks.

Courtesy of *50birds.com.*

and outbuildings, including a crude museum, were destroyed by fire. Allan succeeded in saving most of his bird skins, but ten years' worth of his notes and all his paintings were destroyed.[6] In 1891 his father sold this farm and moved back to Ontario.

Allan worked on the farm in Ontario for three years, studying birds on the side. Finally, he decided once and for all to give up farming and pursue his passion for natural history study. He moved back to British Columbia, this time to the Okanagan Valley, from where he made extensive trips into the mountainous area of southern British Columbia. In order to earn a living he trapped fur-bearing animals in the winter and collected and preserved rare bird eggs in the summer, selling them to museums and private collectors. The pay for collecting was poor, but Brooks loved the wilds so much he continued to do it.

Brooks began to send sketches to several of the customers who had purchased his skins or eggs. At this time he began to consider sketching as a secondary source of income. He received a letter from William Leon Dawson in 1904 concerning contributing notes for *The Birds of*

Washington. Brooks enclosed with his reply a black-and-white sketch of a Black-throated Gray Warbler, asking Dawson if he could use anything like that. Dawson wrote: "My blood leaped at sight of it, for I had not known that anything of that quality was being produced in the West. We arranged at once for forty black-and-whites, and later were able to stage the colour-plates, which have given Brooks a favorable introduction to the world of bird-lovers."[7]

In 1905 Brooks bought an acre of land at Okanagan Landing and built a cabin there, which was to serve thereafter as his home, study, and laboratory. In the following years, he made many field trips in Canada to the Gold Range, the Selkirks, and across the Rockies into Alberta. In 1911 and 1912, in connection with working on *Birds of California* with William Dawson, he travelled into various parts of California in order to familiarize himself with the California birds and their habitats. When he returned to the Okanagan, he completed his work for Dawson, and also did much work for the National Association of Audubon Societies.

Allan Brooks's first show was in 1911 at the International Sportsmen Exhibition in Vienna, Austria, where by the request of the provincial government of British Columbia he contributed nine pieces. With a hint at humour, William Dawson observed about one of Brooks's paintings at this exhibition: "By the conditions of the loan the sale of these paintings was not permitted; but one of the best of them, a magnificent Golden Eagle, was stolen — stolen, too, gossip has it, by one high in official position. (Poor fellow! One scarcely blames him. What else could he do if they wouldn't let him buy it?)"[8]

The accuracy, quality, and appeal of Allan Brooks's bird paintings are universally appreciated. The knowledge behind his paintings is immense. He had to rely on his expert memory for the exact information as to plumage colours and the form of birds in their natural setting, which he had observed in the field through binoculars. He could refer to the skins in his collection, but he had to provide light and shade, balance, texture, and perspective, as well as showing the bird natural in its true environment. A great compliment was paid to his art by another great artist, Louis Agassiz Fuertes, as recounted by Harry Harris:

There is recalled the first A.O.U. [American Ornithologists' Union] meeting held in Chicago where an extensive loan collection of bird pictures had been assembled for exhibition in the Field Museum. The writer had sneaked out of the formal meeting to examine the pictures unhindered by the crowd. Louis Fuertes was of the same mind and was found seated cross-legged on the floor in deep study before a Brooks picture that had been hung low down on a crowded screen. The friendly artist entered into an illuminating discussion of Brooks' work, which he greatly admired. He said he envied Allan's facility in handling accessories, and remarked that his compositions without the birds would still be good pictures.[9]

In 1920 Brooks attended his first annual meeting of the AOU held in Washington, D.C., and shortly afterwards he visited Louis Fuertes in Ithaca, New York. The two worked together in Fuertes's studio, and when several years later Fuertes was killed in an automobile accident, Brooks completed Fuertes's last project, the plates for *Birds of Massachusetts*.

Allan Brooks was an excellent rifle shooter, and in 1914 he trained with the First Canadian Expeditionary Force at Valcartier, Quebec, and then went overseas in October, not returning to Canada until April 1919. He had been rapidly promoted to the rank of major in the Canadian Expeditionary Force. His primary role in the First World War was as a sniper. He was mentioned in three dispatches (all signed by Winston Churchill), and won a Distinguished Service Order:

Capt. Allan Brooks, Nov. 30th, 1915. French.
Major Allan Brooks, Nov. 13th, 1916. Haig.
Major Allan Brooks, Mar. 16th, 1919. Haig.
The Citation: Deed of Action. Dated Feb. 1st, 1919.
Major A. Brooks
7th Canadian Infantry Battalion
Distinguished Service Order.

For conspicuous gallantry in the operations of 2nd and 3rd September in front of Arras. As brigade observing officer he showed great daring and initiative, pushing forward at all times with the most advanced troops under the heaviest fire. Taking a wire with him, he kept brigade headquarters well informed of the situation, and enabled the commander to make decisions that saved many lives. When the enemy were retiring he pushed forward over 500 yards in front of the infantry and telephoned back information from a long distance in front of our advance. During the two days he personally killed twenty of the enemy by sniping shots.[10]

During his time overseas, Brooks continued to observe and sketch wildlife from the trenches. For most of the time, he recorded in a diary and wrote about birds observed in France. In his diary, "One has to search for references to war and when they come it is obliquely as in noting the 'effect of shell fire on birds and mammals.'"[11]

In the 1920s, Brooks's paintings began to attract serious attention and he started receiving numerous orders for his work. In February 1926, he received an order for "illustrating 'Anderson's Arctic Coast Volume' – eleven birds, 12" X 9" in colour, at $40 each – to be delivered before March 31."[12]

In the spring of 1926, Allan married Marjorie, daughter of the late Mr. and Mrs. Richard Holmes of Arundel, England. They were blessed with one son, Allan Cecil Brooks. The family continued to travel widely, gathering material and information for Allan's bird studies and commissions.

Allan Brooks was always a perfect gentleman. Dawson writes about him: "Modesty is Brooks' most conspicuous trait.... Such a mental state is fortunately unconquerable. It simply refuses to believe half the good words said of it, and humbly tries to be worthy of the other half.... Brooks' modesty [comes] from a clear vision of high ideals, high ideals of art, of conduct, and of scientific attainment, before which those who are wise are always humble."[13]

An example of Brooks's modesty occurred on the night of the annual banquet of the American Ornithologists' Union in Ottawa in 1926.

Brooks was seated at the head of the table and was about to receive a gold medal award of merit for his bird paintings. He had just listened to a long introduction of himself by friend and poet Wallace Havelock Robb. "Brooks was never one for speeches and, upon introduction by Robb, he rose from his chair, took the medal from Robb's hand, stuffed it in his pocket, said 'Not Guilty!', and promptly sat down."[14]

Brooks was generous with his time and often instructed young naturalists when they came to visit him in his studio. He was in the habit of giving away his paintings as gifts to friends at Christmas, or as a token of appreciation.

To the children of Okanagan Landing, Allan Brooks was "The Bird-Man." Marguerite Hodgson wrote about the spontaneous visits she and her friends used to make to see Allan in his studio in the 1920s:

> Major Allan Brooks was a naturalist, outdoorsman, and artist. His military training was pronounced in his sturdy and upright figure. He was a handsome man with the ruddy complexion that the outdoors gives to fair people. A short trim moustache complimented his very English features. His blue eyes were warm and friendly and twinkled with the zest for living. We children would go in a group and knock on the door of the small house nestled among the trees a few hundred yards from the shores of Okanagan Lake. Allan Brooks would greet us with a warm friendly smile and invite us into his already crowded study. He never seemed to tire of our endless visits for he loved children and we sensed this. He would settle us down, handing out peppermints or other hard candy to munch on while he questioned us about the birds we had seen since our last visit.... Next he would ask what we remembered him telling us about the big birds mounted and standing on top of his cupboards — their names, habitats, and characteristics. Then he would have us, in turn, choose one of the many drawers in the cupboards. Each would pull out his drawer and try to name

the little birds lying in precise rows within its depths, racking his brains to remember other information that Major Brooks had given him on previous visits.[15]

Allan Brooks also wrote many scientific papers, the last of which was titled "The Under-Water Actions of Diving Ducks" in *The Auk*, October 1945. In this paper, he wrote about the observations he made, from a house on the east side of Vancouver Island, on the actions of various diving ducks when submerged. He found that most species hold their wings tight to the sides when diving, but there was an exception with White-winged Scoters and Surf Scoters. He wrote:

> Here the house in which I resided was built into the rocky shoreline in such a way that from the front windows numbers of ducks of 12 different species could be seen diving for food directly below and not more than 25 feet away for most of the species observed. Best of all, the bottom was mostly composed of broken clam shell, clear white under the crystal clear water. Never before had such an opportunity presented itself and I spent hours with a good binocular watching the unsuspecting ducks. Under such conditions, actions that had never before been clearly apparent were noted with absolute certainty. The most notable of these was the rigid extension of the alula[16] in certain species.... Of all the diving ducks the Surf Scoter has given me the best opportunities for observation; also it was the first to clearly display the extended alula. When first I saw the small, sharp-pointed wings held stiffly extended and pointing decidedly downward I thought I was looking at the entire wing and that the diminution was caused by refraction of the water. Eventually the actual condition became evident and the primaries could be plainly seen held tight to the body with the alula extended to its fullest, pointing outward and downward. It has a slight rowing movement at the commencement

of the dive, but not afterwards when the appearance is of small, sharp-pointed wings held rigidly extended and pointed slightly forward and downward while the bird explores the bottom. The winglets are still extended when the duck shoots to the surface at an angle of 45°.[17]

When Allan Brooks passed on in 1946, he left a great legacy to ornithology. His well-preserved bird skins, which had served as studio models, created a collection that had grown to over eight thousand items, representing every bird found in North America north of the Mexican border, with all major variations in plumage included. This collection was offered to the Royal British Columbia Museum in Victoria, which was unable to house it at that time, and it now resides at the Museum of Vertebrate Zoology at the University of California at Berkeley, California. Allan Brooks also left twenty-five volumes of detailed notes on birds, largely his observations in British Columbia; a bibliography of eighty-five publications; and a legacy of illustrations and paintings done in meticulous, awe-inspiring detail.

Chapter Nine

Cordelia Stanwood
(1865-1958)

"When the bird lover has once mastered the vocabulary of the feathered people he begins to be truly in touch with them.... Then as he steps into the woods, it seems as if an invisible curtain drops down behind him and he is in another sphere."

— Cordelia Stanwood in *Beyond the Spring: Cordelia Stanwood of Birdsacre* by Chandler S. Richmond, 1989.

Cordelia Stanwood did not become an ornithologist until she was in her early forties. However, during the last fifty years of her life, she was devoted to the study of birds, and became known as "Ellsworth's Famous Birdwoman." She was a perfectionist in everything she did, and this showed in her scientific writing and photographs of baby birds and nests.

The bane of Cordelia's life was never being able to make enough money to be financially secure. In working as a teacher from 1887 to 1904, the most she was able to earn was $750 a year (equivalent to about $16,500 in today's dollars). As a writer, she calculated that she earned from all her published writing over her lifetime only $1,500 (about $33,000 today). Cordelia supplemented this income by selling her bird photographs and handmade crafts. A proud and independent woman, she refused to accept any kind of charity. In spite of financial hardship, Cordelia Stanwood became a respected ornithologist through ingenuity and perseverance.

*Cordelia Stanwood at
the age of twenty-nine.*

Courtesy of the Stanwood
Homestead Museum and Stanwood
Wildlife Sanctuary.

Cordelia Stanwood was born in 1865 at the Stanwood homestead in Ellsworth, Maine. She was the eldest of five children. Cordelia was a rather frail child and she did not attend school regularly until after her eighth birthday.[1] In 1859, when she was fourteen, she went to live with her wealthy and childless aunt and uncle in Providence, Rhode Island. It was a great opportunity for the young Cordelia to acquire a higher level of education. She rapidly made up for her prior lack of schooling once she began to attend the schools in Providence. At the age of twenty-one, she graduated sixth in a class of sixty from the Girls' High School of Providence.[2] The following year she graduated from the Providence Training School for Teachers, and began to teach. From 1887-93, she taught the third to fifth grades in the Providence school system, becoming the principal of the Plain Street School in 1892.

In 1890, Cordelia went to a lecture given by Dr. Henry Turner Bailey, who was an artist, author, and teacher, and in the summers of 1891 and

1892 she attended summer school where she took art courses from Dr. Bailey. When he suggested to her that she should seriously consider becoming a full-time art teacher, she decided to give up her position at the Plain Street School. During 1893-94 she attended the Normal Arts School in Boston, where she completed the two-year course in one year. For the next ten years she had a succession of positions in various cities teaching art and supervising art classes. At that time, she was already interested in nature, and she often used plant specimens and flowers as drawing objects in her classes.

Although she was a very good teacher and enjoyed teaching the children as much as they enjoyed learning from her, during that time Cordelia became disillusioned and unhappy with her life. What she was doing was physically and emotionally draining. She was poorly paid and was working several evenings a week teaching drawing in order to supplement her income. She was living in a succession of boarding houses as she changed teaching positions. In 1904 Cordelia had a nervous breakdown.[3] She felt she needed a rest.

In November 1904, Cordelia returned to her parents' home in Ellsworth, Maine. Over the next two years she recovered by spending much time outdoors. At the age of thirty-nine, Cordelia began to become a serious ornithologist. She wrote:

> We bring back from the woods what we carry to it — give little and we get little in return.... The outer world does not exist to one who steeps himself in thoughts of self. Give undivided attention to that outer world and one's own affairs sink into insignificance.... Intimacy with nature is acquired slowly. It comes not with one year out of doors or with two. You look and listen, bewail your stupidity, feel that you have acquired little new information; yet, are determined never to despair or give up. All at once you know what you never dreamed you knew before.... In the beginning, the study of the feathered folk is a delightful torture. There are such a variety of calls and melodies and so many songsters to become familiar with that the novice

confounds the call notes and airs of one bird with those
of another. If he is content to know just the robin, blue-
bird, song sparrow and a few others by sight and song, he
gets a mild sort of pleasure from his intercourse with the
birds, but if he wishes really to lose himself in this world,
he must not only work, but work intelligently.[4]

Cordelia became strongly committed to the study of birds and began
to write field notebooks that became the sources of her many published
articles. Between 1905 and 1917 she added significantly to ornithological
knowledge. In the beginning, many of the birds she observed she found
at a place on the Stanwood homestead called the "Boiling Spring." This
spring is "always over-flowing; its cold water steams a glass on the hot-
test summer day and it has never been known to ice over in winter."[5]
Birds were drawn to the spring to drink and bathe. Cordelia herself always
drank the water from this spring, as opposed to that drawn from the well.
In summer and winter, and in all kinds of weather, this is where she came
for her drinking water.

Cordelia's specialty was studying the nests and young of the birds.
She provided detailed studies of nesting life. Within three years, from
1905 to 1908, "she had located the active nests of nearly a hundred species
of birds, and with infinite patience followed every aspect of their histories,
from construction and incubation, to the first timid attempts of the fledglings in flight."[6] During the nesting season, she built brush blinds close to
nests so that she might observe them.

Cordelia could write about how the singing of Hermit Thrushes had
inspired her, and yet she also could write scientifically, accurately, thoroughly, and precisely. She wrote the following sentiments upon listening
to the singing of Hermit Thrushes:

Stand in the dim aisles of the forest in the twilight when
the sun shows orange and crimson through dim vistas of
interlacing branches and listen to the Hermit Thrushes.
They perch at different heights on the side of the woods
illuminated by the setting sun, and vie with each other in

MORE THAN BIRDS

hymning the glories of the universe. Each peal of melody
is more indescribably perfect.... To know and love the
Hermit Thrush — the Voice of the Northern Woods — and
to receive his benediction in the twilight is one of the priv-
ileges Nature confers on those who worship at her shrine.[7]

Yet she also wrote up her scientific observations about the nests of the
Magnolia Warbler in *The Auk* in 1910:

All these nests were composed of similar materials — hay,
stems of cinquefoil, a plant fiber resembling hair, horse-
hair, plant down and spider's silk, yet each one had a
character of its own, due to the greater proportion of
one or other of the materials used in the nest, and the
way in which the nest was placed in the tree.... In three
nests there were four cream-white eggs in each, with the
pinkish tinge that nearly all freshly laid eggs have, spot-
ted in a ring around the larger end with reddish brown,
umber, and black. There were minute specks over the
entire egg. In the first nest, which was unique in many
respects, the eggs were marked with burnt umber all over
the larger end, as if a person had scrawled over them
with a Japanese brush.[8]

Beginning in 1910 and lasting until 1917, Cordelia published twenty
bird life histories in the periodicals *Journal of the Maine Ornithological Society,
The Auk, Bird-Lore, Nature Magazine,* and *Wilson Bulletin.* Photographs of
birds on the nest, illustrations of habitats and her blind, or parent birds
feeding the young were in some of these articles. The articles were introduced by a narrative, and included facts on the length of time to lay a
complete clutch of eggs, the duration of incubation, hatching, diet of the
young, and the time of fledging. Cordelia freely sent her notes on many
of the birds she had studied to Arthur Cleveland Bent for inclusion in his
extensive work on the *Life Histories of North American Birds,* which was published in a twenty-one volume series from 1919 to 1968. Bent's life histories

remained the primary source of life history information for ornithologists up to the recent publishing of the *Birds of North America: Life Histories for the 21st Century*, a ten-year project completed in 2002. Bent quotes Cordelia's notes in the life histories of the Hermit Thrush, Golden-crowned Kinglet, Dark-eyed Junco, and Red-breasted Nuthatch, among others.

Cordelia was probably the first woman bird photographer. Her specialty, again, was nests and fledglings. At first, she gathered the fledglings at the right time and carried them into downtown Ellsworth to the local photographer. Once they had had their pictures taken, Cordelia carefully and safely returned the little birds to their nest.

Over time Cordelia was dissatisfied with these photos and felt she could take better pictures from a blind in the field. She researched

Three young Red-eyed Vireos (Vireo olivaceus) and their nest. This is one of the photographs made for Cordelia Stanwood in the studio of Ellsworth photographer Embert C. Osgood before 1916.

Courtesy of the Stanwood Homestead Museum and Stanwood Wildlife Sanctuary.

Photograph of Black-capped Chickadee nestlings, taken by Cordelia Stanwood.

Courtesy of the Stanwood Homestead Museum and Stanwood Wildlife Sanctuary.

what would be necessary to do her own bird photography at the nest. In his book, *Bird Studies with a Camera*, Frank Chapman had listed the recommended equipment for taking certain kinds of photographs of birds. The smaller cameras using roll film that had recently popularized photography were not suitable for bird photography. Bird photography required a camera that would carry a 4x5 plate for portrayal of the bird, its nest, and eggs. The requisite 5x7 camera, made of wood and metal, along with a tripod and accessories, was very heavy to carry, but it was necessary in order to provide the good depth of field necessary to show the habitat in the background. Cordelia subsequently mastered her photographic apparatus and took it into the field, sometimes with the assistance of local children to help carry the heavy equipment. Cordelia's pictures were outstanding. However, to obtain them, she suffered through sitting in blinds for hours, being bitten by mosquitoes and black flies, and being bothered by ants. She was able to sell her amazing photographs to ornithological and popular magazines. She could also reuse her pictures, selling them again and again to different publishers and collectors.

Photograph of immature Yellow-bellied Flycatchers, taken by Cordelia Stanwood.

Courtesy of the Stanwood Homestead Museum and Stanwood Wildlife Sanctuary.

As a lover of birds and nature, Cordelia was well aware of the issues surrounding the use of feathers and whole birds on women's hats. She was committed to supporting a ban against the importation of wild birds and the trade in feathers and skins of wild birds. After a morning of shopping, she wrote:

> I hid under a big pine and listened to the Black-throated Green Warbler that sings and feeds among its branches.... I feel rested, soothed, delighted with the world and myself. To be sure, I did not put off that trip to the Milliners this morning but I have found my trip to the wood much more satisfactory. A hummingbird in the bush is much more to my taste than a dozen stuffed, wired hummingbirds, parrots or a multitude of wings made of feathers."[9]

Cordelia played an active role in supporting the ban, as was confirmed in an article in the local paper on October 8, 1913, that said "No one was more active in this section in bringing about the desired result than Miss C.J. Stanwood, the well-known ornithologist of this city."[10]

Cordelia also raised a variety of young birds in her home. One winter two children she knew had trapped an injured Great-horned Owl. Cordelia photographed it, and then she and the children fed and cared for it for nine days until it was healed and flew away.[11] She also raised what she thought was a pet Crow. He was actually a Raven, but Cordelia did not realize this as Ravens did not normally live in her area at that time. She found him in the summer of 1918 and took many photographs of him. She wrote in her notebooks about his clever and sometimes irritating behaviour, which included snatching clean clothes from the neighbours' clotheslines.[12] In May 1919, he disappeared, and Cordelia found his body days later in the barn. Someone had shot him.

Each of Cordelia's bird notebooks was carefully dated, and for many years the temperature, time and weather conditions were noted. In her early years of field study, she simultaneously kept several different notebooks, recording her nest encounters in one, and lists of birds seen and heard in another. Each year she kept a running tally of species seen and heard, and nest studies that she had conducted.[13] Around 1917 she ceased her careful bird studies. After that time, although she continued to go out into the field and write in her notebooks, she was more interested in gathering ideas for short stories and sketches that would be appropriate for popular audiences. However, she did gather census and breeding bird information that she sent to the Breeding Bird Biological Survey.

Cordelia kept field notebooks until 1953 when she was eighty-seven years old. The next-to-last entry of her field notebooks in May 1953, reads:

> I went through the kitchen. The door was open because I had been sitting on my camp stool in the sun in the shed this afternoon, picking over feathers for a pillow. As I returned from an errand in the other part of the house, I heard a peculiar loud buzzing. Lifting a curtain I saw a hummingbird trying to get out through a pane of glass. I got a chair and put it in place slowly, and so slowly, raised the curtain. I put my hand over the hummer and he offered

no resistance as I got down. One bright eye regarded me from behind my thumb. Holding my hand against my face I hastened to the japonica with its gorgeous blooms, opened my hand, kissed the exquisite creature on the top of its head and expected him to fly into the japonica. He had each little leg curled up in his soft, white feathers, but made no effort to stand up. Suddenly, the wings began to buzz. Then the dainty mite soared one hundred feet into the air and disappeared into space.[14]

Cordelia died of cancer in a state nursing home on November 20, 1958, at the age of ninety-three. Although some people had found her behaviour and lifestyle eccentric, she was not bothered by it. She felt she had lived a good life. In her unpublished autobiography, *Firs and Feathers*, she stated her philosophy: "One can never tell what delightful surprise is in store for him the moment he loses himself in the big out-of-doors.... Interest and attention are keys that unlock new worlds to us."[15]

Three years after her death, the following citation was sent to the Stanwood Wildlife Foundation[16]:

THE BUREAU OF
SPORT FISHERIES AND WILDLIFE
UNITED STATES
DEPARTMENT OF THE INTERIOR
WASHINGTON, D.C.
Gratefully acknowledges the faithful services of
MISS CORDELIA STANWOOD
in reporting, for use in scientific investigations,
observations on the distribution, migration, and
abundance of North American birds, for 32 years
during the period 1910 to 1946.

Shortly before her death Cordelia signed over her home, now called "Birdsacre," to the Stanwood Birding Club as a nature sanctuary. The members of the club subsequently rehabilitated the Stanwood homestead, making it into a museum. Today, the Stanwood Homestead Museum and the Stanwood Wildlife Sanctuary are open to visitors. The sanctuary is also a migratory bird rehabilitation center. The 130-acre sanctuary is dedicated to "preserving the home and vision of pioneer, ornithologist/photographer Cordelia J. Stanwood, as a living memorial to her achievements in ornithology and life."[17]

Chapter Ten

Jack Miner
(1865–1944)

"I feel that I have passed through the experimental stage and that my bird sanctuary is at last a success. Men who once chuckled with laughter at my foolish idea now grasp my hand and pour out congratulations."

— Jack Miner in *Jack Miner and the Birds*
(and Some Things I Know About Nature), 1925.

Jack Miner was an early pioneer in the science of wildlife conservation. He was neither educated nor initially inclined to be an advocate for wildlife, but through the years he witnessed a decline in the numbers of migrating birds, and he decided to do something about it. Miner turned from being a hunter in order to provide for his family into giving public lectures and influencing politicians and anyone who would listen about the need to protect wildlife. During the process, he came up with innovative ways of attracting wildlife to places where they could be protected, catching and banding birds so as to discover their patterns of migration, building suitable wildlife refuges, improving the landscape through the planting of trees for windbreaks, and including fauna to provide cover and feeding places. He based his conservation ideas on what he witnessed in his daily involvement with wildlife. He invented ways to accomplish his objective of reversing the decline in wildlife and doing something before it was too late to prevent what were formerly abundant species from existing only as museum specimens. His ideas were original and

*Photograph of Jack Miner
by Frank Scott Clark.*

From *Jack Miner and the Birds*, by Jack
Miner, 1923.

far ahead of his time. He was the true inventor of modern conservation practices. Jack Miner is popularly known in North America as the "Father of Conservation."

Jack Miner was born as John Thomas Miner on April 10, 1865, in Westlake, Ohio. He was the fifth of ten children and received no formal education, remaining illiterate until he was an adult. He said he was educated for "ditching, cutting cord-wood, and splitting nails."[1] The outdoors was his classroom and he spent most of his spare time in the woods, studying the habits of wildlife and becoming an excellent outdoorsman.

In 1878, when Jack was thirteen, he and his family moved to a free homestead near Kingsville, Ontario. There his family started a brick and tile manufacturing business from a clay bed on their land. Jack and his older brother Ted became professional trappers and market hunters in order to supplement the family income. Indeed, throughout his life Jack was never completely opposed to hunting, providing it was in moderation and in consideration of the preservation of wildlife.

In 1888 Jack married Laona Wigle and they had a son, Carl, born in 1891, and a daughter, Pearl, born in 1894. Two more sons, Manly and Ted, were born in 1897 and 1900 respectively. Sadly, Pearl died in 1897 at only three years of age. The following year, when Jack, his brother Ted, and another companion were hunting in Northern Quebec, Ted was killed instantly, shot by the accidental discharge of the companion's gun as he was dropping on one knee to dispatch a wounded and charging bull moose.[2] Jack was devastated by the deaths of his daughter and his beloved older brother. In a friend's words: "Until now he had held aloof from church and social life in the community.... Of an exceptionally emotional and sympathetic nature, his grief was overwhelming. Something had to move, or break. Gradually he ... became active in social and Sunday-school work."[3] Jack was to claim that he learned how to read by listening to Sunday school students' recitations from the Bible.

Jack's first experiments with conservation concerned the Northern Bobwhites living on his land. He noticed that they seemed to have a hard time surviving the winter. He erected brushwood shelters and provided grain for them.

> The feed racks did not seem to fill the bill in every way, so in a year or so I decided to try another scheme. I loaded up all the old junk lumber I could find and hauled it to the woods, and in one day another man and I completed ten little bungalows-in-the-rough. They are about one foot high in the rear, and four to five feet high in the front, with from five to six feet ground space.... Then, to complete my experiment, I begged ten bags of weed seed from a neighbor who was hulling clover. I threw a bagful in each house, and then threw in, on top of the weed seed, corn, wheat and buckwheat. In less than a week the birds visited every house, and on a cold, zero day I believe I have seen as high as fifty quail buzz out

of one of these little, unpatented shacks. And best of all, they scratched right down through the grain and ate the weed seeds first. I soon found I had made a hit, as the shacks furnished the birds shelter as well as food in the time of need, and a certain amount of protection from their enemies.[4]

Miner also pioneered the supplying of bird houses to encourage smaller birds to nest. He had noticed a marked decrease in Eastern Bluebirds and decided to try to entice them to nest on his property. Initially he built nests out of wood, and then experimented with six or eight different varieties made out of drain-tile. The birds preferred to build their nests in the "permanent" tile houses, and Jack refined the design, incorporating a removable top that could be left off all winter. The wet and frost would then rid the bird houses of mites and other insects. Jack wrote:

We usually toe-nail their houses on top of the fence posts around our premises. I have never tagged the bluebirds, therefore I have no positive proof of the same one returns year after year, yet I am like the Scotchman who said he was open to conviction but he would like to see the man who could convince him otherwise, for we have several old birds any one of which will permit us to … remove the roof from her house, and when we peep in she will sit there on her eggs, within eight inches of our eyebrows, and, turning her head sidewise she will cover our whole face with her one little eye as much as to say "Beg your pardon, sir, but you should have rapped before you opened the door." If a stranger is permitted to do this, she will fly out, every time, though after I have taken the top off she will permit him to look in and will not fly out.[5]

It was in 1902 and 1903 that Jack Miner conceived the idea of establishing a bird sanctuary on his property, the first of its kind in Canada, if not in North America. Not until 1904 was work on the sanctuary actually started, with excavations made for ponds. Several wing-clipped live decoy Canada Geese were placed on the ponds, and corn was spread around the banks. This was the origination of the waterfowl refuge management system. After four years of waiting, the first eleven migrating Canada Geese landed on the pond. In subsequent years, larger and larger numbers of geese were attracted to the safe haven of Miner's ponds, which also attracted migrating ducks.

Miner was anxious to study and find out where these feathered creatures spent each season of the year, and on August 5, 1909, he "caught a duck and wrapped around its leg a piece of aluminum, on which was stamped his post office address. This was the first time Jack Miner had done such a thing and, incidentally, this record is probably the first of the kind on the continent. Thus not only is Jack Miner's Sanctuary the first of its kind in North America, but he is the pioneer in tagging ducks."[6] Several months later, on January 14, 1910, the duck that bore the first tag was killed in South Carolina. The discovery of where the bird had migrated to caused great excitement and Jack determined to invent a contrivance for catching the ducks in numbers. He accomplished his goal after many months of work. Over succeeding years, by recording the recovery locations of the returned bands, he was able to plot the flights of these migratory birds.

By 1914 hundreds of Canada Geese were coming to Jack Miner's sanctuary for food and protection, and Jack's next ambition was to start catching and tagging them, as he had done with the ducks. However, catching Canada Geese, one of the largest of migratory waterfowl, for tagging was a different proposition than catching ducks. The geese would not go near the network he had devised for ducks.[7] After studying the situation for a year, he came up with a method of having two ponds with a canal connecting them, covered with network, and with a trapdoor at both ends. A smaller catching-pen, only twelve feet square, was at one end, into which a group of geese would be herded, after which a trapdoor was closed to keep them in. In 1915 Jack caught his first wild Canada Goose and placed an aluminum tag on its leg, with the post office address of the sanctuary. In order to increase interest in his tagging system and ensure that more of the tags would be returned to him, he began adding a short verse from the Bible on one side of each tag.

Early in October 1915, Miner received a letter from the Hudson's Bay Company at Moose Factory dated August 19, 1915. The letter contained his first returned tag from a Canada Goose. The goose had been killed by a Native in the Hudson Bay District.

During the ensuing years, a vast store of information about the migrations of Canada Geese and ducks was built up through the returned tags. Hudson's Bay Company agents, missionaries, and agents of the Revillon Fur Company cooperated in collecting these tags from the Natives and Inuits, and returned them to Miner. In 1931 Manly Miner, Jack's son, wrote:

> On one occasion the Reverend W. G. Walton, an Anglican missionary, who had spent between twenty and thirty years among the Indians and Eskimos and had never been out to civilization, came by canoe from Hudson Bay to Cochrane. From there he took the train to Kingsville and the Sanctuary. He brought a pocketful of tags with him, each of which bore a passage of scripture and Jack Miner's post office address. He had collected these from the Indians and Eskimos all the way from the factory at James Bay, along the east coast of Hudson Bay and as far north as Baffin Land. The natives had brought them to him for interpretation of the verse of scripture.[8]

In this way, a lot of valuable information was gathered as to where these birds nest and why they choose these areas. The tags revealed that most of the Canada Geese nest around the shores and islands of eastern Hudson Bay and on Baffin Island, instead of along more inland rivers and streams. The Natives revealed the reasons why. "The geese arrive in that vicinity around the latter part of April and the first part of May. The rivers and all fresh water are all frozen over at that season of the year, but the Hudson Bay is opened up by the incoming ocean current and the geese prefer to nest where there is open water."[9]

MAPS SHOWING THE MIGRATION OF CANADA GEESE

The dots on the maps below show the places from which tags have been returned to Jack Miner, and hence give exceedingly good evidence of the direction taken by the wild geese which have alighted on the Miner estate at Kingsville, Ontario, on their way north and south.

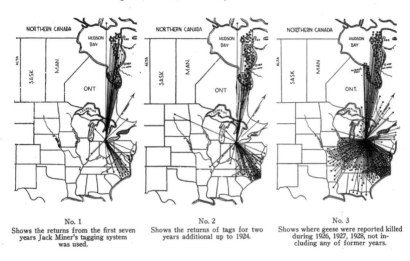

No. 1
Shows the returns from the first seven years Jack Miner's tagging system was used.

No. 2
Shows the returns of tags for two years additional up to 1924.

No. 3
Shows where geese were reported killed during 1926, 1927, 1928, not including any of former years.

Maps showing the places from which Jack Miner's tags were returned.

From *Jack Miner and the Birds,* by Jack Miner, 1923.

Miner's tagging system showed where the geese spent their winters, and also showed that very few geese that visited the sanctuary in the fall visited the following spring. Practically all geese bearing fall tags were killed in the middle states, along the east of the Mississippi River and towards the Gulf of Mexico, while geese that were tagged in the spring wintered along the Atlantic coast, mostly around Currituck Sound, North Carolina. The geese that spent the winter along the Atlantic seaboard nested in the extreme northerly portion of Hudson Bay and Baffin Island. When the fall came, instead of migrating inland, they followed the ocean around by way of Labrador, Newfoundland, and the New England coast, southward to Currituck Sound. In March and early April they left North Carolina, but the Labrador coast and their summer quarters were still frozen over. The geese therefore migrated north from the southern states to the Great Lakes region, where they congregated at the sanctuary during those months.

Over years of studying them, Miner came to greatly respect the Canada Goose and its habits. He wrote:

Canada Geese "with the little ones between."

From *Jack Miner and the Birds,* by Jack Miner, 1923.

Wild geese pair off for life. I never knew them to even make an application for divorce. The male guards his mate on the nest. As soon as the young hatch, he protects them from the side opposite the mother, keeping the babies between the parents. He will leave his family for her and for her only, but he will die in the front ranks for any of them.... I have placed their bushels of corn around one of my mating pairs, and of the thousands of hungry geese that come here, none will interfere with these little plots to take even one kernel.... When travelling in the air, the male Canada Goose leads the way, breaking the air for his sweetheart, who is quartering behind him, and his family travels next to her. In brief, he is one of the most self-sacrificing, godly-principled leaders the human eye ever beheld, and to know him is to love and admire him.[10]

The birds in Jack Miner's sanctuary kept returning to the Sanctuary, year after year, as long as they were able. They knew they could find protection there. They came to know the individual human occupants of the Sanctuary, just as Jack came to know them as individuals. He often found they would come right up to the house when they were injured. He grew to love them and wrote: "Do you wonder at me loving them? Can you blame me for feeding them beyond my means, when this is only a faint, roughly-written picture of their trust and confidence in me? The real home of love is the heart, but the brain is apparently given the power to educate the heart to either love or hate. But any man who does not love those who first love him ... has neither heart nor brains."[11]

Miner became concerned about the future of the native swans, the Trumpeter Swan, and the Tundra Swan, formerly known as the Whistling Swan. During 1923 he made several trips to Niagara Falls to study the wild swans there. On their northward migration, the swans were making their first stopping place at Lake Erie, at a location fifteen miles above the Falls.

> There they would drop down into open water, tuck their heads under their wings, and go to sleep, resting from their long flight. Many, doing so, would be trapped by the swift current of the river, and be carried over the Falls. Some which survived even that experience would succeed in getting out upon the ice-bridge below the Falls, only to become coated over with ice from the freezing spray of the Falls and freeze to death.[12]

Miner consulted with William Hill, known as "The Riverman," and concluded that if the swans were fed and protected near Kingsville, nearly two hundred miles away, they would learn to stay there and not go to their deaths in the Niagara rapids. Miner proceeded to secure several pairs of injured Tundra Swans to serve as decoys at the lakeshore near Kingsville. In the spring of 1924 the first group of swans arrived at the lake near Kingsville. Miner asked James Harkin, Canada's first commissioner of national parks, for help and "in a few hours two mounted policemen arrived and patrolled the shore, forbidding anyone to throw stones at the swans or in any way frighten them."[13] In time thousands of these swans were spending a month to six weeks along the lakeshore at Kingsville, thereby avoiding the deathtrap above the Falls. The government detailed Royal Canadian Mounted Police to protect them day and night.

Jack Miner was also innovative in using flora to protect wildlife. Around his ponds he planted rows of evergreen trees as a windbreak. At the age of forty-five he started planting more trees on his property, until he was planting a thousand a year. He advocated the planting of trees and flora around country homes, saying "in less than ten years you can surround your little country home with a melody of songs of thrushes, cat birds, robins, goldfinches, native song sparrows, and warblers.... It is in reach of every country home financially. I am absolutely certain that the 15 or 20,000 seedling trees and wild shrubs I have planted in the last twenty years have not cost $500 and I doubt very much if they have cost me $300."[14]

Miner held strong opinions, formed by his personal observations, on certain matters. He believed that protection included the eradication of some species that sometimes prey on other birds. He also believed that the Passenger Pigeon was finally exterminated by a contagious disease. To prevent this happening to his flocks of birds, he arranged his ponds on what he called the bathtub system. During the late summer months he let all the water out, and the ponds were allowed to dry up. Then he sowed wheat and rye very thickly in the bottom to purify the soil. He explained: "The overflow pipe is then closed, and when the fall rains come and raise the spring, the [below ground] drain, which is laid from the pond to the spring, floods it over, and preserves the green food in the bottom of the pond for the birds when they arrive, as this green food in the bottom of the pond will not rot but will keep fresh so long as the water remains icy cold."[15]

Jack Miner's conservation activities became widely publicized. Partly to help finance the growing costs of feed for his sanctuary, in 1910 he began lecturing to groups, speaking about wildlife conservation and the need for the establishment of sanctuaries and wildlife refuges. He explained his banding, research, and habitat preservation methods. He encouraged junior bird clubs, advocated to children to build bird houses, and expressed his concern about the declining ecological condition of the Great Lakes. Prominent businessmen and politicians were influenced by his ideas.

In 1913 William Edwin Saunders convinced Jack to visit Point Pelee. After spending a day there and taking in its vast variety of trees and shrubs, Jack was convinced of the need to preserve the place. He proceeded to muster support from prominent local men, as well as two Essex County wildlife protection associations, to support making Point Pelee a national park. Because of his prestige, Jack was chosen to make a personal representation to the Prime Minister of Canada, Sir Robert Borden.[16] This local support, backed by the evidence presented by Percy Taverner and the Great Lakes Ornithological Club, convinced the federal government to create Point Pelee National Park in 1918.

Early data from tagging recoveries instigated by Miner were instrumental in passing the Migratory Bird Treaty between the United States and Canada. This act placed the first restrictions on hunting, giving consideration to future populations of waterfowl. Miner felt that the Migratory Bird Treaty was unfinished and did not go far enough in stopping excessive hunting. In particular, he advocated a shorter open hunting season.

Jack Miner was the true pioneer and leader of the migratory wildlife conservation movement. In 1929 he was awarded the Outdoor Life Gold Medal, "for the greatest achievement in wildlife conservation on the continent." In 1936 he was chosen by Prime Minister Mackenzie King to deliver the around-the-world radio address for King George's twenty-fifth anniversary as monarch. Jack received letters from sixty-five countries following his address. In 1943 he was presented with the Order of the British Empire by King George VI "for the greatest achievement in conservation in the British Empire."

Jack Miner passed away on November 3, 1944. He had banded over fifty thousand wild ducks and forty thousand migratory Canada Geese. Several newspapers in the United States said he was the fifth best-known man in North America, after Henry Ford, Thomas Edison, Charles Lindbergh, and Eddie Rickenbacker. Following his death, the Canadian government desired to create a perpetual memorial to honour him for his pioneering work in wildlife conservation. This had to be postponed until the conclusion of the Second World War. In April 1947, a bill proposing the National Wildlife Week Act was introduced in the House of Commons. By the act, Canada's National Wildlife Week would be observed annually during the week of April 10, Jack Miner's birth date. The bill was passed without any dissenting votes, the first time since Canada's confederation that a bill was passed unaminously.

Jack Miner's life is an incredible success story, displaying what one man is capable of accomplishing when he sees the need for something to be done, and he decides to do something about it.

PART FOUR

Ornithology *as a Science and the Need for Protection*

Chapter Eleven

James Henry Fleming
(1872–1940)

"He was an ornithological historian and what he knew about collectors, collections, expeditions, ornithologists and their work was tremendous. He knew the peculiarity of a collector's 'make' of skin, his labels, handwriting, where and when he had collected, and particularly, what had become of his collection. He could tell many interesting anecdotes concerning the history of individual specimens or of whole collections."

— Lester L. Snyder in *The Auk,* 1941.

James Henry Fleming is acknowledged as the "Dean of Canadian Ornithology."[1] The study of birds was his full-time occupation during his entire lifetime. He acted as a one-man museum and collector of information about birds. With contacts everywhere, little went on in ornithology or adjoining fields that he did not know about and make note of.

Fleming was an ornithological adviser, and at the same time desired to avoid controversy over differing opinions. He was most thoughtful towards others, always answering his large correspondence, acknowledging and reading papers received, and commenting favourably on a piece of work well done. He would often include a relevant news clipping or cartoon along with a brief but appropriate witty comment.

He was not a "private" collector in the true sense of the word. The immense store of material and knowledge he amassed over his lifetime was always intended for the public good, so that Canada might be equipped

James Henry Fleming.

From *The Auk*, 1941.

with the working tools of his profession. His collection and library were open to any qualified inquirer. His advice was always freely given and his work, collections, library, and miscellaneous objects relating to birds were from the beginning intended to be left in a public institution. At the end of his life they were all given without any restricting conditions to the Royal Ontario Museum of Zoology in Toronto.

James Henry Fleming was born in 1872 in Toronto, where his father, a prominent Scottish immigrant, ran a seed growing business on a three-acre plot now marked by Yonge and Elm Streets. He attended public and model schools and Upper Canada College in Toronto. Fleming's interest in study-ing birds seems to have been a spontaneous and self-cultivated one, arising as a hobby when a boy and developing uninterruptedly as his life's work with-out any particular guiding influence from others. It is certain that his interest in birds had become fixed by the age of twelve, as in 1884 he collected and prepared the nest and eggs of the Vesper Sparrow. This specimen is still in his collection. Although other boys of his age also collected specimens, their interest was only a phase and their specimens were soon forgotten and left to decay, while Fleming continued to save and add to his collection.

The idea of building a study collection occurred to Fleming in 1886, at the age of fourteen.[2] From the first, his collection was not merely a local one. His bird skins numbers one and two are specimens of the King-of-the-Paradise-Birds, from New Guinea. It is recorded in Fleming's register that six hummingbirds were purchased in 1884 or 1885 at a bankruptcy sale of millinery stock. He paid ten cents each, the money having been saved out of his school lunch allowance.[3]

Fleming attended the School of Mines in London, England, in 1890 to 1891, and over the next few years he travelled extensively in Europe and also went to British Guiana and the West Indies. On those trips he became more familiar with living birds, and gathered impressions of the regions from which his specimens came or were to come. He also acquired a wide range of ornithological and natural history contacts, with whom he later regularly corresponded. He returned to Europe again in 1895 to visit the British Museum of Natural History and the collection of Walter Rothschild.

In 1897 Fleming married and established a residence in Toronto. His first wife died in 1903 and in 1908 he remarried. His home at 267 Rusholme Road became a familiar destination to ornithologists. Here, Fleming built up his massive library and created his one-man museum, which by 1925 occupied a three-room annex built onto the back of the main house.

Although not an extremely wealthy man, Fleming was able to have enough resources to pursue his ornithological interests without needing to work for someone else by carefully managing the real estate profits from his father's land when Toronto grew. For a time, he supported the operations of a local taxidermy business, mainly for the purpose of having the facilities for the preparation of cabinet specimens. But the taxidermy shop was also a way to keep in touch with events happening in natural history. Sportsmen who came into the shop provided him with information on the annual abundance of animals, on unusual flights of birds, and on the occurrence of rarities. The Yonge Street shop became a kind of ornithological clearing-house where the local naturalists gathered. Among them was Fleming's life-long friend, Percy Taverner, who distinguished himself as a leading ornithologist and who credits the taxidermy establishment with being a "school" where the foundations of scientific ornithology were taught. Taverner stated that "matters of heaven and earth were discussed there, but largely ornithological."[4]

Something of the perseverance, thoroughness, and effectiveness with which Fleming pursued his bird studies is illustrated in the following:

> The only Toronto record of the Curlew Sandpiper was based on a specimen shot about 1886. This bird, a mount, was displayed in a case in a local gun club. Fleming knew it well. Each of two hunters claimed to have shot it. This led to a rather heated dispute between them which one day culminated in a scuffle during which the case was broken into. The bird disappeared. One of the contestants had rather ruthlessly extracted it and when the smoke cleared, part of one leg was discovered attached to the artificial rock-work of the case and the head was found on the floor. The head was taken to the local taxidermist who had mounted the bird. Fleming, who had learned the details of the bird's dismemberment, eventually acquired the head for preservation about 1894. In 1911 Fleming recognized the body of the Curlew Sandpiper in a case of mounted waders in the possession of a man who had obtained it from the shooter who had escaped with it from the gun club. In the meantime the body had acquired a new head and a new leg, apparently from a Red-backed Sandpiper. All trace of this case of birds was lost until 1932, when it was discovered in a local schoolroom. The specimen (mostly Curlew Sandpiper) was still in it. Through proper channels it was removed and transferred to the Fleming collection. Thus were the body and head of the only Ontario specimen of the Curlew Sandpiper reunited after more than forty years, in that haven of rarities, the Fleming collection.[5]

In March 1889, at age sixteen, Fleming had become an associate member of the scientific association, the Royal Canadian Institute, and in

1893 he was elected an associate of the American Ornithologists' Union (AOU). Although there is no record concerning when he first attended an annual meeting of the AOU, from 1906 to 1938 he was absent on only four occasions. He was elected a member of the AOU in 1901, a fellow in 1916, served on council from 1923 to 1926, was vice-president from 1926 to 1932, and was president from 1932 to 1935.[6] Few individuals have served the American Ornithologists' Union so conscientiously. Fleming was also a well-known figure in international ornithological circles. He attended the first International Ornithological Congress in 1905 in London, and subsequently served on its committees and attended their meetings as the official representative of Canada at Copenhagen in 1926, Amsterdam in 1930, Oxford in 1934, and Rouen in 1938.

Fleming was one of the six members of the Great Lakes Ornithological Club, whose beginnings were in about 1900 when a small group of ornithologists living in the region of the Great Lakes became aware of a need for closer cooperation, especially concerning the question of migration routes. Initially they corresponded on key issues through the use of a manuscript bulletin system, whereby a member with an idea relating to birds wrote it out on a sheet of paper and posted it to the club secretary in an especially printed envelope marked "Printer's Mss."[7] The note was circulated to all the club members in rotation with each adding his comments on a separate sheet of paper. The bulletin was then returned to the secretary who recorded any new information. The club soon felt the need to meet, preferably at a place where migration could be studied, and Point Pelee was suggested as the best place.

Point Pelee is the southernmost point of the mainland of Canada and projects some nine miles into the western end of Lake Erie. It is a favourite first landing place for many migrating birds flying across Lake Erie. The Great Lakes Ornithological Club first met at Point Pelee in 1905, and a permanent camp was established in 1908 and occupied at intervals to the end of 1927. During the period of the club's activity, a better understanding of the migration routes and the periodicity of numbers and species was acquired.[8] A detailed journal documenting the numbers of different species of birds observed at Point Pelee was regularly kept. The frequent visits to Point Pelee by the members of the Great Lakes Ornithological

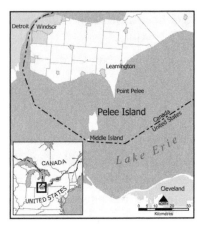

Map of Point Pelee, showing the tip into Lake Erie.

Created by Norman Einstein, 2005.

Club resulted in the publication of "The Birds of Point Pelee," a five-part series in *The Auk* in 1907 and 1908 by Percy Algernon Taverner and Bradshaw Hall Swales, which documented the occurrence of 209 species there. The evidence acquired by the Great Lakes Ornithological Club was influential in convincing the federal government to create Point Pelee National Park in 1918.

Fleming was acknowledged locally and internationally in ornithological circles for his knowledge of systematic ornithology. From 1890 to 1940 he published over ninety papers and notes in ornithological journals and conference proceedings. He was actively involved in local, regional, national, and international ornithological issues.[9]

Fleming's position as an outstanding ornithologist was recognized in many ways. He was elected British Empire Member of the British Ornithological Union, corresponding member of the Zoological Society of London, and member d'honneur étranger Société Ornithologique et Mammalogique de France. The National Museum of Canada made him honourary curator of ornithology in 1913, and in 1927 he was made honourary curator, Division of Birds of the Royal Ontario Museum of Zoology. He also held several honourary member positions in leading Toronto natural history and ornithological groups.

Fleming was active in the study of ornithology right up to the time of his passing. Lester L. Snyder wrote: "On his desk at the moment I am writing ... there is a slip of paper on which is written in pencil: 'June 3, 1940. Connecticut Warbler in greenhouse.' Except for reading letters from his friends which he regretfully could not answer, this memo marked the close of his work with birds and students of birds."[10] James Henry Fleming passed away at his home in Toronto on June 27, 1940.

Fleming always intended to leave his vast storehouse of information on birds to the furthering of Canadian public and ornithological knowledge. He had acquired the world's largest and most comprehensive private ornithological collection.[11] He bequeathed this heritage to the Royal Ontario Museum of Zoology in Toronto. His collection consists of 32,267 bird specimens, containing representatives of nearly all living bird families and more than 6,300 species. It is particularly rich in rare, vanishing, or extinct species, historical specimens, and the more showy types. Fleming also donated his outstanding library of ornithology and zoological travel and research to the Royal Ontario Museum.

Fleming "held a particular niche in Canadian ornithology and, directly or indirectly, was a powerful influence in its development. He was the first Canadian to raise the study from local to a broader interest and to fit Canadian ornithology into the world map."[12]

Chapter Twelve

Percy Algernon Taverner
(1875-1947)

*"He could improvise and make do with the very minimum of
material and tools.... He could make anything! And his work-
bench was a favorite spot.... Metal seemed his strong point and
whenever Percy disappeared in a strange town, he could usually
be found at the nearest tinsmith's. In art work he was at home
with camera, pencil, brush, or clay."*

— Hoyes Lloyd, who was with Taverner in western field
work in 1920 and 1921, writing of Taverner's
mechanical and artistic abilities.

Percy Algernon Taverner performed to the highest possible degree in his
role as Canada's first professional ornithologist. He built up the natural
history collection at the Museum of Geological Survey of Canada, which
later became the National Museum of Canada, then the National Museum
of Natural Sciences, and is now the Canadian Museum of Nature. He
accomplished this through both his own field trips and by organizing one
or more ornithological parties nearly every summer for the investigation of
the avifauna of Canada. Taverner was particularly interested in the migration of birds, and he set up a system of large maps, one for each Canadian
species, showing the times and types of occurrences in Canada for each species. This was linked to a species file, with every reference to a bird on a card.

Taverner produced the comprehensive books *Birds of Eastern Canada*,
Birds of Western Canada, and *Birds of Canada*. These books contributed

greatly to the distribution of knowledge about birds, and served to popularize ornithology in Canada. Taverner also had a major hand in furthering the conservation of birds. He was instrumental in getting Point Pelee established as a national park, as well as Bird Rocks in the Gulf of St. Lawrence, and Percé Rock and Bonaventure Island off the Gaspé Peninsula in Quebec, declared as bird sanctuaries.

Taverner was uniquely prepared to fill such an important role in the development of Canadian ornithology. He was a man of wide talents, skilled at writing, drawing, photography, film-making, carpentry, metal work, wood carving, book binding, gardening, and taxidermy.

Percy Taverner was born in Guelph, Ontario, in 1875. He had an unsettled childhood. His parents' marriage dissolved when he was very young and his mother joined a theatrical company in Toronto, where she met and married another actor, Albert Tavernier, who informally adopted Percy. From 1882 on, his parents owned and operated a theater company and were on the road for much of the year. As a result, Percy temporarily resided and went to schools in Halifax, Nova Scotia; Brooklyn and Highland Falls, New York; and Port Huron and Ann Arbor, Michigan. At times he travelled with the theatrical company, and at others he boarded in various homes. However, almost every summer during his school years was spent at Lake Muskoka, Ontario, where his parents had an island home. His sister writes about Percy and these summers at Lake Muskoka:

> Our summers were very long there in those days for we made a bee-line for the only home we had as soon as the season closed in spring and stayed until it was time to start rehearsals in the fall.... It always seemed to me he could do or make anything. His hands were skilled in every craft — metal work, carpentry, book binding, photography, and a hundred other arts. He was wonderfully adept at small boat handling, could literally sail anything. When in his early teens, he converted a little row-boat of his into a sail-boat, decked it over, put in a center board, called it "The Coffin," and went out in it in any gale.[1]

Percy seems to have been a born naturalist. His earliest definite memories are of a kindergarten at Highland Falls, New York, where he remembered the first flowers of a trailing arbutus in the spring, watching Baltimore Orioles and their nest in a tree in the front yard, and seeing in St. Nicholas Magazine a picture of a Scarlet Tanager.[2] In Ann Arbor, Michigan, he met the taxidermist of the University Museum on the street. The taxidermist proceeded to invite him into his shop where, happy to learn taxidermy and study birds, Percy became a regular visitor and an unpaid assistant. On weekends and holidays he went on bird trips with associates he had met at the shop. Later, on the encouragement of friends, Percy went to Toronto and met James Henry Fleming, whom Taverner described as "the outstanding Canadian ornithologist ... and the only one having more than a parochial view, and in contact with broader fields."[3]

In order to earn a living, Taverner took a correspondence course in architecture and worked in an architectural office. He joined his mother and sister first in Chicago, and then in Detroit. About these years, his sister wrote:

> His room in Detroit was lined with bird cases which he made himself. He had quite a large collection.... Mother and I went on many woods expeditions with him in the outskirts of Chicago and Detroit [where] he brought in everything — lizards, salamanders, snakes, toads, frogs, tadpoles, water beetles, fairy shrimps, etc.... In Detroit we had a tame Wood Duck ... and became familiar with its pretty, conversational, Br-r-r-e-e-e-e-e. Also we had a pet female sparrow hawk [American Kestrel] for several years. Percy bought it from some boys for 10 cents; they had cut its wings. She was very tame, liked to be with us, sitting on a shoulder and running her bill around the convolutions of an ear, snuggling right up to the side of the head.... Falco's wing feathers finally grew but it took several years for her to become fully winged because as the primaries grew out, she ... used to bite them off.... Mr. Fleming

The Great Lakes Ornithological Club. Percy A. Taverner is sitting in front, with L–R: J.S. Wallace, B.H. Swales, W.E. Saunders, and J.H. Fleming.

Canadian Museum of Nature, Neg. No. 60386.

visited us in Chicago in 1902 ... and often ... in Detroit where we were from 1905 to 1911.[4]

It was in Detroit, while working as an architectural draftsman, that Taverner became friends with Bradshaw Hall Swales and the two spent holidays and evenings observing, collecting, and studying birds of the southeastern part of Michigan. Percy and Swales, along with another naturalist, Alfred Brooker Klugh, visited William Edwin Saunders in March 1905. They were greatly impressed by Saunders's description of the spectacular flora and fauna of Point Pelee. Shortly afterwards, the group of naturalists from the Great Lakes area, consisting of Saunders, Klugh,

Fleming, Swales, Taverner, and James Stirton Wallace, formed the Great Lakes Ornithological Club. The group spent much of their free time at Point Pelee in the years 1905 to 1907, intensively studying the ornithology of the area. They continued to meet regularly up to 1927.

Taverner remained in Detroit until 1911. At that time, the post of ornithologist for the Museum of the Geological Survey of Canada was established. Among the other duties of the position, the applicant would need to be able to design and construct natural history exhibits. Taverner's application was supported by strong letters of recommendation from James Henry Fleming, William Edwin Saunders, and Ernest Thompson Seton. With his considerable experience as a draftsman, in taxidermy, and in photography, all of which were considered valuable qualifications in arranging museum exhibits, he won the position and began work in May 1911.

Taverner proceeded to organize ornithological expeditions to investigate the avifauna of Canada. He carried out many field parties himself, as well as employing others to undertake collecting trips for the museum. From 1916 to 1920, after the burning of the parliament buildings, the museum was taken over for use by the Dominion Parliament. However, funds for field work for the geological survey were still available, and Taverner continued organizing the ornithological expeditions. The trips in which he personally took part were to:

> 1913 — Point Pelee, Ontario
> 1914 — Chaleur Bay and Miscou Island, New Brunswick; and Bonaventure Island, Percé Rock, and the Magdalen Islands, Quebec
> 1915 — Percé Rock and Point Pelee
> 1917 — Shoal Lake, Manitoba; Red Deer and Jasper Park, Alberta; and parts of British Columbia
> 1918 and 1919 — Ontario
> 1920 — Alberta and Saskatchewan
> 1921 — Manitoba, Saskatchewan, and British Columbia
> 1922 — British Columbia
> 1924 — Saguenay County, Quebec
> 1925 — Alberta and British Columbia

1926 – Alberta
1928 – Anticosti Island and Canadian Labrador
1929 – Eastern Arctic islands and Greenland on the *Beothic*,
a Dominion patrol boat
1930 – Churchill, Manitoba; and Chesterfield, Keewatin
1936 and 1937 – various localities in western Manitoba[5]

Under Taverner's care, the bird collection at the National Museum grew from less than five thousand to more than thirty thousand specimens. He also organized a system for keeping track of birds seen. It included a species file, with every reference to a bird in Canada on a card, under a species heading. All these records were entered on large maps, one for each species. Different symbols indicated type of occurrence, as summer, winter, breeding, migrant, etc. Each symbol had a key number, and the reference was again entered on a facing page. This gave a summary of species distribution and time of occurrence in Canada. There was also an index to literature, and an author file.[6] The system involved an extraordinary amount of detailed work. It was especially demanding given that Taverner was working for the most part alone, doing most of his own typing, filing, mapping, and even the printing of cards and labels by hand press.

One of the greatest contributions made by Taverner was the extent to which he made the general public aware of the science of ornithology. He made motion picture films of the bird cliffs at Percé Rock and Bonaventure Island in 1913 and 1914, showing the nesting of the Northern Gannet and other sea birds. He also made a film of the wild geese at the Jack Miner Bird Sanctuary. Taverner very successfully made sure that all the findings of the ornithological research expeditions were widely publicized. In 1919, he published *Birds of Eastern Canada*. In the introduction to his first book, he wrote:

> [It] has been written to awaken and, where it already exists, to stimulate an interest both aesthetic and practical, in the study of Canadian birds and to suggest the sentimental, scientific, and economic value of that study; to assist in the identification of native species; and to

furnish the economist with a ready means of determining bird friend from bird foe that he may act intelligently
towards them and to the best interest of himself and
country at large; to present in a readily accessible form
reliable data upon which measures of protective legisla-
tion may be based.[7]

This first book was produced in a French edition, *Les Oiseaux de l'Est du Canada*, in 1922. His second book, *Birds of Western Canada*, was issued in 1926, and the volume *Birds of Canada* was published in 1934. *Birds of Canada* remained the standard work on Canadian birds until the publication of Earl Godfrey's *The Birds of Canada* in 1966. Taverner's books were easy to read and written in a pleasant style, while at the same time providing comprehensive, detailed descriptions of the bird species found in Canada, with abundant information about field marks, nesting, distribution summaries, and sometimes natural history comments or notes on the economic value of the birds. They were highly illustrated, with black-and-white drawings by Taverner, as well as colour plates, mostly done by Allan Brooks. They all had subsequent editions. Two pocket field guides, *Canadian Land Birds* and *Canadian Water Birds*, were also published.

The extent to which Taverner's books on the birds of Canada helped to educate the public about birds, and develop in them an ability to recognize birds, a wish to learn more about them, and thereby indirectly a concern to protect them, is so great that it is beyond measure. It was said that Taverner's three books about birds could be found at the most remote Hudson's Bay Company and Royal Canadian Mounted Police posts, and even in the hands of trappers throughout the vast Canadian wilderness. In the settled districts, they were used as texts in the schools, were handbooks for all bird lovers, and were the accepted works of reference in their field. The plates of the coloured illustrations were lent for people to use in illustrating magazine articles and pamphlets, thus further extending the influence of Taverner's work.[8]

Taverner also made a great impact on Canadian ornithology through his contributions to the conservation of wildlife and its habitat. He was very concerned about conservation and was an instrumental voice in the

*Percy A. Taverner (left)
with Allan C. Brooks.*

Canadian Museum of Nature, Neg.
No. 56275.

creation of bird sanctuaries in Canada. His papers on the birds of Point Pelee, Ontario, were a major influence in the establishment of a national park at Point Pelee.

Prior to this time, the great bird nurseries in eastern Canada were being destroyed. Bird Rocks in the Gulf of St. Lawrence had formerly been the nesting site of as many as one hundred thousand breeding pairs of Northern Gannets, the largest Northern Gannet colony in the world. By 1916, only about 450 pairs remained due to the unbridled clubbing to death of gannets.[9] Also at the time, there was unjustified discrimination against some sea birds. The federal government fisheries department was demanding that the Percé Rock cormorant colony be exterminated, as it was a threat to fish stocks. Taverner and Gordon C. Hewitt, who was the dominion entomologist in the Department of Agriculture and a strong proponent for conservation, advised the Minister of Marine and Fisheries to rescind the order.[10] The minister granted a stay of execution, which allowed Taverner time for a field trip to Percé Rock to evaluate the alleged threat. He found no sign of seabird depredations on the local fishery, but did find ample evidence that local fishermen were wantonly destroying eggs and slaughtering young and adult seabirds in great numbers.

Horrified by what he had seen, Taverner made a report to the federal Commission for Conservation, calling for Percé Rock, Bonaventure Island, and Bird Rocks to be made bird sanctuaries.[11] He supported his recommendations by publishing a study of the stomach contents of the Double-crested Cormorants nesting on Percé.[12] He also made a study of the Northern Gannets nesting on Bonaventure, which contained a strong plea that the island be preserved permanently as a national resource.[13] Taverner succeeded in his cause, and in 1919 all these sites were designated as bird sanctuaries.

Taverner published nearly three hundred articles and books until his retirement in 1942. The ornithological topics he wrote about include distribution in Canada, systematics, taxonomy, nomenclature, vernacular names, migration, banding, conservation, economic aspects, effects of pesticides on birds, behaviour, and numerous book reviews.[14] He was a member and active participant in the affairs of the major North American ornithological societies. In 1926, he accepted the responsibility of hosting the first Canadian meeting of the American Ornithologists' Union in Ottawa. There his book *Birds of Western Canada*, which had just been published, was distributed free to attendees.[15] In addition to his official functions, he encouraged naturalists and ornithologists in the pursuit of their interests, giving many of them sound advice suited to their individual circumstances.

Aside from his ornithological passion, Taverner was "very fond of music and enjoyed the musical evenings at his house.... He liked the old-time songs and his memory of them was truly astounding. He knew the words of all of them.... Rock gardening, photography, and book-binding were his principal hobbies ... for years he made his own Christmas cards, some being drawings carrying an original idea and others photographs, usually of birds."[16]

In summary, Percy Algernon Taverner was the foremost Canadian ornithologist of the first half of the twentieth century. He greatly advanced the science and conservation of birds in Canada, as well as developed the public's appreciation for birds.

Chapter Thirteen

Margaret Morse Nice
(1883-1974)

"The study of nature is a limitless field, the most fascinating adventure in the world. I feel that the study of ornithology is a wonderful game in which strong sympathy and fellowship reign between the serious participants: we are friends and glad to help one another. We have high standards for our science and we want beginners to realize this. We must SEE CLEARLY, RECORD FULLY AND ACCURATELY, and TRY TO UNDERSTAND.... We who love nature, who see and try to understand and interpret, are following the true goal. We have a talisman[1] against the futility of the life of most people. We should try to open the eyes of the unseeing to the beauty and wonder of nature."

— Letter from Margaret Morse Nice to the Margaret Nice Ornithological Club of Toronto, January 30, 1952.

During her very productive lifetime, Margaret Morse Nice rose to the top of her chosen profession of ornithology. She was instrumental in changing the focus of much of the study of nature to one of careful observation and recording of even the smallest details, and attempting to understand the behaviours of other species. Ethology is the branch of zoology that studies the behaviour of animals with emphasis on the behavioural patterns that occur in their natural habitats. Although many naturalists studied aspects of animal behaviour throughout history, the modern discipline of ethology is considered to have begun with the work during the 1930s of the Dutch biologist Nikolaas Tinbergen and the Austrian biologist Konrad Lorenz, who jointly won the 1973 Nobel Prize in medicine.

Konrad Lorenz wrote the forward to Margaret More Nice's posthumously published autobiography and states this about her:

> When I first met Margaret Morse Nice in 1934 at the International Ornithological Congress held in Oxford, I was at once impressed by her deep understanding of ethology, its methods and its approach. Her particular gifts and her attitudes towards nature predestined her to be an ethologist. We happened to sit side by side in a charabanc driving the members of the Congress from Oxford to Tenby in Pembrokeshire; we fell to talking and we have been close friends ever since. At that time, she had already begun her field studies on the Song Sparrow, which occupied her for many years and which turned out to be a major break-through in the methods of studying animal behaviour. Her paper on the Song Sparrow was, to the best of my knowledge, the first long-term field investigation of the individual life of any free-living wild animal. She has been followed by many studies of animal behaviour since and all these "longitudinal" studies of wild animals have proved extremely fruitful.[2]

Margaret Morse was born in Amherst, Massachusetts, in 1883. At an early age, she was interested in exploring nature and the local birds. She said that the most cherished Christmas present she received was the book *Bird-Craft* by Mabel Osgood Wright when she was twelve years old.[3] This book had coloured bird pictures with simple descriptions of the birds and their habits, and Margaret had it memorized.

In September 1901, she entered Mount Holyoke College. The courses she took there in modern languages (French, German and Italian) and in zoology were to prove useful in her later ornithological research. Margaret

The cover of Michael Elsohn Ross's book, Bird Watching with Margaret Morse Nice.

Published by CarolRhoda Books, 1997.

was an avid horseback rider and liked to go off riding or walking in the surrounding area, either alone or with a girlfriend. She was irritated by the rule that girls should not go walking in the woods and fields alone without a man. She suggested to her parents that she buy a revolver to protect herself, and although the suggestion originally met with strong disapproval, she eventually did purchase a rifle (as well as a revolver) in her junior year. The revolver proved to be a comfort to her during her solitary explorations of the Holyoke Range on horseback and on foot. She also carried it many years later on her eight-mile bird censuses in Oklahoma.[4]

After graduating from Mount Holyoke College with a bachelor of arts degree, Margaret returned home and was at odds with what to do with her life. She thought of teaching nature study somewhere, but no opportunities presented themselves. That year the Massachusetts Agricultural College in Amherst started a summer school and she attended. It was here that a visitor who gave two lectures opened her eyes to a whole new direction in life. Dr. Clifton F. Hodge of Clark University in Worcester, Massachusetts, gave a lecture about studying living animals, using the toad as a chief example, including how much and what they ate, and how their activities affected man. Margaret thought that if she could study such things at a university, this would give her life a useful purpose and meaning. Dr. Hodge encouraged her when she asked him about pursuing this possibility, and he volunteered a problem he already had that she could work on — studying the food of farm-raised Bobwhite Quails.

Margaret enthusiastically entered Clark University in 1906 and found her calling. The professors and fellow students showed her there were many unknown problems in nature that needed to be studied and understood. Clark University was devoted entirely to graduate work, with sixteen faculty members and sixty-four students at that time. Margaret was one of the two girl students in the biology department. In her studies on the food of the Bobwhite, Margaret collected many species of weed seeds and insects, and tried to find out how many of these various things the captive Bobwhites would eat in a day. She writes that "one tame hen ate 700 insects, 300 of which were small grasshoppers; another day 1,350 flies (caught in a flytrap), and — proudest day of all — 1,532 insects, 1,000 of them tiny grasshoppers."[5]

In 1909 Margaret married Leonard Blaine Nice, also a graduate student at Clark University. She published a paper on "Food of the Bobwhite" in June 1910 in the *Journal of Economic Entomology*. The article showed that she was already organizing her data into a readable, usable format. It also revealed her patience and ability to concentrate during very long periods while continually observing and recording data — even the minutest details of behaviour.

Margaret purchased three hundred reprints of "The Food of the Bobwhite" for $8.00 and sent them to friends, relatives, and state and government game departments.[6] She was determined that the results of what she had observed would be put to good use. Her feeding tests on the great numbers of insects and weed seeds eaten by Bobwhites were quoted as reasons why the Bobwhite should not be hunted, and cats should be restrained. Margaret was gratified to see that the Bobwhite was put on the songbird list in Ohio in 1912. Gunners were unable to get it removed from this list until 1959 when quail shooting was again legalized, but only on less than 1 percent of the area of the state.

From 1913 to 1927, Margaret and Blaine settled in the prairie town of Norman, Oklahoma, where Blaine was a professor of physiology and pharmacology at the University of Oklahoma. Margaret began a lifetime of observations and studies, and published the results of those studies. She published in learned ornithological journals and societies, including *The Auk, Condor, Bird-Lore, Wilson Bulletin, Bird-Banding, Journal für Ornithologie, Transactions of the Linnaean Society of New York, Oologist, Proceedings of the Oklahoma Academy of Science, Publications of the University of Oklahoma Biological Survey, University of Oklahoma Bulletin, American Midland Naturalist,* and the American Ornithological Union's *Fifty Years Progress of American Ornithology 1883–1933.* Her published books are *The Birds of Oklahoma,* co-authored with her husband, *The Watcher at the Nest,* and *Research Is a Passion With Me,* which is her posthumously published autobiography.

The diligence and thoroughness of Nice's many published observations and results is inferred from her comments about watching a nest of Black-throated Blue Warblers in 1930: "For a week I watched the nest from three to nine and a half hours a day, seeing the male bring 201 meals and his mate 193. I recorded 1,285 songs from him; these were of four different types. It was a triumph on my last day of watching to witness the exit from the nest of the baby birds."[7] Nice allocated a similar devotion of her time and attention to each of her many ornithological studies.

In 1927, Blaine joined the faculty of Ohio State University and the Nice family moved to Columbus, Ohio. There were by then five children in the family: Constance, born in 1910; Marjorie, born in 1912; Barbara, born in 1915; Eleanor, born in 1918; and Janet, born in 1923.[8] Margaret wrote: "Our home at 156 West Patterson Avenue stood a quarter of a mile east of the Olentangy, a half-mile south of the bridge at Dodridge Street and a half-mile north of the bridge at Lane Avenue. I called this wild, neglected piece of flood plain 'Interpont,' that is, 'Between the Bridges.'"[9] It was there that Margaret conducted her famous studies on the Song Sparrow that catapulted her to the attention of the international ornithological world.

On March 26, 1928, Margaret banded her first Song Sparrow, which she later named Uno. This bird, along with another, named 4M, were to become famous. In Interpont she conducted detailed field work over a period of eight years on the life history of the Song Sparrow. By trapping and banding all the adults and nestlings over a relatively large area she was able to follow each one's activities. She began to build a huge compilation of data about their lives, in the process making several original discoveries about this common bird. For instance, she learned that male Song Sparrows begin singing in mid-February and that each male has a repertoire of from six to twenty-four individual songs, which, with a very few exceptions, are possessed by him alone. She wondered as to the origin of their songs. Were the song patterns innate or learned from parents? She discovered that "No son had any song of his father."[10] She later found that Song Sparrows learn their songs in late summer or perhaps early fall, after they have left the territory where they were born. In late winter they experiment with a great variety of phrases, and by early spring develop their own personal repertoire of favored songs.

Margaret also made other discoveries, including finding evidence from banding records that some individuals of the *euphonia*[11] subspecies are resident in regions where most of their kind are migratory, and that some individuals migrate in some years but not in other years.

Margaret banded the Song Sparrow she named 4M in his second year of life and he returned to raise new families each spring for eight years, reaching nine-and-a-half years, a very old age for a Song Sparrow. 4M sang more than any bird she observed. On May 11, 1935, Margaret arose at dawn to record the total number of songs 4M could give in a day. At that time over eight years old, 4M produced an incredible 2,305 songs.[12]

In 1937 Margaret left Ohio and moved to Chicago, where Blaine was head of the physiological and pharmaceutical departments at the Chicago Medical School. She wrote about her feelings on leaving Interpont: "I owe a great deal to Interpont and the opportunity at our doorstep to study such a notable species as the Song Sparrow. Indeed, with its rich variety of individual songs it seems to me the most admirable bird imaginable for an intensive study, for each male is a unique personality. When he dies these songs are lost forever. This is the sorrowful aspect of a study such as mine."[13]

In the years 1937 to 1974, living in Chicago, Margaret's life changed. Between 1920 and 1936 she had spent much of her time out in the field, observing and recording data. Living in the heart of a major city this was not as practical, and after 1936 she spent more time at her desk writing. She completed major works on the population and behaviour studies of the Song Sparrow and other passerines. In 1937, *Studies in the Life History of the Song Sparrow I: A Population Study of the Song Sparrow* was published, followed in 1943 by *Studies in the Life History of the Song Sparrow II.*

At that time, Margaret spoke out concerning some of her ideas on conservation. She advocated that weeds, shrubs, and vines should be left alongside roads and fences to provide adequate bird habitat. In 1944 she pleaded against the use of lead shot in waterfowl hunting. In both correspondence and in print, she condemned the unrestricted use of pesticides, the killing of albatrosses on Midway Island, and the misuse of wildlife refuges.

In the summers of 1951 through 1954, Albert Hochbaum, the scientific director of the Delta Waterfowl Research Station in Manitoba, invited Margaret and her eldest daughter Constance to come to the station as visiting investigators. The Delta Marsh is located at the south end of Lake Manitoba and is a wildlife breeding and migration staging area of major importance. Waterfowl and songbirds are especially abundant in the marsh, either as breeding residents or seasonal migrants. There Margaret and Constance watched many birds, from hatching on, in order to study the stages of behavioural development in precocial[14] birds compared to altricial[15] species. The scientific part of their studies was published in 1962 as "Development of Behaviour in Precocial Birds."

Margaret Morse Nice received many honours during her lifetime.[16] She became a fellow of the American Ornithologists' Union (AOU) in 1937, and later, became a life fellow. In 1942 she received the AOU's prestigious William Brewster Memorial Award for her studies of the Song Sparrow. She served on its committee on research from 1942 until 1953. Margaret became a member of the Wilson Ornithological Club (later Society) in 1921, was a council member from 1929 to 1931, a second vice-president from 1934 to 1936, first vice-president in 1937, and president in 1938 to 1939, thereby becoming the first and only woman to serve as president of any major North American ornithological society. She was an associate editor of *The Wilson Bulletin* from 1939 to 1949.

Margaret joined the Cooper Ornithological Club in 1921, becoming a life member in 1950. In 1922 she and fifty-one other bird banders organized the Inland Bird-Banding Association (IBBA), and between 1935 and 1942, and again from 1946 until her death, she was an associate editor of *IBBA News*. She was president of the Chicago Ornithological Society from 1940 to 1942. She was elected to honourary memberships in the British Ornithological Union, in the Finnish, German, Dutch, and Swiss ornithological societies, and was a corresponding member of the Hungarian Institute for Ornithology. She was an honourary member of seven ornithological or conservation societies, and sponsor of the Hawk Mountain Association and Conservationists United for Long Island. The Margaret Nice Ornithological Club of Toronto was organized in January 1952 and named in her honour. During her fiftieth reunion at Mount Holyoke, her alma mater, she received an honourary doctorate of science and in 1962 she received another from Elmira College.

Chapter Fourteen

Joseph Dewey Soper
(1893-1982)

"Yes indeed, it has been a great experience, especially during the migration, with thousands upon thousands of these birds and others swarming over the snow-free patches of tundra on their way to higher latitudes."

> — Letter from Dewey Soper to
> Percy A. Taverner, July 18, 1929.

When the University of Alberta conferred an honourary doctor of laws degree on Dewey Soper in 1960, Dr. Ralph Nursall concluded the presentation with the words: "Dewey Soper is a man of action and acuity, in a particular sense *l'homme engagé*, second to none as a pioneer of the North whose courage, industry, and initiative inspire us to find our country and extend all its benefits into our lives."[1] Dewey's son, Roland Soper, wrote that these words were a fitting tribute to his father, a man who spent nearly eight years in the early part of his career in Arctic exploration and spent a lifetime in the study of its natural history and the pursuit of scientific knowledge.

The principal enduring theme throughout Dewey Soper's life was the exploration and description of natural history. He recorded his discoveries in prolific writings, some of which were purely scientific and factual, and some of which were in a more narrative vein in that he wrote about what it was like to experience the challenges and wonders of living in the Arctic. His adventures in the Far North were never far from

Dewey Soper in his
northern field clothes.

University of Alberta Archives D. Soper
Collection, No. 79-21-34-175.

his thoughts. In his later years, he wrote more about his Arctic travels and painted two hundred watercolours depicting the northern scenes, which he fondly remembered. Dewey Soper was also a great scientist and zoologist, publishing many articles and reports on the birds and mammals in various regions of Canada. He was of a generation that did not expect life to be easy and full of the conveniences afforded by modern technology. While efficiently and effectively carrying out his assigned duties, he maintained his inner passion for the work he was doing in the wilderness areas.

Dewey was a very observant, intelligent, and empathetic man who could appreciate the struggles of the Natives, mammals, and birds he encountered in his explorations. He was an explorer of nature and her ways throughout his life. His son wrote about him:

> In the years that followed his official retirement, he con-
> tinued to do field work, usually alone and in remote
> wilderness camps.... He enjoyed sketching and waterco-
> lour painting, and much of his art was used to illustrate
> his writing in later life.... He was a robust man and
> appeared that way even in later life.... One quality that set

him apart from so many of his peers was that he retained
his boyish enthusiasm for the natural world to the end
of his life. He only hung up his boots and binoculars for
good when failing health forced him into hospital.[2]

Joseph Dewey Soper was born on a farm near Guelph, Ontario, in
1893. His family moved to agricultural land near Rockwood, Ontario, in
1906. On the farm Dewey pursued his innate interests in wildlife and
natural history. With money earned from trapping, he purchased bird
books and binoculars. In 1908, at age fifteen, he began his first rudimen-
tary, illustrated, naturalist notebook,[3] of the kind that he would write
throughout his scientific career. In 1911 Dewey moved with his family
to Strathcona, which later became a district of Edmonton. By then he
had determined to pursue a career which concerned nature. Working as
a journeyman carpenter in order to pay for his education, he attended
Alberta College and the University of Alberta, majoring in zoology.

In 1920 William Edwin Saunders invited him to a naturalists' meeting at Point Pelee, to investigate spring bird migration. There, Dewey met
Percy Taverner and Rudolph Martin Anderson, the great Arctic explorer
and naturalist. Dewey had always had a desire to visit the Far North, having read about northern explorers. Among the books that had excited
him were John Richardson's *Arctic Search Expedition*, Fridtjof Nansen's *In
Northern Mists*, and Vilhjalmur Stefannsson's *Hunters of the Great North*. In
Dewey's own book, *Canadian Arctic Recollections*, he wrote: "I seem to have
been born with this longing for boreal latitudes."[4]

Meeting Rudolph Martin Anderson in person and listening to stories
about his experiences in the Arctic ignited Dewey's desire to see the north
firsthand even more. Dr. Anderson was then head of the Natural History
Division of the Victoria Memorial Museum (now the Canadian Museum
of Nature). In 1923 Anderson offered Soper a summer assignment to
travel on the government's annual patrol boat to the Arctic, with instructions to gather specimens of birds and plants for the museum's collection.
At thirty years of age, Soper began the first of his three expeditions and
eight years in the Far North. He went on explorations in the Arctic in
1923, from 1924 to 1926, and from 1928 to 1931.

In July 1923 Soper left from Quebec City on the government patrol boat, the *Arctic*. They sailed up the west coast of Greenland to Melville Bay and north to within eleven degrees of the North Pole. Impeded by ice, the ship turned south towards Cape Sabine, entered Lancaster Sound, and stopped briefly at Cornwallis Island and then Beechley. In Beechley Soper saw the Arctic's best known landmark, the graves from the Franklin expedition of 1845. At Pond Inlet and other stops along the way, Soper collected specimens for the museum and made his initial observations of Inuit life. Finally, before returning home, the ship visited Pangnirtung in Cumberland Sound.[5]

One of Soper's objectives on this first voyage was to try to discover the nesting grounds of the Blue Goose. (The Blue Goose has since been determined to be the dark morph form of the Snow Goose species.) Soper wrote: "I resolved then to devote myself to the discovery of the Blue Goose nesting grounds insofar as I was empowered to do so. During the course of that voyage of some 7,000 miles information was sought everywhere as to the possible occurrence and movements of the Blue Goose, and Lesser Snow Goose, which habitually associate during migration."[6]

In 1924 the National Museum again retained Soper, this time for a two-year expedition to Baffin Island. Soper's main camp was at Pangnirtung, Cumberland Sound, where he stayed at a Royal Canadian Mounted Police base that also served as a centre of operations for the Hudson's Bay Company. Soper described the Arctic upon his arrival at the height of the brief Arctic summer in July 1924 as: "a veritable Paradise of warm sunny days, blue skies, and sparkling waters, which attracted wild fowl in multitudes.... Against the background of austere terrain ... one may ... watch the careless flight of bumble bees and butterflies and gaze on gaudy beds of small exquisite Arctic flowers that exist only in polar lands."[7]

With his warm and friendly manner, Soper befriended the Inuit at Pangnirtung and began to learn their ways, language, and skills. He met Akatuga, a clever and experienced hunter, whom Soper described as "the finest and most reliable of all the men I had ever known in the North."[8] Akatuga's wife, Unga, prepared an entire winter wardrobe for Soper, consisting of "outer and inner *kuletaks* (parkas), trousers, knee-high boots, and double mittens, long caribou socks, duffels, caribou skin ground robes and more."[9] Soper wrote about the Inuit dwellings which were made in the same way as they had been for thousands of years. The Inuit built sealskin *tupiks*, or tents. The use of duck canvas for tents was still relatively unknown. Other dwellings, which were always temporary, used materials that were at hand. The igloo was the structure that "best demonstrated the Inuit's brilliant survival skills. Large or small, the igloo's geodesic dome was simply the most appropriate shelter especially during the treacherous polar winter. It could be built in less than an hour by someone well-trained and experienced in the art. Inside, a seal oil fire could quickly provide warmth to a person clothed properly in caribou robes."[10]

Soper had to wait until after Christmas or the New Year for the snow to be sufficiently deep to build igloos. Only then could he begin the extended journeys by sledge, pulled by dog-teams, into the unknown interior of Baffin Island. During the 1924 to 1926 period, Soper covered many thousands of miles by dogsled, boat, and canoe. He mapped territory unknown to the white man, and brought out "4,600 scientific specimens, including mammals, birds, insects, fishes, plants, and ethnological material."[11] Soper had intentionally selected southern Baffin Island as the place for his field work, largely because its interior was unknown. While his primary objective was biological, he also was prepared to travel widely and make simple surveys. For several months of each year, his work was principally of geographical interest.[12]

In August 1984, an archaeological survey party discovered an Arctic stone record cairn or Inuksuit that had been erected by Soper in the winter of 1926. They described the cairn and its contents as follows:

> The cairn is approximately 1 m high and built on a small promontory at an elevation of about 15 m above lake level.... The record, which was folded and placed into a small metal container (Sterno can), was not found in the cairn but 10 m to the southwest, against a narrow rock ledge. The container is covered with surface rust but fortunately was well sealed, leaving the contents dry and in excellent condition. Many cairns and Inuksuit were located in our survey of Mirage Bay; however, the

proximity of the record to this particular feature, suggests that it is the one built by Soper and his Inuit companions in 1926.[13]

The text of the note is reproduced as follows:

Record deposited by J. Dewey Soper, Naturalist, of the Geological Survey of Canada, February 6th, 1926. Left Pangnirtung Fiord, Cumberland Gulf, with four natives, Akatuga, Newkequak, Pasjoon and Koonaloosee on January 9th to make a traverse to Fox Channel via Nettilling Lake. The two latter natives were engaged as extras to freight dog-feed to the east side of Nettilling Lake, from which point they were sent back on the morning of January 28. I successfully reached Fox Channel at a point approx. magnetic north from the exit of the Koukdjuak in the forenoon of February 2nd. The coast here is many miles farther east than is shown on the latest maps. Leaving Fox Channel the following day I adopted a course southeast, then east, true, until Nettilling Lake was reached, after which its west coast was followed and mapped to this point. Today I start back for Pangnirtung, following and mapping the north coast of Nettilling Lake enroute. Dogfeed low and no game. All well.

J. Dewey Soper
Northern extremity of Nettilling Lake,
Baffin Land
February 6, 1926.[14]

This note was deposited on the return leg of a 1,050-kilometer sled journey from Pangnirtung across Baffin Island to Foxe Basin, undertaken to determine the longitude of the Baffin coast there, which Soper felt had erroneously been mapped at about 75°W. The investigation supported his hypothesis. By completing the crossing, Soper became only the second white man to successfully traverse Baffin Island from east to west, being preceded in this achievement by the German scientist, Bernard Hantzsch, who perished from fever and starvation on the island's west coast in 1911 before he could make the return trip.[15]

The hardships that were involved in that journey, as well as Soper's own courage and resolve, are reflected in his writings: "I still feel extraordinary admiration for the splendid efforts of Akatuga and Newkequak who endured so much fatigue and suffering without a murmur, and what seemed the incredible hardship for the dogs. It is impossible to forget the frightful cold of 70° below zero as we forged our way over the frozen Lake Nettilling and across the Great Plain of the Koukdjuak to Foxe Basin and back to the east coast."[16]

Although Soper was a sturdy and experienced outdoorsman, and he was accompanied on his journeys by the best Inuit men, he wrote that the Arctic was rarely a hospitable place except during its brief summers. He found Stefansson's book *The Friendly Arctic* totally unrealistic, and wrote: "There is altogether too much hardship, suffering, slow starvation and death most of the year to believe that such a 'friendly' land could exist in the high latitudes. Lesser or greater misadventures will continue to threaten man at times as long as these 'lands forlorn remain.'"[17]

Just before Soper's return to Ottawa in August 1926, an old Inuit hunter from the Tikoot Islands, off the southern coast of Baffin Island, told him that the Blue Goose could be found in Bowman Bay, northeast of Foxe Peninsula. This information was independently confirmed later when Soper returned to the North in 1928. This time, while based at Cape Dorset, Soper met two Gordon Bay Inuit who, some years before, had hunted caribou over the great tundras of northern Foxe Land and along the west coast of Baffin Island to within about one degree of the Arctic Circle. These men had a local reputation among their own people for having stumbled upon the breeding grounds of the Blue Goose. They were thoroughly questioned, and encouraged to impart all the information they possessed respecting the Blue Goose on its summer range.

The earnestness and candor of their account and the perfect agreement of their separate statements were entirely convincing. There appeared but one possible conclusion — that the chief breeding grounds of the Blue Goose had been definitely indicated at last, after nearly three years of close search and about 4,000 miles of personal travel by dog team and small boat in and about Baffin Island. Routes were discussed with the Gordon Bay Inuits for reaching the grounds and even a rough map was prepared indicating the area in which the species was reputed to nest.[18]

After Soper had returned from the North in 1926, he visited his sister in Wetaskiwin, Alberta, where he met and married Carolyn ("Carrie") Freeman, a graduate nurse. From June to November 1927, he continued to work for the National Museum, conducting a survey of the mammals along the International Boundary in Canada. Because the National Museum was unable to provide him with permanent employment, Soper accepted an offer for a third Arctic expedition, this time under the direction of the Northwest Territories and Yukon branch of the Department of the Interior. He spent the winter of 1928 to 1929 travelling over and mapping Foxe Land and the west coast of Baffin Island north to 67°40', near the point where the ornithologist Hantzsch had perished.

On May 17, 1929, Soper left Cape Dorset for the Blue Goose grounds with four sleds, forty-two dogs, and five Inuit drivers, carrying sufficient food and equipment to cover a period of three months in the interior.

After eight days of unremitting and hard travel we reached the proposed site of our summer camp on the banks of a tundra river near Foxe basin in latitude 65°35' North. This was named Camp Kungovik after the Eskimo name for the Blue Goose. Now that we were located well within the designated breeding area of the Blue Goose, we had but to be patient, make ourselves as comfortable as possible, await the retreat of winter and the arrival of the birds.[19]

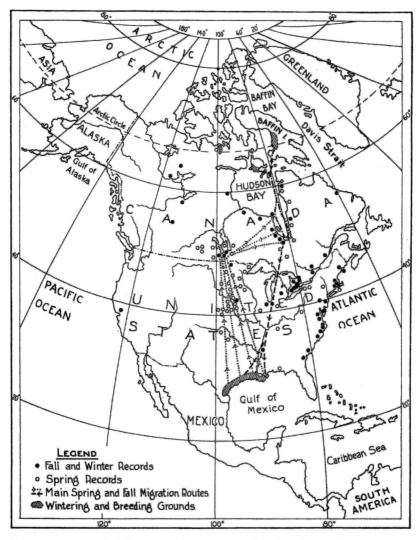

Sketch map showing the fall, winter, and spring records of the Blue Goose (Chen caerulescens), its wintering and breeding grounds, and main spring and fall migration routes.

From J. Dewey Soper, *Life History of the Blue Goose*, 1942.

In early June the geese started arriving, and in July Soper was able to verify this area as a major breeding ground of the Blue Goose.

The passion and enthusiasm that filled Soper at this time is revealed in a letter written to Percy Taverner on July 18, 1929, from southern Baffin Island:

As a bird migration route and breeding grounds [this] eclipses by far anything I have ever beheld in the past. Think of a region swarming with Blue Geese ... and around camp to have such birds commonly nesting as Red Phalarope, White-rumped Sandpiper, Parasitic and Long-tailed Jaeger, Black-bellied and Semipalmated Plover, Ruddy Turnstone, King Eider, Black-throated Loon, Sabine's Gull and – a little removed, Blue and Snow Geese![20]

While waiting at Camp Kungovik for the appearance of the Blue Goose, Soper described the presence of Willow Ptarmigan about the camp. From time to time a flock of these birds would land near the tents, their curiosity aroused by this unusual sight. Provided no one appeared and everything was quiet, they would noisily go about inspecting everything in camp. On these occasions it was common to see fifty to one hundred birds within a few feet of the tent and excellent photographs of them could be taken through a slit in the front flap of the tent.[21]

Soper wrote concerning the varied distribution of bird life in the Arctic. He said that comparatively few naturalists have a clear conception of the manner in which birds are locally distributed in the Arctic regions and that many mistakenly believe that the polar lands support a paucity of terrestrial life. He wrote that while this may be true for numerous localities, it was not for others, as there is a huge difference in bird occupancy often within very narrow limits. There are many areas in polar lands which support a huge wealth and diversity of bird life. Soper wrote that some of the most spectacular aggregations of Arctic birds are to be found on coastal islands and cliffs of the mainland. These include colonies of King and Northern Eiders, Black Guillemots, and Thick-billed Murres. Aside from these highly localized colonies, some of the greatest concentrations of breeding birds in the Arctic are found on flat, grass-tundra plains in various parts of the Canadian Arctic islands. He found that the northern Foxe Peninsula on Baffin Island, north along the Foxe Basin coast nearly to Hantzsch River, then east to Nettilling Lake, is an especially high-quality breeding area.

The grass-tundra plain bordering Foxe Basin on the western side of the island, especially, is visited by vast numbers of geese, Brant, waders and Eider Ducks, which either breed locally, or pass on to more northern latitudes. A great part of this western Baffin Island territory is of extraordinary interest and fascination to a naturalist.... In the light of present knowledge these plains, at large, stand in a class by themselves; avifaunally rich as they are in summer, they are especially notable for a line of migration which, for concentrated volume and persistence, probably has no counterpart in the whole of the eastern portion of the Canadian Arctic.[22]

Soper stayed in the North for several more years after 1929. In the summer of 1930 he brought his wife and infant son, Roland, to Lake Harbour on Baffin Island where he and his Inuit helpers built a house. Soper wrote that during his stay in the Arctic, he had travelled a total approximate distance of 30,300 miles.[23]

During the Depression, federal funding for arctic expeditions stopped and Soper was assigned to do a two-year wildlife study of Wood Buffalo National Park. Located in northeastern Alberta and the southern Northwest Territories, Wood Buffalo National Park is the largest national park in Canada. It contains the only natural nesting habitat for the endangered Whooping Crane, and is representative of Canada's northern boreal plains.

In 1934 a daughter, Mary Lou, was added to the family. In July 1934, Soper was appointed as the first federal chief migratory bird officer for the prairie provinces, one of four such officers at that time. His headquarters were in Winnipeg and he spent the next fourteen years there fostering the protection and conservation of migratory birds. In 1947 the Canadian Wildlife Service was established and, in the expansion of staff that followed, Soper was transferred in 1948 to Edmonton as the federal chief migratory bird officer for Alberta, the Yukon, and the Northwest Territories. In 1949 to 1951, he travelled extensively throughout these areas. In August 1951, he visited Kendall Island in the Northwest Territories to observe the Snow Goose colony there.

In 1952 Soper officially retired at age fifty-nine. Unofficially, he continued with his field work. In the spring of 1960, the University of Alberta's department of zoology commissioned him under the title honourary research assistant to conduct mammal investigations for the department's museum. During those years Soper produced over twenty volumes of field notes, twenty-three volumes of "bird notebooks," twenty-one day journals, and thousands of illustrations, maps, and photographs.[24]

Dewey Soper was a prolific writer throughout his lifetime. He wrote books, reports, and newspaper articles and published papers. From 1917 through 1981 he published more than one hundred articles and reports, forty of them on birds. Inventories of the birds and mammals of Prince Albert, Elk Island, and Riding Mountain National Parks, which had been prepared by him, were published as *Wildlife Management Bulletins* by the Canadian Wildlife Service. These bulletins marked the beginnings of the Canadian Wildlife Service's tradition of in-house scientific publications.[25]

In 1957 the government of Canada established the Dewey Soper Bird Sanctuary. This sanctuary is located near Bowman Bay, where Dewey had patiently awaited the arrival of the Blue Geese in 1929, and which he had emphasized was a major migratory and breeding bird habitat. Soper's contribution to the exploration of Baffin Island was further recognized by the Canadian Committee on Geographic Names in the naming of Soper River and Soper Lake (near Lake Harbour), and Soper Highlands (near the northwest shore of Nettilling Lake). In 1978 Soper received the Northwest Territory Commissioner's Award in recognition of his contribution to the Northwest Territories in the fields of science and exploration. In 1980 the Canadian Nature Federation presented him with the Douglas H. Pimlott Conservation Award. Dewey Soper was a fellow of the Arctic Institute of North America, a charter member of the American Society of Mammalogists, and a fellow of the American Ornithologists' Union.[26] The J. Dewey Soper Award, the highest honour of the Alberta Society of Professional Biologists, is given periodically to a Canadian biologist who makes significant contributions to the field of biology.

Dewey Soper is a source of inspiration to any young biologist seeking to learn more about the natural world. The enthusiasm and common sense approach which he brought to his scientific studies allowed him to make great contributions in the field. His ability to write, both scientifically as well as narratively, added to the world's knowledge. That his experiences in the far northern regions were always held very close to his heart can be seen through his watercolour paintings of the Arctic, done in his later years.

PART FIVE

Thirst For Knowledge

Chapter Fifteen

Louise de Kiriline Lawrence
(1894-1992)

"In the beginning, the feeding station was to me just a nice place in which the birds of the forest could be attracted to please the eye. But soon the fascination of watching superseded all other pleasures derived from it. The rare bird and the strange animal still continued to provide their moments of special thrills, but what the ordinary bird did proved to be far more exciting and challenging.... And I wanted to be able to 'read' these moves and attitudes and learn something about how [the bird] felt and the motivations behind these acts. So I began to watch in a different way and, naturally, the more I watched, the more I saw. A realization of the immense importance of the finest detail of each movement in relation to the prevailing situation began to dawn upon me. Very gradually I learned to read the signs and to decode the mysteries and it is quite amazing how far into the essential things of life this watching leads the watcher."

— Louise de Kiriline Lawrence in *The Lovely and the Wild.*

Louise de Kiriline Lawrence was an incredibly smart, independent, and empathetic lady. She is internationally known as an expert in the diverse fields of medicine and nursing, nature writing, and behavioural ornithology. Her accomplishments in each of these fields are enough to establish her at the top of the respective profession.

Louise de Kiriline Lawrence.

Courtesy of Pat McGrath.

She became a very skilled nurse, proving her ability in the emergency room of a major city, in rehabilitation hospitals during war, and as head nurse ensuring the survival of all five of the Dionne quintuplets during the first year of their lives. She then turned to writing and realized her great talent and ability to write non-fiction that is more exciting than any work of fiction. Finally, from being a novice naturalist, she took advice from the best people in the field of ornithology, and became a great behavioural ornithologist, in the traditions of Konrad Lorenz and Margaret Nice.

Louise was born in 1894 in Sweden into an aristocratic family. She was named after her godmother, Princess Louise of Denmark, who was a good friend of her mother. She grew up on the family estate called Svensksund overlooking the fjord of Braviken, which cuts in from the Baltic Sea on the east coast of Sweden. In the spring, a vast assortment of shorebirds arrived there to breed during the brief northern summer. Louise wrote that "The lapwings etched themselves most deeply upon my memory, these beautiful birds with their black fronts and iridescent backs, and their spectacular crests curving over their foreheads and crowns to a long upswept end."[1]

Louise's father, Sixten Flach, was a university-trained naturalist and conservationist. Visitors to the family estate included Bruno Liljefors, one of the world's finest painters of birds and nature, and the ornithologist Einar Lönnberg. Louise listened in on the long discussions between her father and these other naturalists, and the significance of nature began to leave a deep impression on her. However, the untimely death of her father when she was seventeen led to her mother's decision to leave Svensksund and move the family into the city. This led to her temporary removal from a life surrounded by nature.

Louise soon grew impatient with the leisurely life of the Swedish and Danish aristocracies, and she determined to do something meaningful with her life. In 1914 at the age of twenty she entered nursing school and she became a very skilled and efficient nurse. After graduation she wanted to gain challenging work where she could make good use of her acquired skills, and she became a Swedish Red Cross nurse. She accepted a post as a nurse in charge of one of the barracks of tubercular Russian soldiers at Horseröd in Denmark. At the time Louise knew Swedish, Danish, English, and French. At this camp she was impressed by the spirit of the Russian soldiers, and in particular by one officer, Lieutenant Gleb Nikolayevich Kirilin. The men of the Kirilin family belonged to the famed regiments of the Imperial Guards, into whose safekeeping the lives of the Russian Tsar and his family were entrusted. Gleb's father was a general, and while Gleb had been wounded, his brothers had been killed in the First World War fighting against Germany. Gleb taught Russian to Louise and they fell in love and were married in 1918. In 1919 Lieutenant Kirilin returned to Russia and Louise joined him there. The Bolshevik Revolution had begun in 1917. In 1919 the English, French, and American Allies, along with Russian officers of the White Army, were mounting a counter-offensive against the Bolsheviks from northern Russia at Archangel.

Suddenly, on September 27, 1919, the Allies surreptitiously pulled out all their men and equipment, leaving the Russian officers stranded. Louise

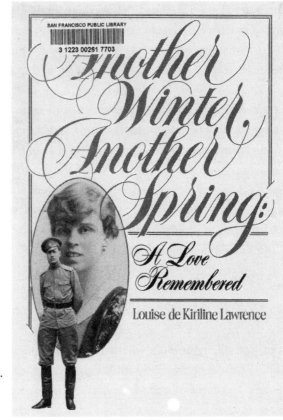

Another Winter, Another Spring: A Love Remembered

Louise de Kiriline Lawrence

Cover of Louise de Kiriline's book on her life in Sweden and Russia, showing Louise and her first husband, Lieutenant Gleb Nikolayevich Kirilin.

Published by McGraw-Hill, 1977.

and Gleb fled Archangel just before it fell to the Bolsheviks. They went with a party of other officers and their wives, by horse and sleigh, closely pursued by the Red Army. After many days, with their exhausted horses fallen by the wayside in the heavy snow, they were captured by the Bolsheviks, herded into boxcars, and sent to concentration camps. Eventually they were moved to Moscow, where Louise, because of her Swedish citizenship, was freed. Gleb was returned to Archangel for trial and Louise never saw him again. Many years later, it was confirmed that her husband was one of the many hundreds of Russian officers shot at Archangel by the revolutionists.[2]

Louise stayed in Russia for several more years, working as a nurse. Eventually she returned to Sweden, and then in 1927 came to Canada where she hoped to begin a new life. She joined the Canadian Red Cross's outpost service in northern Ontario, and worked as a district nurse in

Bonfield (previously called Callander Station) east of North Bay, Ontario. In the early 1930s she was a school nurse and "travelled by dogsled in the winter, and Model-A in summer, and taught using a hand puppet to get her story across."[3]

In 1934 Louise was hired by Dr. Allan Roy Dafoe and became famous as the head nurse in charge of the Dionne quintuplets during their first year of life. For her dedication and skill in this task she was awarded the Jubilee Medal from King George V. Louise retired from nursing in 1935. Although she was in demand to give lectures on the raising of children, she did not like the way the girls were being "exploited" and she sought a simpler life. In 1936 she wrote a book called *The Quintuplets First Year*, and bought a property on Pimisi Bay, forty kilometers east of North Bay. In 1939 she met and married Len Lawrence, and the two built a log house on the property, which became known as "The Loghouse Nest."

There, in the relative solitude of Pimisi Bay, between North Bay and Mattawa in the Canadian Shield, she became immersed in the world of birds. Louise was always a great observer and a natural-born scientist, who was always trying to understand the "why" behind certain behaviours. After a friend gave her a copy of Percy Taverner's *Birds of Canada*, Louise wrote to the ornithologist asking him what she could do in order to better interpret the actions of the birds. Thus began a regular correspondence between the two naturalists. It was Taverner who suggested that she take up bird-banding, and Louise later recorded in her files over twenty-five thousand birds that she had banded. Besides the influence of Mr. Taverner, Louise gave special credit for her development as an expert ornithologist to Doris and Murray Speirs, who visited Pimisi Bay on a bird-watching trip and became her good friends. They introduced her to Margaret Nice, who also influenced the direction of her work with birds. Throughout the rest of her life, Louise corresponded with similarly minded naturalists.

Louise always recorded her observations and findings accurately and in the minutest detail. She later wrote up her notebook recordings for professional journals. She published nearly twenty scientific articles in the *Canadian Field-Naturalist*, *The Wilson Bulletin*, and *The Auk*, as well as more than forty popular articles in *Audubon* and other magazines.

Robert W. Nero and Louise de Kiriline Lawrence, taken in Pimisi Bay, Ontario.

Courtesy of Iola Price.

The exactness and detail with which Louise conducted her life-history studies is demonstrated in "A Comparative Life-History Study of Four Species of Woodpeckers," a monograph published in 1967 by the American Ornithologists' Union.[4] In it she discusses the behaviour of the Yellow-bellied Sapsucker, Northern Flicker, Hairy Woodpecker, and Downy Woodpecker. She studied these birds intensively over a period of seven years. Most of the birds studied were colour-banded. She described in detail the year-to-year activities, including changes of territories and mates, which illustrate the variation in behaviour that may occur among individuals. She made a strong case that close cooperation between a pair is essential for breeding success, and expands on the previously available knowledge about means of communication and the functions of various types of drumming and tapping.

Louise also conducted detailed field studies of Red-eyed Vireo mating behaviour, the reverse migration in Snow Geese, hoarding behaviour in

Gray Jays, and the comparative nesting behaviour of Chestnut-sided and Nashville Warblers.[5]

In her book *The Lovely and the Wild*, Louise commented on the declining numbers of songbirds. She wrote: "A study of my daily counts and breeding censuses conducted over the past twenty to twenty-five years reveals that the decline began in 1949–50 and concerned nearly all species of the migratory woodland birds."[6]

The spring of 1956 was a disastrous one for the woodland birds migrating north. Compelled by their inner clocks to move northward to their breeding grounds, they continued on despite extremely cold weather, which persisted through to the end of May. Multitudes froze or starved. Up to that time, there had been a declining trend in numbers which Louise had not paid much attention to. But after 1956 she began to realize the songbirds were not in the woods in such numbers as she had previously seen and recorded. In 1968 she wrote:

> The decline of the Red-eyed Vireo began slowly at first in 1950. Thereafter it gathered momentum until of late only about fifteen pairs or less may be found where twenty-five to thirty-five used to nest regularly twenty years ago on a hundred acres of land.... The population of thirteen warblers are similar; only the start of the decline varies slightly, with nearly half of them already showing signs of it in 1947 and the rest over the following years up to 1951. The decline is gradual up to 1956, but after that the number drops sharply in all but the most common, the Chestnut-sided Warbler, whose population low occurs two years later.... In four — the Chest-sided, Mourning, and Canada Warblers, and the Common Yellowthroat — the total decline of each represents a drop of about 70 to 80 percent of their former abundance; in the rest 10% or less. The changes wrought in the environment, for the most part natural, should not affect these thirteen warblers to any marked degree....[7]

From the point of view of natural balance, less fortunate population increases have taken place among the blackbirds — the Red-winged Blackbird, the Common Grackle, and the Brown-headed Cowbird — which are spreading into the forested areas during the nesting season.... I have often wondered, considering the difference that ignorance would have made - if I had never seen the unassuming elegance of the Red-eyed Vireo, the vivid guise of the Blackburnian Warbler, the American Redstart's ethereal displays or heard the singing of the Veery and the Hermit Thrush; if I had never known the vast variety of woodland songbirds — might I not have looked quite differently upon these other innocents, the red-wing with its scarlet epaulets, the grackle in its rich iridescence, and even on the cowbird in softest beaver-brown and shiny black? Might I not then have thought them birds of striking beauty and overlooked the stridor of their voices? And having no others to compare them with, would I not then willingly have conceded their roles to be as important as those of any other birds and beasts in nature's scheme of self-preserving balance?[8]

This philosophical question is typical of Louise's inborn desire to understand and explain what has occurred. In her writings, she goes beyond descriptions of reality to try to comprehend the true meaning of what has happened and its consequences and implications.

Louise de Kiriline Lawrence was an extremely skilled writer. Seven of her books were published: *The Quintuplets First Year* (1936), *The Loghouse Nest* (1945), *A Comparative Life History Study of Four Species of Woodpeckers* (1967), *The Lovely and the Wild* (1968), *Mar: A Glimpse into the Natural Life of a Bird* (1976), *Another Winter, Another Spring: A Love Remembered* (1977), and *To Whom the Wilderness Speaks* (1980). Her last book was published when she was eighty-six years old. In 1991 Les Line, then-editor of the National Audubon Society's magazine *Audubon*, called her the "greatest and perhaps the last of a cadre of nature writers fast disappearing from the

North American scene."[9] In 1969, Louise de Kiriline Lawrence became the first Canadian to receive the prestigious John Burroughs Medal for distinguished natural history writing for her book *The Lovely and the Wild*. In the same year she received the Sir G.D. Roberts Special Award from the Canadian Authors Association.

Louise's scientific career was acknowledged as early as 1954 when she became the first Canadian woman to become an Elective Member of the American Ornithologists' Union. In 1970 she received an honourary doctorate from Laurentian University in Sudbury, Ontario, where there is a scholarship in her name. In 1980 she was the recipient of the Francis H. Kortright Outdoor Writing Award, and in 1991 she received the Doris Huestis Speirs Award from the Society of Canadian Ornithologists.

Louise passed on from this world in 1992 at the age of ninety-eight, after contributing much new knowledge in the fields of medicine and behavioural ornithology. She left a legacy of splendid and perceptive nature and other non-fiction writing.

Chapter Sixteen

Doris Huestis Speirs
(1894–1989)
and J. Murray Speirs
(1909–2001)

"How can anyone have one favourite bird species? Anyone who has studied any species in detail will know the endless satisfaction that is derived from learning about the behaviour, the migrations, even the great variety in plumage and structure that go to make up a single species."

— Murray Speirs in the introduction to *Birds of Ontario*.

Doris Huestis Speirs was a remarkable woman who became well-known as a self-taught ornithologist. The most prestigious award given by the Society of Canadian Ornithologists is the Doris Huestis Speirs Award, presented annually to an individual who has made outstanding lifetime contributions to Canadian ornithology. As a serious ornithologist, Doris was good friends with Margaret Morse Nice. She edited Nice's posthumously published autobiography *Research Is a Passion With Me*. In the early 1950s ornithology in Canada was still considered to be the domain of men, and women were excluded from belonging to the Toronto Ornithological Club. This did not seem appropriate considering the major contributions in ornithology by women doing extensive bird studies. Doris made up her mind to organize a group where women with a passionate interest in ornithology could meet regularly. She named this first women's group devoted to bird study the Margaret Nice Ornithological Club, which was founded in 1952 and immediately became affiliated with the Federation of Ontario Naturalists. In Doris's words, the aims of the club were:

To gain a better knowledge and appreciation of bird life through a study of the birds in the field; a further understanding of the bird's habitat or environment; to record all species of birds observed and numbers seen on each field trip and also phenological[1] data. The club makes possible the meeting of ornithologists at regular intervals, for mutual encouragement and a certain joyous fellowship. We discuss, review and report on topics of natural history interest and ecological significance furthering a more scientific understanding of ornithology.[2]

Before she was a serious ornithologist, Doris became engrossed in the area of Canadian art. She was a close friend of several members of the Group of Seven artists and was an invited contributor to their exhibitions from 1926-31.[3] Her involvement with the Group of Seven began when a friend invited her to see a Tom Thomson memorial exhibition and she subsequently met Lawren Harris and A.Y. Jackson. In 1919 she and several friends pioneered the picture rental system, whereby they approached members of the Group of Seven to lend out pictures to them for a period of time. Doris and her friends would then exchange the pictures after having them in their homes for several months. The *Toronto Star* wrote an article about this rental system, and public relations attention was thereby given to the Group of Seven, who were not well known at that time. Doris herself had a natural affinity for art, and beginning in 1926 she exhibited with the Group of Seven, and continued to do so with the Canadian Group of Painters. Although her work appeared in later exhibitions and eleven of her paintings are in Canadian and international galleries, Doris stopped painting in 1937 as she turned her attention towards the in-depth study of birds. However, throughout her life, she continued to hold a conviction to and promotion of Canadian art and artists.

Doris was always attracted to the world of nature. As early as 1916, when she was twenty-two years old, she described herself as a bird watcher and in that year she identified fifty-six species in and around Toronto.[4] It was in 1936 that she began to keep a regular diary, recording her observations of bird behaviour and in 1937 she began to seriously study birds.

In that year she saw her first Evening Grosbeaks, which she described as: "They were brilliant as a tree full of parakeets."[5] In her diary she described their plumage and behaviour, and did an oil sketch of one seen from a window. Doris was to spend years studying the behaviour of the Evening Grosbeak. In the process of her detailed studies, she became an expert self-taught ornithologist and went on to write the section for Evening Grosbeak in Arthur Cleveland Bent's *Life Histories of Familiar North American Birds*, published by the Smithsonian Institution in 1968.

From the time of their marriage in 1939 on, Doris and John Murray Speirs often worked together as a team in their bird studies, conducting detailed studies of Evening Grosbeaks, American Robins, Black-capped Chickadees, and Lincoln Sparrows. They co-authored the account of the Lincoln's Sparrow in Arthur Bent's *Life Histories*.

Doris and Murray Speirs out birding.

Courtesy of Rosemary Speirs and the Pickering Township Historical Society.

Murray Speirs was a leading ornithologist in Ontario for over sixty-five years. His many accomplishments include publishing two large volumes entitled *Birds of Ontario* in 1985. Murray was a born naturalist and bird lover and once said: "There's nothing more alive than a bird."[6] He first became fascinated with birds at age six, watching a Ruby-crowned Kinglet as it passed through his parents' Toronto city garden in migration.

As a teenager he found some friends who had a similar interest in birds, one of whom lived near the well-known ornithologist James Henry Fleming. Murray says "Mr. Fleming had a fabulous library and collection of birds, and fostered my interest in ornithology."[7] Murray kept detailed daily sighting notebooks from the age of fifteen. In 1931 at age twenty-two he joined the Wilson Ornithological Society, one of many such groups he became involved in.

Murray obtained his masters degree from the University of Toronto, and in 1939 signed up for war duty. He had a bad leg and could not go overseas, but the Royal Canadian Air Force trained him as a meteorologist, and he was stationed at North Bay, Ontario, during the war. His job was to inform the pilots whether it was safe to go out. Here, Doris says: "we were just living on snowshoes and everything there in North Bay because you couldn't get petrol or gasoline."[8] On one of their birding outings during this time, Doris and Murray called in on Louise de Kiriline Lawrence, also living in the area, and thus began a long friendship with a mutually shared interest in nature and birds.

At the end of the war, Murray completed his Ph.D. at the University of Illinois in 1946. His thesis topic was "Local and migratory movements of the American Robin in eastern North America." While doing his thesis he became interested in quadrant studies of bird populations and territories. This method is used to measure the abundance of birds in a given area. The number of established bird territories on a sized area is found by a series of daily walks through the study area during the breeding season. Murray said that "For species that have faint songs or that avoid highways (such as Bay-breasted Warblers and Henslow's Sparrows), these give a better picture of abundance than do the roadside counts used for the Breeding Bird Surveys."[9] Murray was a strong believer in this field research method and he subsequently taught it to all his students in the department of zoology at the University of Toronto, where he taught for forty years.

In 1948 Murray and Doris purchased a cobblestone house in Pickering, Ontario, east of Toronto. The location allowed for the sun to be at his back during his commutes into and out of the city. The property became known as "Cobble Hill."[10]

Both Murray and Doris Speirs were known for their meticulous recording of ornithological information. Some idea of the extent to which Doris pursued her ornithological studies is given in her accounts of Evening Grosbeaks in Bent's *Life Histories*. She wrote:

> Louise de Kiriline Lawrence, my husband, and I found a nest near a forest edge in Lauder Township, Nipissing District, Ontario, on June 21, 1945. The nest was fifty-five feet up in a white pine and very well concealed. It contained at least three young and through a 47X telescope we were able to watch the young being fed. I spent three days observing this nesting. After the young left we collected the nest, which is now in the Royal Ontario Museum of Zoology and Palaeontology....

> One morning in North Bay, Ontario, when the temperature was 35 degrees below zero, anxious to find out what the grosbeaks did on an extremely cold day, I went out. A flock of twelve were located, feeding on Manitoba maples. Above each bill, the breath of the bird could be seen like a little wreath. All were males. My notes read: 'I noted that they looked noticeably larger than usual, as their feathers were fluffed out as far from the body as possible, so that they were encased in warmth. Their feet were tucked into the warm down and could not be seen at all. One of them reached far out for a pair of the winged seeds, and broke through the silver ice, with which the seeds were encrusted, with a loud snap. In spite of the icy frosting over the trees and seeds, apparently they were

getting all the food they needed, and even piped prettily, *choo-wee, chorr-wee*, to each other....

In April 1940 I received a pair of live Evening Grosbeaks from Norwood, Manitoba. After a few days I noticed how early they roosted for the night. I then noted their times of retirement and measured the light intensity with a Weston illuminometer. In May they roosted on an average forty five minutes before sunset.... In autumn I made daily observations. About November first the birds roosted on an average of fifty seven minutes before sunset.... In December, January, and February the pair often retired shortly after 1 p.m. and hid in their spruce, sound asleep throughout the afternoon and evening. Rarely did they ever leave their roosting place unless badly disturbed.[11]

Doris and Murray Speirs had a large influence on other ornithologists, naturalists, and artists. Robert Bateman first met Doris and Murray Speirs in 1947 when he was seventeen and working at the Wildlife Research Camp at Algonquin Park, where they came as visiting scientists. Thirty-eight years later he wrote about them:

I usually think of the Speirs as a unit. They are one of the most inspiring team relationships I know. My most vivid memory from that 1947 day in Algonquin Park was the auspicious flock of Evening Grosbeaks which lifted off from the central open area of the camp just as the Speirs arrived. The enthusiastic exclamations of Doris were my first insight into the decades of study of that bird by Doris and Murray.... Through the years I learned their great depth of skill in research and tireless efforts in learning more of these birds and other birds in Ontario. As I grew older and became involved with organizations such as the Federation of Ontario Naturalists, I observed

Evening Grosbeaks, *1980.*

Courtesy of and copyright Robert Bateman.

the great esteem which all of the top people in natural history and conservation had and still have for Murray Speirs. When he spoke, you knew that you were listening to a voice of wisdom.[12]

Murray became known as the "Quiet Giant" of Ontario ornithology and he was the recipient of the Ontario Field Ornithologists' Distinguished Ornithologist Award. He had a phenomenal ear for bird songs and calls, and could imitate bird calls with accurate whistles and clicks. Although his main focus was with birds, he was really an all-round biologist who was very interested in conservation. His niece, Rosemary Speirs, commented that "He regarded [birds] as a symptom of the general environment. If the birds were doing all right, the rest of the system was probably healthy."[13] Wildlife artist Barry Kent MacKay wrote about Murray that "He was a consummate teacher. If you came into his sphere you learned wonderful things about the intricacies of how all creatures interrelate to one another."[14]

In 1995 Murray donated 2.8 hectares of the property at Altona Road in Pickering to the Altona Forest to be used as a bird habitat and conservation area. The Altona Forest is a very special place given that it is located within an urban centre. The southwestern section of the forest has been designated for research and is called the J. Murray Speirs Ecological Reserve. In 2000 the Governor General of Canada, Adrienne Clarkson, visited Murray at his home in Pickering to invest him in the Order of Canada for his work as a conservationist.

For her work in ornithology, Doris received a number of honours during her lifetime. In 1974 she and her husband were jointly awarded the Ontario Conservation Trophy by the Federation of Ontario Naturalists, and Doris was again honoured by the federation in 1977. In 1975 she was one of nineteen Canadian women honoured for their scientific contributions in an exhibition at the National Museum of Natural Sciences (now the Canadian Museum of Nature) in Ottawa.

Chapter Seventeen

Roger Tory Peterson
(1908-1996)

"Forty years ago, in 1953, when my English friend James Fisher
and I made our special trip around the perimeter of the continent,
we saw a bird that has since become extinct – the dusky seaside
sparrow. Indeed we saw quite a few...Extinction is forever."

— Roger Tory Peterson in
All Things Reconsidered: My Birding Adventures.

After that of John James Audubon, the name people think of most when they consider those who are prominent in the world of birds is Roger Tory Peterson. He revolutionized the science and art of recognizing and learning about birds. First as an artist and educator, and then as a writer, photographer, and conservationist, he led North America into a new era of appreciating the world of birds.

Roger Tory Peterson was born in 1908 in Jamestown in southwestern New York State. He attended school there, graduating from high school at age seventeen. As a boy, he found his most faithful friends in books. He had skipped the second grade, and as such was a year younger than his classmates.[1] Peterson credits two experiences growing up which sparked his undying fascination with birds. One was a Northern Flicker he saw at age eleven, which he describes:

We came across a flicker, just a few feet off the ground on the trunk of a tree. Its head was tucked under its wing coverts. It was probably exhausted from migration, but we thought it was dead. We stood and stared at it for awhile, examining its beautiful plumage. When I reached out to touch its back it exploded with life — a stunning sight, flying away with its golden underwings and the red crescent on its nape — I can see it now — the way it was transformed from what we thought was death into intense life. I was tremendously excited with the feeling which I have carried ever since, of the intensity of a bird's life, and its apparent freedom, with this wonderful ability to fly.[2]

The second influencing factor was his seventh-grade teacher, Miss Blanche Hornbeck. She had organized a Junior Audubon Club, where children were given ten leaflets, each of which contained a description of a bird, a colour plate of that bird, and an outline drawing to colour in crayons. Roger recalls: "One day Miss Hornbeck brought in a portfolio of *The Birds of New York State*, by the great bird painter Louis Agassiz Fuertes. Each of us was given a small box of watercolours and a colour plate from Fuertes's book to copy. I was given the Blue Jay, and that was my first bird painting."[3] Many years later Miss Hornbeck wrote to Roger saying she remembered a rainy morning bird walk when she had been surprised anyone had shown up and Roger's telling her: "You can count on me, no matter what the weather."[4]

At age thirteen or fourteen Peterson bought his first camera, a Primo No. 9, to take pictures of birds. He had delivered the *Jamestown Morning Post* on his bicycle, getting up at 3:30 a.m. to earn the money for it. At that time he also bought a four-power opera glass[5] from an advertisement in *Bird-Lore*, the popular magazine then published by the National Association of Audubon Societies. Peterson soon became interested in and started reading the professional bird journals *The Auk* and *The Condor* as well. He also began to keep lists and daily logs of notes on birds.

In 1925 Peterson graduated from Jamestown High School with distinction in design and mechanical drawing. He accepted a job decorating Chinese lacquer cabinets at the Union-National Furniture Factory in Jamestown. That same year he also published his first article in *Bird-Lore* and submitted two of his first watercolours to the exhibition of bird art at the American Ornithologists' Union annual convention in New York City. He travelled to New York to attend this convention, where he met such ornithological greats as Ludlow Griscom and Louis Agassiz Fuertes. Peterson wrote:

> Ludlow Griscom was the first ornithologist I ever met when, as a lad of seventeen, I came to New York in 1925 to attend my first meeting of the American Ornithologists' Union. I arrived a day early, and to get my membership sponsored I climbed the stairs to the bird department on the top floor of the American Museum, where a well-made young man of thirty-five signed my application. The young man was Ludlow Griscom.[6]

At the convention he also met Louis Agassiz Fuertes, whom Peterson considered one of the two bird artists who most influenced his own paintings (the other being John James Audubon). Fuertes was gracious to the young, aspiring artist and Peterson remembered:

> When we left the hall and descended the stairs, Fuertes reached into his inner jacket pocket and withdrew a handful of watercolour brushes. Picking out a flat red sable about a half inch wide, he handed it to me, saying, 'Take this. You will find it good for laying in background washes.' I thanked him, and before we parted he added, 'And don't hesitate to send your drawings to me from time to time. Just address them to Louis Fuertes, Ithaca, New York.' Actually, I never did send any of my drawings to him for criticism; I had decided to wait until they were worthy of his time. And so, by delaying, I forfeited a priceless opportunity, for less than two years later, in 1927, Fuertes met his death at a railroad crossing while driving home to Ithaca.[7]

It was Peterson's wish at this time to attend Cornell University and study ornithology, but he lacked the funds as well as any financial backing from his father.[8] His boss at the furniture-decorating company encouraged him to leave Jamestown to study art in New York City.

Peterson arrived in New York in 1926 at age eighteen. He managed to find work decorating furniture at Deutsch Bros. Furniture in the Bronx. For three years his mornings were spent decorating furniture to earn money for food and tuition, while in the afternoons he attended art classes, first at the Arts Student League and then at the National Academy of Design. Peterson spent all his free time observing birds in the New York City area. Once a week he went to the Bronx Zoo to draw its birds. He said: "There were two that I constantly drew. They were the Shoebilled Stork and the Eagle Owl, which is like our Great Horned Owl. I drew them because they never moved a muscle. They would sit for ten minutes at a time."[9] He attended bimonthly meetings of the Linnaean Society, where he met members of the Bronx County Bird Club, a group of young, enthusiastic amateur ornithologists.

The Bronx County Bird Club had the then original idea of finding and identifying as many different species of birds as they could. They put their money together to buy an old Buick so they could go chasing birds all over the Bronx and they raced anywhere birds could be found, including sewer outfalls and garbage dumps. Peterson said, "We were addicted to the Hunts Point Dump, and one winter we found four Snowy Owls feeding on rats."[10]

The club's mentor was Ludlow Griscom, whose extraordinary ability to identify living birds at a distance influenced the development of Peterson's later first field identification guide book to birds. Peterson described this method of quick field identification as follows:

> The mind of a good field observer works just like a kaleidoscope, the gadget of our childhood, wherein loose fragments of coloured glass fall quickly into symmetrical patterns. We see a bird. With an instinctive movement we center it in our glass. All the thousands of fragments we know about birds, locality, season, habitat, voice, actions,

field marks and likelihood of occurrence flash across the mirrors of the mind and fall into place — and we have the name of our bird.[11]

Peterson described a couple of his birding experiences in New York City as follows:

On some misty evenings hundreds of small birds can be seen fluttering through the brilliant lights that illuminate the tall towers of Radio City.... On autumn nights, when the wind is in the northwest, I sometimes take the elevator to the observation platform, sixty-odd stories above the street. There, far below, the city lights are strung like jewels to the hazy horizon, while close about me in the blackness I can hear the small voices of southbound migrants. For a few brief moments I feel as if I were one of them.

On a warm fall day a number of years ago a southbound Hermit Thrush, weary of picking its way through the bewildering canyons of New York, descended to the sidewalk on Madison Avenue at the southeast corner of 63rd Street. The display of palms and flowers in the shop of Christatos & Koster must have suggested to the thrush its tropical destination, and it flew in through the open transom, taking refuge in a secluded corner. All through the winter the bird led a happy existence and finally became so tame it would alight on anyone's hand to secure a meal worm. Marco, as he was christened for no accountable reason, had many admirers who used to drop in to pay their respects. The following spring he was restless and one day, when the transom windows were open, he departed. His friends hoped that he had gotten safely out of New York and joined his fellow Hermit Thrushes in their flight to the cool northern woods. Two years later, during the fall migration, a

Hermit Thrush appeared in front of the very same shop. He allowed himself to be picked up and brought in, and the proprietor and his employees insisted it was Marco who had returned. I myself saw the bird and it really seemed as though it must have been the same Marco, for he had already fallen into his old habits and came to the hand for food. Furthermore, it is well known from banded birds, that many individuals return to the same spot each winter. If this was Marco, why did he skip a year before returning?[12]

Roger Tory Peterson first acquired his teaching skills while acting as a counsellor of nature study at a YMCA camp in Michigan for one summer, and then at Camp Chewonki in Maine for five summers. The Peterson-led field trips at Camp Chewonki were vigorous and sometimes risky outings. They became very popular among the campers, and nature study became as respected an activity as athletic games.[13]

In 1931 Peterson realized that with the deepening Great Depression he was faced with having to leave New York, and end his Bronx birding. Deutsch Bros. Furniture had gone under and Peterson was thinking of returning to Jamestown. Then Clarence Allen, the founder of Camp Chewonki, who was now headmaster at Rivers School, a private school for boys in Brookline, Massachusetts, offered him a position teaching natural history and art. Here, Peterson occupied a tiny room above the Rivers Administration building, and received a small salary, weekly meals, and free room and board.

He became a popular teacher at Rivers School, and from 1931–34, he worked diligently in the evenings on the plates and descriptions for his book *A Field Guide to the Birds*. He was close to the Boston Museum of Science, and the Museum of Comparative Zoology in Cambridge, from where he could obtain study skins. At Rivers, Peterson "found a cache of mounted birds – including an Eskimo Curlew and a Heath Hen – in an attic and commandeered an unused room for a museum." In 1932 he published three articles on duck identification in *Field and Stream*, using the type of schematic illustrations which would later be typically used in his first field guide.[14] At the graduation ceremony of his last year at Rivers, Peterson was presented with a plaque with the following inscription: "Roger Tory Peterson – June 7, 1934. From the boys and masters of The Rivers School – A tribute to friendship, industry, and skill and an acknowledgement of our pride in *A Field Guide to the Birds*."[15]

In April 1934, in the midst of the Great Depression, Houghton Mifflin published *A Field Guide to the Birds*. The first printing of two thousand copies was sold out in a few weeks and the book immediately went to a second printing. The field guide was the first to simplify and clarify the identifying characteristics of similar species. Peterson credits the original concept back to his reading as a boy of Ernest Thompson Seton's *Two Little Savages*, wherein the hero Yan learns how to identify ducks at a distance by looking at the key characteristics of ducks in a showcase. He then lays out the ducks all together on a page, showing each one's unique shape and colour pattern. To this concept, Peterson added his own invention – that of adding arrows to highlight the key identifying characteristics of each species. This method became known as "The Peterson Identification System" and was used in subsequent field guides of birds and other nature subjects.

Following the publication of his field guide, Peterson began to gain national and international recognition. In 1934 he moved back to New York City to take a full-time position as a member of the administrative staff of the National Association of Audubon Societies. Shortly afterwards he was named educational director, as well as art director of *Bird-Lore* (now *Audubon*). As education director he rewrote the Junior Audubon leaflets for school children, wrote bulletins on nature study for educators and also wrote articles of general interest. At this time Amy Clampett wrote: "The thing I remember most about Roger Tory Peterson is this: In mid-conversation about mundane matters at the busy headquarters of the Audubon Society in the middle of New York City (not far from the reservoir in Central Park), Roger would pause, hearing the call of a bird, and say: 'Ah, that's a Laughing Gull.'"[16]

In February 1943, Peterson signed up for the army. In July 1943, he married Barbara Coulter. They were married for over thirty-two years and had two sons, Tory and Lee. In 1945 Peterson was transferred to the Air

Corps in Orlando, Florida, where he was involved in early pioneering research on the effects of DDT on wildlife.

Peterson normally considered himself an advocate for conservation through his writing. He said: "I'm not an activist in the sense of bothering my Congressman. I'm an opinion-maker in my writing and my painting. I'm a publicizer. I like to give people information, and over the years I've written a great many articles for magazines. Activists sometimes work on information that's not valid."[17] Nevertheless, Peterson was not afraid to speak out and inform people about atrocities against birds. He publicly condemned the harmful effects of DDT on wildlife later in his career, after being presented with irrefutable facts collected by his wife Barbara and research student Peter Ames on the effects of DDT on the eggs of Ospreys near his Connecticut home. In August 1962, he wrote to fellow ornithologist Carl Buchheister:

> I realize that we have got to fight like hell in the years
> to come and that we have been playing at conservation
> most of us. I for one am going to become a very nasty
> fellow as the years go on because I see the disintegration
> in so many ways.... We have got to be far more militant,
> and I am afraid that biologists as a whole have got to be
> a bit more aggressive from now on. The [people] who are
> destroying America are very aggressive as you know.[18]

In 1964 Peterson testified before a subcommittee of the United States Senate Committee on government operations, presenting the facts and explaining the effects of DDT up the food chain. DDT was finally banned in 1972.

Peterson recounts an interesting experience during the war years:

> The European Goldfinch, a little tan bird with a red
> face and a yellow wing patch, which we see so often in
> medieval paintings (it was a symbol of the soul and resur-
> rection) was imported in droves by homesick Europeans.
> One lot, liberated in Hoboken in 1878, prospered. They

became common around Englewood and in Central Park, and they appeared on Long Island. Then they vanished. Yet during those years there must have been a few holding onto the thin thread of existence somewhere, for in the 30's they again made their appearance; and for a few years many nested in Seaford, Massapequa and other towns along the south shore of Long Island.

Edwin Way Teale and I made a special trip to see them there. We searched about the spot where John Elliott, the local authority on these birds, had seen one the day before. A suspicious bird darted into a maple. I hurried over, and there, its red face peering at me from among the green leaves, was my first European Goldfinch – sitting on a nest! The species had never been photographed on this side of the Atlantic, so it was worth a try. An old door placed across two sawhorses made a platform for my tripod and Graflex. Standing on a tall stepladder, I focused on the nest and wired a remote control release to my flash equipment. The motorcar patriots driving along the Sunrise Highway that Sunday had reported my suspicious operations to the Seaford police, and a patrol car pulled up just as I was waiting for the bird to come back. In those early war years everyone was nervous about spies along the South Shore. Only a week before several German spies had been captured after landing from a submarine a few miles to the east.

When I told the officer I was after goldfinches he inquired, "British or American?"

"British," I gasped in astonishment.

He then told me he knew all about these birds. He had picked up a man and his wife earlier in the day, and to explain their actions they showed him a book that said Seaford was the best place to look for British goldfinches. The book was a copy of my *Field Guide!*[19]

In 1950 Peterson published *Birds Over America*, a series of essays describing "some of the ornithological spectacles I have seen."[20] This book won the John Burroughs Medal for best nature writing. In *Birds Over America* he wrote of one of his experiences on Mount Rainier:

> Once as we came down the cloud-shrouded slopes of Rainier where we had been looking for White-tailed Ptarmigan, the little arctic chickens that live among its bleak boulder fields, a sudden storm swept in from the low peaks to the west. There was no shelter where we were, so we hurried the last few hundred yards to a ranger's cabin at timber line. As we waited on the porch for the black clouds to break, a chorus of Varied Thrushes, the robins of the rain forest, made cathedral music with their eerie harmonic whistles in the dark firs below. When the first big drops fell one thrush hopped from its shelter in the shadows, and as the downpour increased in tempo, flew from branch to branch until it perched on the tip of the tallest tree. There it sang, as I have seldom heard a bird sing, while the rain pelted down. Never have I seen a bird express such oneness with the elements, nor in such a setting, for to face the fresh breeze on Rainier is to blow the cobwebs from one's soul.[21]

On one of his pelagic trips, Peterson saw as many as fifteen albatrosses gathered around his boat to gobble up the oil and greasy suet thrown out for them. He said: "We even tossed squid to them, which they caught in their great horny hooked bills, just as we would throw bread to the tame ducks in a city park... I took a hundred pictures and Stackpole [Peter Stackpole, a *Life* magazine photographer] snapped twice that many. There was a gentle dignified look about them as they watched us with seeming curiosity."[22]

Roger Tory Peterson did a series of paintings for *Life* magazine from 1938 to 1948. In the 1950s, he was responsible for producing some of the Red Rose Tea cards — tiny one-and-a-half inch high by two-and-three-quarter inch long cards that came free in packages of Red Rose Tea and

Blue Ribbon Coffee. Many of his paintings were reproduced on the front of these cards and he wrote the text for the back of each bird card. These cards were collected by children and adults and were an educational source for learning about the natural world. At this time he was also producing paintings of birds and their landscape backgrounds, intended for the general public, which appeared on calendars, postcards and books. In 1950 Peterson accepted the position of Art Director for the National Wildlife Federation conservation stamp program, where for years he planned the stamp sheets and albums, recruited artists and assigned subjects, wrote captions, and contributed numerous paintings.[23]

Peterson was also involved in making films for the Audubon Screen Tours, including *Wild America*, a full-colour, ninety-minute nature film in 1955. This silent film was shown to audiences with Peterson providing the audio commentary. Although he had a script, he modified it depending on the audience. His 1960 film *Wild Europe* was also silent. This was followed by the sound films *Wild Eden* about the Galapagos in 1967 and *Wild Africa* in 1972.

Peterson did a tremendous amount of travelling, both nationally and internationally, related to his work with birds. He became good friends with James Fisher, Britain's best-known ornithologist, and in 1953 carefully planned out a transcontinental birding tour of North America for the two of them.

In 1968 Peterson first joined Lindblad Travel on an expedition to Antarctica. This was the first of many trips he made with Lars-Eric Lindblad to Antarctica, the Arctic, Europe, Asia, South America, and Africa. Peterson emphasized the need for conservation worldwide. He recalled:

> It was largely because of our mutual friend Lars-Eric Lindblad, and his great ship the *Explorer*, that Peter [Scott, son of Antarctic explorer Captain Robert Scott] and I became such frequent companions, sharing our delight in the wild places of six continents.... Whenever there was a convention of any environmental significance, Peter was always there. At a World Wildlife Fund meeting at Buckingham Palace, he even introduced me

Roger Tory Peterson (middle) with Robert Bateman and Peter Scott.
Courtesy of Birgit Freybe Bateman.

to Queen Elizabeth. When she asked me how many kinds of birds there were in the world, I answered "About 8,600, Your Majesty."[24]

For the last forty-one years of his life, Peterson chose to make his home base in Old Lyme, Connecticut. As he said, "As an artist and writer, I need New York for the American Museum of Natural History and Boston for Houghton Mifflin, my publisher. But as a naturalist I prefer to live as far from either city as I can manage. So I chose a midway point in Connecticut — Old Lyme — near the mouth of the Connecticut River, and I have lived there almost half my life."[25]

The breadth and calibre of the awards presented to Roger Tory Peterson indicate the wide extent of his work. They include the William Brewster Memorial Award, the highest honour of the American Ornithologists' Union, for his contributions to ornithology (1944); the John Burroughs Medal for nature writing (1950); the Geoffrey St. Hilaire Gold Medal from the French Natural History Society (1954); the Gold Medal of the

New York Zoological Society (1961); the Conservation Medal of the National Audubon Society (1971); the Gold Medal of the World Wildlife Fund (1972); the Joseph Wood Krutch Medal from the Humane Society of the United States (1973); the Explorers Medal from the Explorers Club (1974); the Linnaeus Gold Medal of the Royal Swedish Academy of Sciences (1976); the Order of the Golden Ark from the Netherlands (1978); the Presidential Medal of Freedom, the highest honour awarded to an American civilian (1980); the Ludlow Griscom Award from the American Birding Association for excellence in field birding (1980); and the James Smithson Bicentennial Medal from the Smithsonian Institution (1984). He received twenty-two honourary doctorate degrees.[26]

From 1984 to 1996 Peterson published a column called "All Things Reconsidered" in the bimonthly *Bird Watcher's Digest*. In 1993 the Roger Tory Peterson Institute of Natural History building opened in Jamestown, New York. Its mission is "to inform society about the natural world through the study and teaching of natural history."[27]

Roger Tory Peterson never stopped working strenuously on his many projects. The output from his extensive work in the fields of art, photography, writing, education, and conservation is astounding. He managed to accomplish all this through keeping up an intense pace which could be compared to the high metabolism of the birds he studied and loved. His work was his life and his life was with birds. He always wanted to be where the birds were. S. Dillon Ripley, Secretary Emeritus of the Smithsonian Institution, described Roger Tory Peterson as follows: "In my mind's eye I can see Roger as a perennial Norseman, striding along cliff edges or on rocky promontories washed by pounding surf, white hair tossing in the wind, binoculars clutched at the ready, he represents an undying enthusiasm for all the works of nature."[28]

Chapter Eighteen

Hans Albert Hochbaum
(1911-1988)

"It is their destiny to ride the wind that carries them to faraway places. They leave at sundown, dark against the blaze, pursuing their course by measures man does not yet comprehend. This annual rhythm of travel has been the way of waterfowl from the beginning of their time, one hundred million years before Homo sapiens evolved as a human being."

— H. Albert Hochbaum in *To Ride the Wind*.

The majority of Albert Hochbaum's life was spent in the scientific study of waterfowl — North American ducks, geese, and swans of the family *Anatidae*. He first came to Delta Waterfowl Research Station at Delta Marsh on Lake Manitoba in 1938, and later became its research director, a position he held until his retirement in 1970. He was a scientist and conservationist who interacted regularly with sportsmen, but first and foremost promoted what was in the best interests of the waterfowl.

Hochbaum realized that very little was really known about the lives and habits of the various species of waterfowl, and he encouraged scientific studies to discover more about them. He spent a lifetime studying waterfowl and describing their actions in books. In these books, he wrote about some of the conclusions he had arrived at as a result of his scientific studies. His books are so well-written that they received numerous awards. *The Canvasback on a Prairie Marsh* (1944) won the William Brewster Memorial Award in 1945. The Brewster Award is given by the

H. Albert Hochbaum.

Courtesy of C. Stuart Houston.

American Ornithologists' Union for an exceptional body of work on birds of the Western Hemisphere and consists of a medal and an honourarium. This book also won the 1944 Literary Award of The Wildlife Society, which recognizes accomplishments in wildlife publications, management science, and professionalism. Hochbaum's book *Travels and Traditions of Waterfowl* (1955) won him a second Literary Award in 1956.

Besides being a scientist and writer, Albert Hochbaum was also an artist and painter. He illustrated his own books, as well as those of others. His paintings are owned by many private individuals, corporations, and museums, including the Smithsonian Institution and the Canadian Museum of Nature. One of his paintings was presented to Queen Elizabeth II during her visit to Manitoba in 1970.

Albert Hochbaum was born in 1911 at Greeley, Colorado, and went to school in Boise, Idaho, and Washington, D.C. He studied at Cornell University and received a bachelor of science in zoology. Then he worked

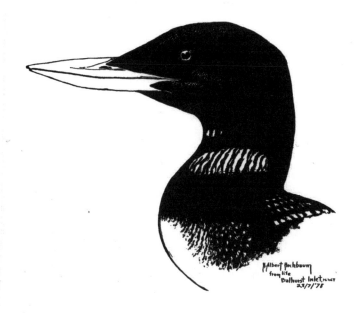

Drawing of a Yellow-billed Loon, by H. Albert Hochbaum.

Courtesy of C. Stuart Houston.

for three years as a wildlife technician with the United States National Park Service. He became a graduate student working under Aldo Leopold at the University of Wisconsin in Madison, and this is what first brought him to the Manitoba Delta Marsh.

The origin and history of the Manitoba Delta Marsh are especially interesting. James Ford Bell, who was the founder of General Mills, became unhappy with the declining waterfowl conditions at his hunting grounds in Minnesota and began to look around for better sites. He was attracted by the large fall flights at Manitoba's Delta Marsh. According to Joan Hochbaum, Albert's wife, "He got off the train and met a Dr. Fred Cadham, who owned all the land where the [Delta Marsh Research] station is now. Bell bought his first holdings from Cadham and he got another company in Winnipeg to put together the rest of the holdings."[1]

In 1923 Bell purchased additional holdings on the southern shores of Lake Manitoba, which included York Lodge, which became his home during his hunting trips. Bell wrote about this area: "When I first went to the Delta, there were no limits except those which were self-imposed. Despite this freedom, we did set limits as to the amount and to the number of shells to be used in getting that limit. Still it troubled me to think we were destroying without making some effort at replenishment."[2]

Bell thought there might be a way for man to hand raise wild waterfowl and thereby replenish the local population. In 1926 he hired Edward Ward as his groundskeeper and manager of the hunting lodge. Edward Ward had snowshoed across a frozen portion of Lake Manitoba from the Inter-Lake region to apply for the position.[3] Ward was the son of a Scottish gameskeeper and he had worked for several seasons with Percy Algernon Taverner, the ornithologist. Taverner had recommended Ward who, because of his understanding of waterfowl, would be best able to assist with Bell's plan to hand raise wild ducks. With government permits, eggs from wild Mallards in the marsh were gathered and artificially incubated and reared, with the plan to reintroduce them into the wild. Bell and Ward learned many things doing this, but Bell wrote:

> Then came a realization that we must go deeper into the matter and have an understanding of the various phases of their lives and the dangers to which the species were exposed. In other words: What could we expect in the way of propagation from an ordinary pair of ducks, not over a single year, but over a sufficient term of years to cover the cycle of their lives? What was the incidence of botulism? What was the incidence of shooting? What was the incidence of predators? What was the incidence of climate? What was the impact of a growing population upon the various ground areas which formed their natural habitat? etc.[4]

Bell decided that the best qualified person to form a waterfowl research program at the Delta Marsh was the renowned naturalist Aldo Leopold. After some initial misgivings, Leopold became convinced that Bell was serious about offering his property for any research useful to waterfowl conservation, and not just for raising ducks. Leopold applied to the technical committee of the American Wildlife Institute and received a $1,000 grant to support a graduate student to work at Delta Marsh. Albert Hochbaum, then a graduate student of Leopold's at the University of Wisconsin, was appointed to spend June through November conducting research at the facilities provided by James Ford Bell. Peter Ward, Edward Ward's son, became his research assistant. Upon his arrival at Delta Marsh, Albert Hochbaum is said to have exclaimed: "This is the place I have always dreamed of."[5]

Working in the summers at Delta Marsh and in the winters at Madison, Hochbaum earned his Master of Science in Wildlife Management degree in 1941. In 1939, he had married Eleanor Joan Ward, the daughter of Edward Ward, the game warden at Delta. They were to have four children, three boys and a girl. Under Albert Hochbaum's leadership as Research Director, the Delta Research Station became the temporary home to students from all over North America doing their Master's or Ph.D. research. It also attracted well-known ornithologists such as Margaret Nice, who conducted waterfowl research studies there.

Albert Hochbaum spent over thirty years studying waterfowl at the Delta Marsh field station. The Delta Marsh is one of the largest in the Canadian wheat belt. Nineteen miles long east and west, and as much as five miles wide between lake ridge and wheat prairie, it includes about 36,000 acres. It is the largest of several marshland units in the Lake Manitoba basin, and is one of the finest waterfowl breeding places on the Canadian Prairies. Lake Manitoba itself is about 115 miles long north and south, and about thirty-two miles wide at its southern end, which is a broad, unbroken expanse of water. The lake is slightly larger than the Great Salt Lake of Utah, and is shallow, its depth not exceeding twenty-six feet.[6]

The Delta Marsh is more than just a breeding place for waterfowl. Ducks do come to Delta Marsh to nest and rear their young, but it is also a home for wildfowl from the first breakup of the ice in the spring until the ice returns in the autumn. Ducks are present more than half of the year. Some species may rarely nest there but spend the period of their flightless molt in the marsh. The brief period in which ducks are paired at Delta covers only late April, May, and June. Shortly after that, crowds of newly flying young roam about the marsh, some of which were born locally, while others have come in from other regions.

Albert Hochbaum studied the habits and movements of the different species over many years. Among his many observations are some notes on the nesting preferences of ducks that breed in the Delta region:

> The species of ducks that breed in the Delta region may be classed broadly in two groups, those that nest on dry land away from the water, and those that nest over water. All of the river ducks, as well as two diving ducks, the Lesser Scaup and the White-winged Scoter, are land-nesters. The Redhead, the Canvasback, and the Ruddy Duck are water-nesters. The American Golden-Eye, an uncommon species in summer at Delta, represents a third group, those that nest in hollow trees.... In all species there are occasional departures from normal behaviour.[7]

Hochbaum described how the eyes of ducks have evolved to serve their needs for long-distance flights and predator avoidance:

> It is impossible, with our binocular vision and narrow visual field, to imagine how the world appears to a duck.... Unless, of course, you can imagine your eyes the size of grapefruits and stuck about where your ears presently reside.... Compared to a duck's visual abilities, in fact, we human vertebrates have tunnel vision and a nearsighted, blurred view of the world.... Unlike the human eye, which is oval-shaped, like an olive, a duck's eye is flattened, its cross-sectional share lenticular. So structured, the duck's eye serves like a super wide-angle lens on a camera, capturing a wide field of vision. This eye shape, along with its large size, allows the duck in one glance to see close and distant objects in sharp focus (great depth of field, in photographers' terminology) over a large part of the horizon. Thus, with one eye pointed outward on each side

of its head, a duck can survey an extremely wide field of view. The common pigeon, which has similarly shaped and positioned eyes, enjoys a total visual field of about 340 degrees. This means that a duck or pigeon, except for a narrow wedge of blind spot immediately behind its body, can sharply view objects near and far in almost a full circle around and above itself without having to turn its head.... So what advantage does a duck receive from having large, wide-set eyes and largely monocular, instead of largely binocular vision? First, when flying at high altitudes, ducks need little depth perception. When on the ground or paddling on the water, where they are most susceptible to predators, their wide-set eyes and sharp monocular vision allows ducks to better detect predators above and around them.... In other words, a duck's optical equipment and visual abilities are adaptations best suited to serve the bird's lifestyle.... It has been repeated for years that waterfowl vision is 50 to 100 times more acute than that of humans.... These birds can discern colour, and they are always on the lookout for movement, which to them, signals danger.[8]

In his books on waterfowl, Hochbaum emphasized the need for further careful research and study into many unknowns that may be impacting waterfowl. He stated: "On my bookshelf, which is essentially a waterfowl library, I have ten pounds of literature on farm game management for every ounce on ducks. And I can find more of the life history facts on the Song Sparrow than on the Redhead or Ruddy Duck, neither of which has yet fully recovered from their dangerous position of the last decade."[9]

One topic that he says deserves further research is the existence of an excess of males in the populations of North American waterfowl.[10] In careful counts he made during the 1941 and 1942 migrations, he saw 329 male Ruddy Ducks and thirty-five females, nine drakes for every hen. Although this greater number of males undoubtedly was influenced to a certain extent by the earlier arrival of drakes in this species, he still found a noticeable excess of males throughout the breeding season. In mid-June, when most females are nesting and still are attended by their mates, he witnessed hundreds of loose, unattached males paddling through the marsh.[11] This unequal sex ratio means that the potential breeding population of a species is considerably less than indicated by a census. In a population of 100,000 ducks, with a male-female ratio of 65:35, instead of a potential breeding population of 50,000 pairs, there actually can be no more than 35,000 pairs at the very most. With some females not breeding their first year and others harassed by the heavy excess of unmated males, the number probably would be considerably less. In such populations a species might not be able to reproduce its numbers in a season, much less increase.

A possible reason given for the preponderance of males and scarcity of females is female deaths during incubation when a ground-nesting female, bearing the full task of incubation by herself, is more vulnerable to predators and fires than the drake. Whenever ducks are shot on northern breeding grounds, a larger kill of adult females will prevail, due to the midsummer departure of the drakes and the delayed wing molt of the females. Also drought conditions may take a heavy toll of flightless young and the females who remain with them.

In his *Travels and Traditions of Waterfowl*, Albert Hochbaum expressed what he meant by "tradition." He wrote: "However alike two ducks may be in their physical structure, however similar may be the innate behaviour of one duck to that of its specific companions, each individual bird is different from all others of its kind by virtue of its unique experiences."[12]

He explains that unlike the Canada Geese at Delta, where adults and young-of-the-year may depart southward together in November and return still as a united group the next April, in North American ducks there is quite a different arrangement. The father leaves his mate before the young are hatched, leaving the nesting area to join other males, which, like himself, are molting. The mother usually stays with her ducklings until they are on the wing and then she leaves them to undergo her own flight feather molt. The young ducks are then completely on their own, and there is no further bond of kinship between parent and juvenile. Young ducks wander during the summer, gain their own knowledge and experience of varied surroundings, and eventually join with larger groups, which also contain experienced adults. The ducks seek out other ducks and learn from their companions, but each duck has an individual store of knowledge and experience, which is supplemented by the traditions which it picks up from its companions. This is not an innate, but rather a learned behaviour.

Hochbaum provided an example of a successful attempt to transplant ducks as breeding populations into ranges where the original populations have been extinguished.

> In the summer of 1951 a crate of young Pintails trav-eled to New York State by rail. These ducklings had been hatched at Delta from eggs taken from wild nests in nearby stubble and meadowland. They were half-grown when they left Delta and had seen no countryside beyond the narrow view from the hatchery window. Their travels ended in central New York, where they were banded and released on Spicer's Marsh. Next spring, a survivor of the first autumn and winter, identified by her leg band, migrated back from the southland to nest and rear her young on Spicer's Marsh. This place had not known nesting Pintails in modern times. With all the wide northland to visit, she was faithful to the marsh of her maidenhood.[13]

This has implications for restoring populations of such species as Redhead or Gadwall to ranges where they had previously been wiped out. Young birds that have their first flight experience at these sites may return to breed there and eventually begin a new tradition.

Hochbaum also writes about the effects of "broken traditions," where birds are exterminated from a local area. He explained that once all the local breeders from an area are destroyed, there are none to return to these areas to breed. Historically, settlers may have thought there was no harm in taking a modest harvest of local birds every year, especially considering the great flights that passed through in the spring and fall. However, in a few years, this predation gradually thinned local nesters down to a few widely-scattered birds. When the last families were taken, their traditions were dead. The lakes, with their "rushy borders, and the muskrats upon whose houses these wildfowl nested, have survived to please the settlers' grandchildren; but the native geese and swans are gone."[14] By annually taking a few from the home marsh, eventually no local breeding birds were left. Although many ducks continued to pass by in spring migrations, once the native birds with local breeding traditions were killed, few or none stopped to nest in these localities.

Albert Hochbaum, known by many as "Man of the Marsh,"[15] died in 1988 at Portage la Prairie, Manitoba. His writings have a profound way of teaching classic lessons of life by writing about simple truths, food chains, the battle for survival, and what happens when this delicate balance is disrupted. He opens our eyes to the complex natural world around us.[16]

During his lifetime, Albert Hochbaum's dedication to waterfowl, his immense talents, and his lifetime of accomplishments were acknowledged in many ways. He received a John Simon Guggenheim Fellowship (1961), the Manitoba Golden Boy Award (1962), an honourary doctorate from the University of Manitoba (1962), a fellowship of the American Ornithologists' Union, the Manitoba Centennial Medal of Honour (1970), the Crandall Conservation Award (1975), a Canada Council Explorations fellowship (1975), membership in the Order of Canada (1978), the Aldo Leopold Wildlife Conservation Award (1980), a Special Conservation Achievement Award of the National Wildlife Federation (1986), the Distinguished Naturalist Award (Seton Medal) from the Manitoba Naturalists' Society (1986), and the Professional Wildlife Conservation Award of the Province of Manitoba (1987).

Epilogue

The bays are closed with ice; the ducks are gone. Where blue-bills rode a week ago, a Snowy Owl now sits in the middle of an ice field. The ducks are gone; for five months to come there will be only the music of the north wind in the maples. It is winter and rough winter every day, until sometime in late March when Georgie Storey will strain with hand in air from the last seat in the last row of the little building housing the marsh-side school.

"Yes, George?"

"I seen four Mallards this morning."

"SAW, George. I SAW four Mallards. The past participle is —"

The lesson is never finished. From far away comes the bark of geese. The children run for the schoolyard, the teacher for the stoop.

"There they are! There they are! Canada Grays over Slacks' bluff!"

Over by the shed the men stop their work and step into the sun to watch the birds in silence. They see them swing over the bay, flare above the schoolyard, then head north across the frozen lake. Old Ernie Cook, gravely taking pipe from mouth, says, "A week early."

There is no sound except of geese and the south wind in the maples, the coming of another spring.[17]

PART SIX

Conservation and Preservation of Species

Chapter Nineteen

Robert W. Nero
(1922–)

"We probably can never really know any other creature fully. Though we catalog its comings and goings, measure and photograph its performances, count its numbers, and write endlessly about it, still, the true character of this 'different race of creatures' eludes us."

— Robert W. Nero in *The Great Gray Owl:*
Phantom of the Northern Forest.

In Robert Nero, there is a unique blending of scientific field study of unsurpassed excellence, with the eloquent and poetic expression of what this study means. He has been able to effectively combine his passions for birds, wildlife, conservation, and archeology with his talents for writing and poetry. Robert Nero is a great naturalist at heart and has completed extensive field studies of the life histories of the Red-winged Blackbird and the Great Gray Owl. He has investigated the status of the Cougar in the Prairie Provinces, and made in-depth scientific studies of birds and other animals of Saskatchewan and Manitoba. Behind his scientific work, there is always a realization of the importance of understanding a species, and of conservation. His enthusiasm and passion for natural history studies is infectious and is passed on to everyone he encounters personally, as well as through his writing and poetry.

Robert Nero was born and raised in Wisconsin. During the Second World War he interrupted his university studies to become a corporal in a

United States mortar company, fighting against Japan on Leyte and Luzon in the Philippines. When in June 1945, the war suddenly ended, he wrote about his feelings in a poem called "Bird," which was later published in his book *Spring Again: And Other Poems*. He "was enjoying a new freedom. Walking fearlessly outside our camp for the first time in many months, duties largely suspended, everything had great appeal for me. Suddenly, I had time on my hands, and access to a typewriter! Swallows flying low over fields near our camp one breezy morning caught my attention — a simple scene. I can still recall the elation I felt."[1] Following the war. Robert Nero obtained his master's and Ph.D. degrees at the University of Wisconsin in Madison, majoring in zoology with a minor in wildlife management.

While trying to decide on a thesis topic, a fellow graduate student, James R. Beer, who was studying muskrats at a marsh near the university, suggested to him a Red-winged Blackbird study in the same marsh, and Nero's major professor, John T. Emlen, Jr., agreed to the project. The Wingra Marsh, which is a two and one-quarter acre cattail marsh about three miles south of the Madison campus, became Bob's main study area from 1948 to 1953. He began by observing the behaviour of one territorial male in great detail, recording on maps the movements of his bird with the length of time it spent at each location. He wrote:

> To stand and watch a single bird, hour after hour, day after day, its own behaviour, interactions with other males and other species, all carefully recorded in this first lesson in watching birds — it was a revelation.... Redwings, it turned out, were not just scattered randomly across the marsh; rather, the males moved within definite systems. I had no idea things were so formalized. What I had earlier perceived as a marsh ringing with the sounds of exuberant birdlife turned out to be a tense, regulated series of actions and reactions — compelling, structured, and effective.[2]

In June 1948, Bob married Ruth, who became a constant companion and assistant in his field work. Every day during the summer of that year,

Robert Nero walking along a trail in Wingra Marsh in spring, circa 1951.

Photograph by Hugh Wilmar from Robert W. Nero, Redwings, Smithsonian Institution Press 1984.

they rode their bicycles from the campus to the marsh, leaving before dawn to set traps for Redwings. Nero wrote: "I was determined to colour-band as many birds as possible in order to better understand their behaviour."[3] With the help of several fellow graduate students, in 1950 Nero built two observation towers twelve feet above the water out in the marsh. He had to wear hip waders to get out to them, but once settled there he was able to look down on the marsh and see everything that was going on. In order to better understand the behaviour of individual birds, he banded 282 birds, including 175 nestlings or fledglings, during the years 1948 to 1952.

Nero says that by the end of his first year of studying Redwing behaviour, he thought he had it fairly well figured out. However, by 1953, he found that almost all of his early rules of behaviour had been broken and his field notes indicated much variation among individual birds. He wrote:

> One of the professors on my thesis committee ... suggested that I was over-emphasizing "abnormal behaviour." Surely there must be something that they all do in the same way ... but birds do show a great deal of individual behaviour, and the longer I watched Redwings the more of this I saw. I suspect this is so for all the species. Only in short-term studies are behaviour patterns simple and regular.[4]

Because of his close involvement with Redwings, Nero has respect for them and empathy with their lives. He also understands the great damage these birds can inflict on crops in the fall when they gather into large flocks. He comments that the annual overall loss from various types of blackbird damage to farm crops in southern Manitoba alone has been estimated at two million dollars, and that various methods are used to try to control the damage. However, he writes:

> Somewhere in my files I have a clipping from *Life* magazine from many years ago showing a full-page photo of about a dozen adult male Redwings trapped by freezing spray on the edge of open water on one of the Great Lakes. The birds had probably been foraging along the ice when they became frozen to its surface and then engulfed. Only their heads and sharp bills showed above the shiny, translucent globules of ice in which each was trapped alive. There was no sign of alarm in their eyes. State conservation officials were shown in other photos

carefully chopping loose the ice-encased birds and then thawing them out under a car heater, prior to releasing them. The Redwings in their balls of ice made a dramatic sight and one had to admire the tender care with which they were being rescued. Wildlife officials at all levels are confronted ... with problems of blackbird crop depredation and winter roosts of millions of birds. Still, I like to think of that picture of the men freeing the ice-trapped Redwings as a good example of the crucial relationship between man and nature.[5]

During his years at the University of Wisconsin, Nero also worked for the Zoological Museum, collecting and preparing bird and mammal specimens. Shortly after he got his Ph.D., he and his family moved to Regina, Saskatchewan, where he was the assistant director of the province's new museum of natural history, which is now called the Royal Saskatchewan Museum. There he was directly responsible for supervising and directing the educational programs, organizing field activities, supervising specimen collection, and helping to design displays and exhibitions.[6] He was also asked to develop a small archaeological program for the museum, as archaeology would be necessary to establish its professional reputation and to provide new exhibits. Robert Nero was well prepared for this type of fieldwork. A year after arriving at the museum, he teamed up with paleontologist Bruce McCorquodale to conduct a small archaeological operation at an eroding bank below a dam on the Souris River near Oxbow in southeastern Saskatchewan. The small side-notched arrowheads they unearthed there turned out to be the oldest known points of that type in North America.[7] They called the site the Oxbow Dam site, and subsequently that type of projectile point became known as the Oxbow Point, and hence the Oxbow Culture.

In the summer of 1960 Nero set off to study birds in the extreme northwestern part of Saskatchewan, close to the Northwest Territories. He kept notes on all the birds he saw, as well as collected, and prepared bird and mammal specimens. He also collected artifacts. With his characteristic humour, he wrote: "Being almost equally interested in ornithology and archaeology, at times in the field I have been forced to choose between looking up or looking down."[8]

Nero's sense of humour is again recorded in the following description from the museum in Regina:

> His sense of humor was appreciated by many visitors to the Museum, especially in 1956, when he made a display case of lost and found items, including professional, museum-quality labels. Entitled "What's New," the display included items like gloves, mittens, earrings, belts and scarves. A collection of mittens was labeled "Gloves from Several Tribes," and a collection of keys was designated by a tag that reads "Use of Metallic Minerals." A lone pair of earmuffs received the honour of being designated a "Ceremonial Headdress."[9]

While working at the museum, Nero began the Prairie Nest Record Scheme in 1958, which was a response to the concern over decreasing bird populations. This program to record information on bird nests quickly spread throughout the Prairies. The long-term data sets allow researchers to determine trends in such areas as population dynamics of birds, and the impact of climate change.

Robert Nero was assistant professor of biology at the Regina campus of the University of Saskatchewan from 1960 to 1966. During that period he made several summer trips to the Lake Athabasca region, combining searches for birds of the area with searches for archaeological artifacts. He published *Birds of the Lake Athabasca Region, Saskatchewan* as a special publication of the Saskatchewan Natural History Society in 1963. Nero found the Athabasca Sand Dunes on the south shore of this large lake a particularly productive area for discovering artifacts, as well as an interesting ecological place. He wrote in a letter to his wife Ruth in July 1960, that "The south shore was more like a wilderness than any other part — and wide open — like expecting to see an Arab on a camel."[10]

In his report on birds of the region, he wrote in an article describing how he and two other naturalists had discovered Arctic Terns nesting in the sand dunes on the south shore of Lake Athabasca: "Archaeological remains are often found uncovered in sand dunes and it was mainly in a search for such sites that we hastily set out from camp late in the afternoon.... A few minutes later, while examining firestones and flint chips in a prehistoric camp-site, which we found about 150 yards away, we made the then astonishing discovery of two brown eggs, unmistakably tern eggs, lying in a shallow depression on the bare sand." The caption under the photograph of that scene in another report reads: "Site of an Arctic Tern nest (and, incidentally, a prehistoric camp site) in the dunes about five miles west of Beaver Point."[11]

The sand dunes of Lake Athabasca so impressed Nero that he continued to speak of it publicly. In 1983 he gave a talk to the Manitoba Naturalists Society about this area of Canada. Following the presentation, Edith Williams, then president of the society, was so impressed that she wrote in a letter to John Roberts, the Minister of Environment:

> In the evening of January 3, 1983 ... we were treated to an extremely enlightening illustrated talk on the vast sand dune area on the south shore of Lake Athabasca.... Nero spoke to approximately 350 members ... a lucid and exciting overview of the origin of the sand dunes, the archaeology, geology, botany, ornithology, and especially, their beauty. It was a dramatic and impressive visual experience. There seems little doubt that there is no more unique, fragile and beautiful natural area in Canada than the Lake Athabasca sand dunes; there is nothing comparable on the Canadian mainland. There is also no question that this area has great scientific value and should be given a high degree of protection from development. As a unique land feature and botanically significant site it merits full protection.[12]

In 1966 Robert Nero accepted a position with the new Manitoba Museum of Man and Nature, and moved to Winnipeg, Manitoba. For the next four years, he was occupied helping to plan the new museum's exhibits and programs. However, he still found time to stay on top of area developments in ornithology and zoology. In 1970 he moved to the Wildlife Branch of the Manitoba Department of Natural Resources (now called Manitoba Conservation). Initially hired as a writer, he later became involved with wetland development and a program for endangered species management. In 1971, while under contract as a writer with the Manitoba Conservation Education Branch, he was asked to write a booklet on the polar bear. With his usual truthfulness, Nero describes this experience: "I thought about it for awhile, then went back to my boss to point out that since I'd never seen a polar bear in the wild, perhaps he'd authorize a trip for me to Churchill. [His boss] said unhesitatingly: 'Dr. Nero, a true writer draws his inspiration from within – back to your desk.' [Nero's booklet] *The Great White Bears* is still being distributed by the Manitoba government."[13]

With the intention of getting the Cougar afforded better protection by the Manitoba government, Robert Nero initiated a program at the Wildlife Branch to compile records of Cougar sightings in Manitoba and adjacent areas. In 1982 he and Robert Wrigley of the Assiniboine Park Zoo in Winnipeg published on the status of this animal in Manitoba, under the title *Manitoba's Big Cat: The Story of the Cougar in Manitoba*. Nero researched records and encouraged amateur naturalists and other people around the province to report sightings to him. In Manitoba, sightings of two or more animals at the same time, some with kittens, were reported over fourteen times. This presence of females with young would confirm the existence of a resident population in Manitoba, since only after a Cougar has established a home range does it quit its transient phase and enter into the reproductive phase of its life.[14] Nero and Wrigley worked hard to gather data to show that the Cougar should be recognized as an endangered species in Manitoba.

Robert Nero's relationship with the Great Gray Owl began in 1968. In April of that year, he and wildlife photographer Robert R. Taylor trudged through deep, wet snow carrying equipment to build a photography tower at an active Great Gray Owl nest, north of The Pas, six hundred kilometers north of Winnipeg. This nest was only the third one known in Manitoba. Then, in the fall of 1968, large numbers of Great Gray Owls suddenly appeared southeast of Winnipeg. Several years later,

Nero discovered that they were nesting in this area. The Great Gray Owl breeding area is within or close to the boundaries of the Boreal Forest Zone. In the southeastern corner of Manitoba, there is an area of black spruce and tamarack-muskeg habitat which can accommodate the nesting requirements of the Great Gray Owl. In this area, Robert Nero was able to observe a resident population every year since 1968 during both summer and winter.

Nero describes the Boreal Forest as follows:

> There is comfort in the heavy mass of spruce that surrounds us as we ski through the woods, comfort in the absence of wind, and in the close contact with winter birds that approach us with curiosity. A flock of Boreal Chickadees, briefly pausing in their prying inspection of limbs and twigs, repeatedly call: "Dee-dee!" — fluttering about us when we softly squeak to draw them close. Gray Jays, light as down and fluffed out like thistle heads, come to visit us, dropping down in slow, almost motionless glides, then loosely hopping from one perch to another, whistling and chattering.... Though it is thirty degrees below zero, a sudden, sharp sense of springtime bird song halts us: a Pine Grosbeak in cheerful red plumage, perched on a wiry black spruce spire, delivers his sweet, flutelike call. How, we wonder, do these winter birds find enough food to sustain themselves? Moving lightly and quickly, they seem without cares; but they are constantly on the move, searching for food as they go through the forest, and this is part of their adaptation to long, cold winters.[15]

For years Nero searched for and banded Great Gray Owls, in the process learning much about their ways and needs. He and his partner, Herbert W.R. Copland, worked closely together in the field over many years, constructing nest platforms for them. The famous owl, Lady Grayl, came from one of the platform nests which Bob and Herb had built. In the spring of 1984 they were assisted in their work on several days by Renate Scriven, who at age seventeen was already an experienced bird rehabilitator and a raptor enthusiast. At one nest, they found three under-sized and weak chicks who were clearly not getting sufficient quantities of food. The youngest chick had two severe cuts on its head, presumably made by its older, larger nest-mates.

Great Gray Owls begin laying as early as mid-March, when temperatures are frequently very low. Keeping the eggs at close to ninety-eight degrees Fahrenheit, when the temperature may be as much as thirty or forty degrees below zero, is a full-time job for the female owl. Unlike waterfowl, whose females surround their eggs with down when they leave the nest, there is no such covering for owl eggs, and the female has little opportunity to leave the nest. The incubation period is about thirty days, but the period from the laying of the first egg to the hatching of the last egg can be from thirty to fifty days. Over this long period, the male owl must bring a great supply of food to the nest to feed both the female and chicks.[16] Sometimes the male is unable to find enough food.

On a later visit to the nest containing the three chicks, the youngest chick was barely able to hold up its head. Renate suggested that she take the injured chick and try to raise it. At first Nero was inclined to let nature take its course, but then he made up his mind to try to save the chick. From the beginning, the intent was to rehabilitate this owlet, not for release back into the wild, but to assist in education and fundraising efforts in connection with the Wildlife Branch project. An owl imprinted on humans could not be turned loose in the wild, as Nero later explained about Lady Grayl:

> There are several reasons why this bird can't be turned loose. For one thing, Grayl is afraid of owls or anything that looks like an owl! Because she is so strongly imprinted on people, owl creatures are outside her area of interest. Also, she has no experience whatsoever in hunting, and would probably have difficulty maintaining herself in the wild. The strongest reason for not giving her freedom in the wild, however, is that she is a hazard to humans. Turned loose in a strange world, she'd

probably fly to the nearest person as soon as she became hungry, expecting to be fed. Landing on the shoulder or head of an unsuspecting person could lead to accidental injury. For that reason alone, we would not dare to turn her loose. We knew all this, of course, well in advance of bringing her home. You can't take a young raptor from the wild, raise it with people, and then release it. A tame, human-imprinted raptor is a non-releasable bird.[17]

Renate, who held a provincial permit to rehabilitate wildlife, took the owlet into her home and skillfully cared for it, which was a major undertaking. Robert Nero then took over custody of Lady Grayl. One of Grayl's first public appearances was when Bob took her to an adult education class at Red River Community College. He talked about Gray Owl attributes, the research project, and the need for funding. Afterwards, as he headed for the car with Grayl on his arm, he was approached by one of the ladies from the class who asked if her five-year-old daughter could please see the bird. Nero relates: "I stooped down so that the child could get a good look, but I hadn't counted on the girl rushing forward and hugging the bird; she even kissed it on the bill! I was shocked, but the owl neither flinched nor showed any sign of annoyance. This was my first indication of the tolerance Grayl has for small people."[18]

The first marathon public appearance by Lady Grayl was in April 1985, at a Winnipeg shopping mall, where she sat in front of a Natural Resources display of large mounted photos of Great Gray Owl field studies for up to twelve hours a day for six days in a row. The owl display was one of about thirty exhibits organized for National Wildlife Week.[19] Nero took Lady Grayl out in public on many hundreds of public occasions after this. She enjoyed riding in the back of the car and seemed to like these outings. She always maintained her lenient attitude towards people. She made appearances at occasions ranging from press conferences to clubs to nursing homes, and she took it all in her stride, with never-ending grace. She was especially a great hit at schools as she related so well to young people. Lady Grayl was instrumental in having the Great Gray Owl named the provincial bird of Manitoba on July 16, 1987.

Robert Nero and Lady Grayl.

Photo by Alan Forrest.

Bob Nero officially retired from Manitoba Conservation in 1991, but he continues to hold the title of volunteer senior ecologist. He continued to take Lady Grayl to elementary schools, in order:

> To help get students to study birds of prey, not just to worry about fractions and adverbs, but to embrace the world of the owl as well, that is what is behind all this business of taking an owl to school.... When I look back over my life and try to identify things or situations that encouraged my interest in birds, one that stands out in my memory is sitting and looking at a mounted Barn Owl on top of a bookcase. This happened when I was eight or nine years old. I was living in an orphanage and was being punished for some silly thing I'd done or not done, and was forced to sit by myself in a seldom-used parlour. So I had time to look at the Barn Owl, lots of time. I like to compare that incident with now, when

youngsters get to see this live, tame owl. Who knows how the experience of meeting this bird may affect them?[20]

Lady Grayl lived for twenty-one years and touched the lives of thousands of people. She left the world on October 13, 2005. In her memory, the Lady Grayl Fund was established to help fund research, conservation, and education projects directly relating to owls and other wildlife.

Robert Nero has already received numerous honours for his life work in nature study, conservation, and education. He was awarded the 1995 Doris Huestis Speirs Award from the Society of Canadian Ornithologists. He has won awards throughout his career from Nature Saskatchewan, the Manitoba Naturalists Society, the Ottawa Field-Naturalists' Club, and the Wildlife Society. He received the Champion of Owls Award in March of 2006.

He has published several volumes of his poetry, including *Woman by the Shore and Other Poems: A Tribute to Louise de Kiriline Lawrence*, *The Mulch Pile*, *Spring Again*, *Growing Old Together* (which celebrates his marriage to Ruth), and *Out With the Dog: Poems for Dog-Lovers*.

Perhaps Bob Nero's most endearing quality is his ability to arouse in others an awareness and interest in the natural world through communicating his own knowledge and enthusiasm about nature. His daughter, Lorrel Beth Onosson, wrote a poem for him in 1997 for Father's Day:

TEACHER

How many country roads
we discovered on my
father's journeys — he
intent on finding artifacts
getting sore when our
childish minds paid no
heed to those lessons of
bird-lore he was anxious
to impart.

Robert and Ruth Nero with Lady Grayl on the cover of Robert Nero's book.

Copyright Birch Nero. Cover design by Neil Thorne.

He didn't know then
the storehouse of memories
developing as we took
to other adventures in
our secret children's minds —
those rutted muddy roads
are well-imprinted on my
brain — the texture, colour
and feel of well-packed,
drying, Saskatchewan gumbo.

Perhaps we fought a lot
all crowded in the back

of that old green Rambler
but what swells up in my mind
is the smell of wheat,
dry and dusty plains, the
excitement of another
lost farmhouse to explore;
the surprise — favourite to me
of small pebbled streams
found in the middle of nowhere.

Hence my fondness now
for long solitary walks
in forest, field or, yes
even a city railroad track —
I know the offering well —
I learned my lessons of
observation even if we
didn't seem to pay attention.

My knowledge surprises
me at times — after Spring's
flood waters have receded
I happen upon a frantic
female Redwing — helplessly
flapping — she is bound by
pink wool left by

Winter's sledding children —
I quickly grasp the flailing
bird and free her as her mate
circles around.
How did I know so well —
with not a second's hesitation
the art of approach and proper
hold to calm and free

this desperate thing — to
feel my own heart's joy?[21]

Robert Nero's intensive studies of various species of birds and other animals have instilled in him a great respect for and empathy with these creatures. Similar feelings are no doubt often held by other naturalists who have lived very closely with creatures found in nature and have come to a sympathy with them. However, Robert Nero is one of the very few scientist-naturalists who can so eloquently put these feelings into words. He concludes his book *The Great Gray Owl: Phantom of the Northern Forest* with these thoughts:

> In my own pursuit of the owl, I crave further understanding of its relationship to the spruce-tamarack bog and all it contains. What holds meaning for the owl? Being part of the bog, it relates to this environment in ways we'll probably never know.... The owl has superior vision and hearing, but what does it perceive in its surroundings? In sky, forest, flowers, and birds, we humans see patterns of light and colour, hear a medley of sounds, perceive various elements according to our individual insights, sharing some, but not all. But ah! If we could perceive the world of the owl, what strange sounds and beautiful forms we might enjoy![22]

Robert Nero wrote a poem called "The Owl's Gift":

> In the dark rainy night
> I consult with this oracle
> reaching through soft feathers
> to feel her warm throat
> the fabric of her being
> is mere thin skin stretched
> over braced bones and flesh
> a fragile assemblage
> to so command our attention.

So then where's the spirit of
this comforting creature that
ceaselessly charms us all?
It must be in her mind
(do birds have minds?)
it's in her attitude, the way
she trusts us and accepts us;
she comes from her owl-being
to meet us in her time
gravely allowing us a
glimpse of her world
a gift of tender tolerance
we do well to honour.[23]

Chapter Twenty

Robert Bateman
(1930–)

"I can't conceive of anything being more varied and rich and hand-some than the planet Earth. And its crowning beauty is the natural world ... I want to soak it up, to understand it as well as I can, and to absorb it. And then I'd like to put it together and express it in my painting. This is the way I want to dedicate my life."

— Robert Bateman.

Robert Bateman has united his extensive knowledge and understanding of the natural world with his equally encompassing knowledge of art and painting, to become one of the world's foremost and most celebrated wildlife artists. In many of his paintings, the bird or animal he depicts is at the edge, rather than at the centre, of the composition, and is often almost invisible. But this is what it is really like in the true world of nature! His paintings evoke in the observer a sense of being outdoors and experiencing the scene as it would actually happen in nature. His subjects are not staged and represent the bird or other animal from its own point of view, either looking at or ignoring us as human beings.

Robert Bateman was born in Toronto, Ontario, in 1930. At a very early age, he became immersed in the nature near his family home at that time. Below the backyard was a ravine which was filled with migrating birds, and he drew every one of them. His talent for drawing with precise accuracy, and his having such empathy with the bird or other animal that he is able to convey its true nature, seem to have been in-born characteristics.

Afternoon Glow: Snowy Owl (detail), 1977. Robert Bateman wrote about this painting: "I have portrayed this owl at the end of the day in the rich glow preceding sunset. White light is made up of all the colours of the spectrum. On a winter evening, these colours seem to separate and radiate a shimmer of every hue. I have echoed the bounds and curves of the grasses in the form of the bird and in the wind-sculpted snow."

Courtesy of and copyright Robert Bateman.

As a boy he rode his bicycle to places outside of the city and explored the woods for hawks, owls, and birds' nests. He was joined in his birding adventures by enthusiastic, like-minded friends. Bateman began to learn the names and characteristics of the birds and wrote:

> In my childhood birding days, [Northern Saw-whet Owls] would sometimes gather during migration on the islands in Toronto's harbor — one of my favorite birding haunts. My friends and I would take the ferry to that bird haven on autumn weekends and spot the saw-whets in the dense undergrowth at the island's edge, their lemon-yellow eyes staring right back at us through a patch of wild grapes or dogwood.[1]

Northern Reflections: Loon Family, *1981. Robert Bateman was commissioned to do this painting by the Government of Canada as a wedding present for H.R.H. the Prince of Wales Charles and Lady Diana Spencer when they were married in 1981.*

Courtesy of and copyright Robert Bateman.

Bateman became involved with other serious naturalists in his early teens when he spent Saturday mornings at the Junior Field Naturalists Club at the Royal Ontario Museum in Toronto. Here he was influenced by Terence Shortt, the dean of Canadian wildlife artists, whom Bateman felt knew more about wildlife than anyone he had ever met. After Bateman and some friends had outgrown the Junior Naturalists, they started the Intermediate Naturalists Club.[2] By the age of seventeen Bateman had acquired an excellent general knowledge about North American bird, mammal, and plant life.

In 1947 Robert spent the first of three summers at a wildlife research camp in Algonquin Provincial Park in northern Ontario, where he mingled with scientists studying natural ecosystems. Later, during his university years and after, he was with biological and geological field parties in such places as Newfoundland, the Ungava Peninsula in northern Quebec, and the tundra near Churchill, Manitoba. One summer he did fieldwork at the treeline near Churchill with J. Bristol Foster, his friend from the Royal Ontario Museum days. Foster subsequently completed a doctorate in biology at the University of British Columbia and is known for "Foster's Rule," which is a principle in evolutionary biology that members of a species get smaller or bigger depending on the resources available to them in the environment. This principle is at the heart of the study of island biogeography.[3]

Bateman recalls:

> One day as we were crossing the lichen-textured tundra, we heard a lyrical whistle and knew we'd come upon a Golden Plover.... We scoured every patch of ground, hoping to find a nest — and finally saw the female fly up at my approach.... We remained only a short while [so as not to draw the attention of potential predators] and set a twig in the ground to mark the spot.... When we returned some time later, we were surprised to see that, in spite of our caution, the eggs had completely disappeared.... Then our eyes caught an emerging pattern — revealing four tiny chicks, right between my feet! Their camouflage was so effective that I could easily have stepped right on them without noticing.[4]

During the five years Bateman was earning his honours degree in geography from Victoria College at the University of Toronto, followed by his high-school teaching certificate, he also travelled with friends to British Columbia, Mexico, England, France, and northern Europe. Travel, with a focus on wildlife biology, became, and still continues to be, important to him. Wherever he goes, he constantly sketches and takes photographs from real life, for later reference when painting.

In 1956 Bristol Foster proposed that the two of them take a trip around the world during the summer in a Land Rover. At first "Bob was incredulous," but "[w]ithin a week they were planning the trip with a school atlas."[5] They started from England in 1957 and went by sea to Ghana. From there they drove eastward across equatorial Africa, meeting tribal people along the way and visiting the great animal parks of East

Robert Bateman and a Gentoo Penguin.

Courtesy of Birgit Freybe Bateman.

Africa. One of the highlights of the journey was spending five days with the "Pygmies" in the Belgian Congo. Then they travelled on to India, Burma, Thailand, Malaya, and by ship to Australia.

In 1955 Bateman had begun teaching high school art and geography in a high school near Toronto. This was a career which sustained him and his growing family for the next twenty years until 1976. He says about his years of teaching high school: "Although my degree was in geography, I decided to teach art, because this engagement allows one to get to know the students at a deeper level. I loved sharing ideas with teenagers, many of whom became lifelong friends."[6]

Painting and nature were never far from Bateman's mind. From the age of eighteen he was starting to think of himself as an artist, not necessarily a professional artist, but a person who was seriously interested in art. He began reading art books and magazines and visiting art galleries. He experimented with impressionism and was influenced by the works of Paul Cézanne, especially as to the composition of a painting. He recalls: "Ever since then, I've treated painting as an assemblage that an artist puts together on purpose. He recreates nature, so to speak, and every element in the painting is selected and has a purpose."[7] Bateman also experimented with Cubism[8] and Abstract Expressionism. During the twentieth century, the art world had evolved away from subject matter into abstraction. Therefore, Bateman painted nature as abstract colour and form. At the same time he was increasingly active as an adult naturalist.

In 1962 Bateman had a revelation when he first saw the work of Andrew Wyeth at an art exhibition in Buffalo, New York. For the first time he saw that it was possible to combine abstract art forms with the particularity of the real world in paintings. From that time on, Bateman returned to realistic painting, while at times continuing to employ subtle abstract shapes, Cubist techniques, and patterns of shape and colour from other art forms in his paintings.

In 1963 he went to Nigeria for two years to teach advanced level geography at Government College in Umuahia under a Canadian external aid program. At that time Bristol Foster was in Kenya, teaching wildlife management at the University of Nairobi, and the two spent time in the game reserves. Foster acted as Bateman's informal agent when a local gallery became interested in exhibiting Bateman's paintings of African wildlife. These paintings elicited serious public interest and Bateman developed a reputation and following in Nairobi and London before he became well known in North America. During this time, Roger Tory Peterson was passing through Nairobi and visiting Bristol Foster, when he first saw a painting done by Bateman, which was hanging above Foster's mantelpiece. Peterson was greatly impressed with the work. Roger Tory Peterson and Robert Bateman met in person years later, and became good friends, travelling in various places together. Roger Tory Peterson has said about Bateman's work that: "He has looked at his subject so long that he can almost think like a deer or an antelope or whatever the species may be"[9] and "[his] paintings have a third dimensional activity, a movement in space, that many wildlife artists fail to master."[10]

Upon returning to Nelson High School in Burlington, Ontario, to teach, Bateman created a special project for himself for Canada's centennial year in 1967. He decided to do a series of paintings based on those things in his home county of Halton, Ontario, which had been

Roger Tory Peterson (left) and Robert Bateman.

Courtesy of Birgit Freybe Bateman.

there since at least 1867 — in other words natural and human heritage. He thought it would be fun to have these paintings exhibited where his friends and family could see them in a show at the local art gallery. The result of this experiment was a sell-out on the first night. Bateman notes that although much of the human heritage had lasted over one hundred years, most of it was wiped out in the next ten.[11] This art show was the start of his career as a professional artist.

Since the late 1970s Bateman has become recognized as one of the world's most outstanding artists in the field of nature and animal art. Although most of his paintings are in private collections and public art museums, many of the originals are seen by the public in the enormously popular retrospective exhibitions of his work, where paintings are temporarily lent out and later returned to their owners. Some of these one-man major exhibitions were the 1975 Tryon Gallery show in London, England, the 1987 Smithsonian show in Washington, D.C., and the 2009–10 shows in St. Petersburg and in Moscow at the State Russian Museum. Bateman's paintings are in tremendous demand. In order to allow his work to become accessible to more of the public, he agreed to a proposal by Mill Pond Press to produce limited-edition reproductions of his work. He personally checks the colour proofs of each edition in intense detail before signing them.

When they travel together on birding expeditions, Robert and his wife Birgit usually head off the beaten track, using detailed bird-finding guides to look for less well-known nesting and feeding grounds. Bateman says: "It takes longer to arrive at our final destination, but that is one of the beauties of birding. Looking for birds gives you a reason to slow down and enjoy the natural world."[12]

On one such side trip, they visited the Last Mountain Lake Bird Sanctuary, north of Regina, Saskatchewan in early October in the late 1970s. Last Mountain Lake Bird Sanctuary became the first ever designated bird sanctuary in North America in 1887. It is a crucial gathering and stopover place for many species of migrating birds, and in the fall flocks of cranes, geese, and ducks, often numbering in the tens of thousands, can be observed.[13]

Bateman describes their experience at this protected site:

> We ... came upon a flock of two or three thousand Sandhill Cranes feeding in a field not far from the lake itself. As I peered through my binoculars at this great assembly of tall gray birds, two white figures stood out like giant statues. For a moment my heart stopped. It was almost like seeing a pair of ghosts. But there was no mistaking the two tall Whooping Cranes with their crimson crowns and their wings tipped with black feathers. We watched them for a long time [as] they continued grazing placidly, oblivious to their fame and our continuing concern for their survival.[14]

Bateman's concern about decreasing biological diversity and the reckless way in which humans are treating the earth has led him to become a spokesperson for the conservation of both our natural and human heritage. He donates much of his time and money to causes advancing the preservation of biological diversity. With his great knowledge and appreciation of nature, he is always willing to speak out on behalf of the preservation of our natural and human heritage, which he sees is rapidly diminishing and being replaced by a more uniform, sterile environment.

Bateman has used his artwork and limited edition prints in fund-raising efforts to provide millions of dollars for organizations involved in environmental and preservation issues. The National Audubon Society made this remark in 1998 when including Robert Bateman as "One of the Twentieth Century's One Hundred Champions of Conservation": "With his evocative images of animals in their native habitat, [he] is one of the world's best-known contemporary wildlife artists. His paintings have brought a heightened awareness of nature to countless people ... Rather than rest on his reputation, Bateman constantly uses his popularity to speak out for the environment."[15]

Robert Bateman built a home on Salt Spring Island, British Columbia, between the mainland and Vancouver Island, and he and his family have lived there for many years. He has received twelve honourary doctorate degrees and is affiliated with, and a member of numerous naturalist and conservation groups. Bateman is the recipient of numerous major honours and awards, including the Queen Elizabeth Silver Jubilee Medal (1977); Officer of the Order of Canada (1984); Member of Honour Award of the World Wildlife Fund, presented by HRH The Prince Philip (1985); Governor General Award for Conservation (1987); Rachel Carson Award (1996); Golden Plate Award of the American Academy of Achievement (1998); National Audubon Society's "One of the Twentieth Century's One Hundred Champions of Conservation" (1998); Queen's Jubilee Medal (2002); Roland Michener Conservation Award of the Canadian Wildlife Federation (2003); and the Niagara Escarpment Lifetime Achievement Award (2009).[16] In 2010 the Society of Animal Artists gave him their Lifetime Achievement Award.

In 2007 Robert and Birgit Bateman gifted Royal Roads University near Victoria, British Columbia, with original art, photographs, sketch books, and artifacts to be housed in the Robert Bateman Centre, which is to be an education centre with a range of relevant and accessible programming emphasizing stewardship of place and the sustainability of the natural environment.

Robert Bateman's children and grandchildren have all been brought up experiencing nature, and in their own ways they carry on the heritage of art and nature. His recent concern and campaign is helping to bring the present generation of North-American young people back to experiencing nature as a balance to their damaging preoccupation with the electronic screen. He says: "Our society runs the risk of suffering from nature deficit disorder."[17]

Chapter Twenty-One

Kenn Kaufman
(1954-)

"The sheer aliveness of birds has to appeal to people. Most birds live at a level of intensity that we can't match. Watching a bird I'm often reminded of just what an intense experience life can be."

— Kenn Kaufman in an interview, May 17, 1997.

Kenn Kaufman is one of the world's best-known experts on birds. He has led birding and natural history tours on all seven continents and has made a special study of nearly all the North-American birds. He is fascinated with the lives of birds and goes to great extremes to find out more about them. He is an educator who believes that the greater the number of people who know something about birds and their lives, the greater will be the pressure exerted on governments and industries to protect them and facilitate their survival. Through his writings in books, periodicals, and field guides, as well as presentations at conferences, symposiums, and workshops, he shares the knowledge he has gained. Because he has learned so much about birds and their natural world and has the ability to pass this knowledge on to others, he is their true advocate.

Kenn Kaufman was born in South Bend, Indiana, in 1954. In his earliest childhood he was captivated with picture books on nature, and by the time he was six he had already focused his attention on birds. His hero was Roger Tory Peterson, whose books he borrowed from the local branch library, reading them over and over again and studying all of Peterson's

Kenn Kaufman in the forest in Nicaragua in January 2011.

Courtesy of Kimberly Kaufman.

bird paintings. His childhood interest in birds came to dominate his thoughts, to the point where all he could think about was to be able to go out into the world and see for himself the birds whose pictures he so admired. On his ninth birthday his family moved to Wichita, Kansas, where he first discovered the Western Kingbird. He wrote:

> One day when I was walking home from school I saw a bird the size of a robin, but patterned in pale yellow and gray, perched on a wire near my house. Running home, I grabbed my ... Peterson's ... bird guide ... and rushed back to find the bird still there. Squinting first at the bird and then at the field guide pictures, I figured out what it was: a Western Kingbird.... In that instant, the Western Kingbird became my favorite bird.... During that summer and the next, I found many kingbird nests. I spent hours watching them and taking notes. I admired the aggressive exploits of the adult birds as they drove away predators or rivals, tried to see what kinds of insects they brought to

feed their young, and watched the actions of the young
birds when they left the nest and learned to fly.[1]

At this time Kenn was birding without any binoculars. When he
was ten-and-a-half he bought a pair of $20 Sears binoculars. In his early
teens he began to dream about the possibility of travelling all over North
America to see all the species of different birds. In 1970, when he turned
sixteen, he worked as a nature instructor at a summer camp. With the
money he had saved from his job, he decided that he would not return
to high school, even though he was a good student, and instead he would
travel to see the birds. His parents agonized over whether or not to allow
him to make such a decision affecting his future career, but they finally
relented under the conditions that he keep in touch with them and travel
by public transport.

Kenn tried to obey the latter rule about not hitchhiking and started
out taking a Greyhound bus. But he soon found he needed to walk to the
places where he wanted to go to see the birds, and he could see no good
reason to turn down a passing driver's offer of a ride. In 1970 hitchhiking
was a more common method of travel, especially for impoverished teenagers who wanted to get from one place to another, and there were a lot of
people doing it. Law enforcement generally frowned on it, but in most
places it was legal. It was not uncommon for drivers, especially truck drivers, to pick up hitchhikers to keep them company and keep them awake
while driving at night on the interstate highways.

Over the next year or two Kenn made frequent birding trips, travelling until his money ran out and then returning to Wichita to work at day
jobs until he had enough money to travel again. He says about this time
that "I was always lucky enough to come out unscathed. It was all luck,
too. It was not skill or savvy or world-wise smarts, because I did not have
those things; all I had was dumb luck. I was learning, though. My sole
intention was to learn about birds, but on the way I also learned some
things about the world."[2]

Kenn had joined the American Birding Association at age sixteen, at
about the time it was just beginning and its bi-monthly magazine *Birding*
gave him helpful information on where to find birds. The American

Birding Association also provided him with connections to other birding colleagues and to prime birding hotspots. As he travelled around the continent searching for birds, Kenn looked up other birding enthusiasts, often joining them on excursions to find unusual species. He met up with other such passionate devotees as Rich Stallcup, and the single-minded Ted Parker, whose intense concentration in the field and drive to succeed had earned him a reputation as a genius in the sport of birding.

Anytime he heard of a serious birding activity going on anywhere on the continent, Kenn found he could get there in a few days at the most, travelling day and night. He was so passionate in his endeavour that he did not consider it a hardship to sleep outside in all kinds of weather. For food he bought cans of vegetable soup and perishables marked down for quick sale at grocery stores, and sometimes survived on free refills of coffee, supplemented with lots of cream and sugar, at roadside diners. He had made a commitment to himself to learn as much as possible about the birds and he began to think about trying to break the record for the most species seen in a year. The old record of six hundred North-American species had been broken in 1971 by Ted Parker, who had recorded 626 species. In 1973 Kenn made up his mind to try for the North-American Big Year record.

Travelling tens of thousands of miles, and crisscrossing the North American continent in 1973, Kenn succeeded in recording 671 species, including five from Baja California, which was included in the species checklist area of the American Ornithologists' Union. However, including only the region which became the official checklist area of the American Birding Association, he had 666, while his only close competitor, Floyd Murdoch, had 669 species. However, Kaufman says he "did set one record in 1973 that may never be broken — in the category of 'birds per buck.' My total living and travelling expenses for the year came to less than a thousand dollars, and nearly half of that amount went for a couple of plane flights in Alaska; most of the time I was getting by on less than a dollar per day."[3] Kenn later wrote about his birding adventures during this period in his book *Kingbird Highway: The Biggest Year in the Life of an Extreme Birder.*

Towards the end of his Big Year, Kaufman's interest in listing turned into a desire to study the birds, both common and rare, more carefully to take in all the details of both their appearance and behaviour, to see if he could really get to know them. His success as a birder led to his becoming a leader of international birding tours, first for WINGS and then for Victor Emanuel Nature Tours. He became associate editor of *American Birds*, the field journal of the National Audubon Society, and then field editor for *Audubon*, a position he still holds.

From the age of nine or ten Kenn had wanted to write bird books when he grew up, like his hero Roger Tory Peterson. He wanted not so much to work as an ornithologist, but to interpret birds and nature to the public. One of the methods he uses to accomplish this is to write articles, and he is a regular contributor to every birding magazine, including *Audubon*, *Birding*, and *Birder's World*. He writes a regular column, "After the Spark," in every issue of *Bird Watcher's Digest*. Another method is his keynote presentations at birding and wildlife festivals and birding workshops. But perhaps his most successful method of getting people involved in understanding more about birds and nature is through his books.

Kaufman's first very successful book was the *Peterson Field Guide to Advanced Birding*, published in 1990. This book was sponsored by the National Audubon Society, the National Wildlife Federation, and the Roger Tory Peterson Institute. It was intended to cover the more difficult birding challenges of identifying subtle differences between the similar-looking groups of birds in species such as shorebirds, gulls, and sparrows, as well as how to identify birds in their winter or immature plumages. In the editor's note to the book written by Kenn Kaufman and edited by Roger Tory Peterson, Peterson wrote:

> An effective field guide cannot be written by a large committee. There is too much risk of "flattening-out" of ideas. Therefore, although this book draws on the knowledge of many experts ... most of the text and all the drawings present challenging birds as seen through the eyes of Kenn Kaufman.... Aware of the special needs of less-experienced birders, Kenn Kaufman takes pains to explain basic things thoroughly and clearly....

Kenn Kaufman in the field.

Courtesy of Kimberly Kaufman.

Insights like these could take years to work out on your own, but with this book you can accelerate the learning process.[4]

In 1990, the year his *Advanced Birding* was published, Kaufman began to change direction in his thinking about how to advance knowledge of, and concern for, birds. He realized that suitable bird habitat was disappearing at an alarming rate, and that the best way to preserve this habitat was to get more people interested in nature and birds, thereby generating their desire to save habitats to ensure the birds' survival. When asked recently about his work, Kenn said: "All of my focus is on getting more people interested in nature: not just nature as an abstract idea, but nature as a complex of distinct species interacting in healthy ecosystems. If I give myself a job title, it might be 'recruiter' — always trying to enlist more people to care about biodiversity." Kaufman describes success as creating a world in which every adult and teenager could recognize fifty species of animals and plants native to their own region, and be very concerned about the continued survival of these species.[5]

Kaufman's *Lives of North American Birds*, published in 1996, is a great resource for people interested in birds. It includes a concise but thorough life history of every bird species found in North America, describing their types of summer and winter habitats, feeding diet and behaviour, court-ship behaviour and nesting, defense of nesting territory, nest site and type, eggs, behaviour and care of young, migration areas, and conservation status. All of this information is presented in a well-composed narrative style. Any special behavioural characteristics of each species are noted. The book includes photographs and range maps, but it is the narrative description that most readers are interested in. Once one has identified a bird, he can find out more about its life by reading about it in this book.

Kaufman began working on his own series of nature identification guides, the *Kaufman Field Guides*. His approach is to consider how difficult the process of identification is for a lone individual. He remembers what a long struggle he went through when first starting out in order to identify the birds he saw. So he made the field guides self-contained and easy to use. His first *Kaufman Field Guide* was *Birds of North America* published in 2000. This was followed by *Butterflies of North America* (2003), *Mammals of North America* (2004), *Insects of North America* (2007), and *Advanced Birding* (2011). In 2005 he published a Spanish version of his *Birds of North America* called *Guia de Campo Kaufman: a las Aves Norteamericanas*.

In his field guides, Kaufman uses a medium between photography and painting. He carefully chooses photographs after first studying his field sketches to review the typical postures and poses of the bird. Then he "paints" over the photographs using Adobe Photoshop. He is able to change the images in whatever way he feels is necessary, for example changing the colour, angle, and posture. He can alter the plumage by sleeking down head feathers if the bird was alarmed, or removing out-of-place feathers. He then removes shadows on the underparts as well as any artificial highlights.

Kenn Kaufman is currently recognized as an expert in the lives of birds and the natural world. In 1992 he was honoured by the American Birding Association with the Ludlow Griscom Distinguished Birder Award.

In 2008 he received the Roger Tory Peterson Award from the American Birding Association "for a lifetime of achievements in promoting the cause of birding" — although, as he points out, he isn't finished yet.[6]

In 2005 Kaufman moved to northwestern Ohio and became involved with a local organization called the Black Swamp Bird Observatory (BSBO). The observatory was entering a phase of rapid growth, partly because an energetic young lady named Kimberly was ramping up its educational and outreach programs. Within a year, Kenn and Kimberly were married, and within three years, Kimberly Kaufman had been promoted to Executive Director of BSBO. With her work through the organization and Kenn's work as an independent writer, they are able to support and enhance each other's efforts.

The Kaufmans and BSBO focus much of their attention on Magee Marsh, a place that is becoming known as one of the best places to see migrant warblers in eastern North America. At Magee Marsh it doesn't take a large weather event to bring migrant songbirds down from their northward migrations. Night migrants moving north across Ohio in the spring, and, reaching the southern end of Lake Erie at first morning light, are likely to come down there rather than continue across the

Kenn and Kimberly Kaufman in Trinidad in July 2009.

Courtesy of Kenn and Kimberly Kaufman.

lake. Finding good foraging areas, they may stop over for several days to refuel. A boardwalk at Magee Marsh meanders for a mile through the woods and is a popular place from where to observe the warblers in their flashy spring plumages. Kaufman says: "With human activity confined to a predictable corridor, birds seem willing to approach the boardwalk closely, and the views of the migrants are often phenomenal. I suspect that many people have had a casual interest in nature converted to passionate commitment by the experience here, so the effect on conservation must extend far beyond this seven-acre woodlot."[7]

Kaufman is never concerned about having too many birders. He says:

> When we find a ... Magee Marsh — a place that will support a lot of birding traffic — we should use those opportunities to recruit more bird watchers and attract more attention. There is no danger that we will wind up with "too many birders." There's no such thing. With luck, we might wind up with enough birders to make a difference, to make our voices heard, to protect more bird habitat for future generations.[8]

Chapter Twenty-Two

David Allen Sibley
(1961-)

"There are a lot of threats to birds [today], and all are related to bigger environmental and societal issues, especially the fact that humans are taking up more space and using more of the Earth's resources.... The long-term solution to environmental problems is to control our own consumption and reduce the demand; otherwise, there simply won't be anything left for the birds."

— David Allen Sibley in *Birding*.

David Allen Sibley is acknowledged as one of North America's most well-known bird illustrators and he has published some of the best-selling nature field books of all time. Sibley has a deep concern for habitat preservation and environmental health. He was born in 1961 in Plattsburgh, New York. His father, Fred Sibley, a notable ornithologist who was a director of the Point Reyes Bird Observatory in California and later was a curator at the Peabody Museum of Natural History at Yale University, was active in the early phases of the recovery efforts of the condor in California.[1]

Growing up surrounded by biologists, David naturally acquired a more scientific approach to the study of nature. He often did not have to search in field guide books for the answers to his questions about the identities of various birds and other objects in nature because there were people around him who could immediately provide the answers. When his family went on weekend hikes and picnics, his father and father's

David Allen Sibley.

Courtesy of Erinn Hartman.

friends pointed out birds, snakes, insects, and everything else. David was interested in all of it, but his primary focus quickly became the birds.

David started drawing birds as soon as he could draw, at about five or six years of age. His house was filled with books about birds and David taught himself to draw by tracing and copying pictures by such illustrators as Arthur Singer in *Birds of the World*. When he was seven, and his father was director of Point Reyes Bird Observatory, David learned to band birds. Being able to hold birds in his hands, see them up close, and feel them, gave him a sense of how alive and individually unique they are, an experience which was much more real than looking at them through binoculars.[2]

At first David considered following his father's academic path to become an ornithologist and he spent two semesters at Cornell University in Ithaca, New York. Then he decided to strike out on his own looking for birds and worked at the Cape May Bird Observatory in New Jersey observing and counting hawks for several years. Leaving Cape May, he travelled throughout North America in his pickup truck, constantly watching and studying birds, sketching them, and making notes about them, all the while sleeping in the back of his truck. By his mid-to-late twenties, Sibley had become acknowledged as an expert on birds. He became the leader of birding tours all across the country, as well as internationally, for WINGS, the birding tour organization.

Sibley wrote and illustrated articles on bird identification for *Birding* and *American Birds*, as well as regional publications and books, including *Hawks in Flight*. In the forward to *Hawks in Flight: The Flight Identification of North American Migrant Raptors*, published in 1988, Roger Tory Peterson wrote: "David Sibley, an artist and leader of international tours for WINGS, is one of the most perceptive field birders in North America. His drawings are graphic replications of what hawk watchers truly see in the field. His sense of flight and shape are unparalleled."[3]

David finds that in order to draw a bird realistically, incorporating characteristic posture, shape, and movement, one must gain a real familiarity with it by watching it for many hours as it goes about living in its environment. To Sibley, the two activities of watching and drawing birds have always been closely related. While in the field watching birds, he is constantly thinking about drawing them and making sketches, and when he is drawing birds, he is constantly recalling his field experiences. Thus his talent for drawing birds accurately and realistically has been honed by years of study and practice. For Sibley, birding gets more interesting the more one gets into it. Greater expertise just leads to more interesting questions. He says: "I approach birding in an academic or scientific way, asking questions and testing hypotheses."[4] Sometimes when he goes birding, he sets himself a specific goal to study scientifically, such as the way the neck feathers move, or the tail movements of all the small passerines he sees, or the bill colour of fall warblers, or the way the wings fold over the tail. In this way, he has steadily built up an expert knowledge of the birds.

By the age of twelve David had already made up his mind that he was going to do his own field guide to the birds. During the more than fifteen years when Sibley was in the field with binoculars and telescope, watching and sketching live birds in the wild, in the back of his mind there was always the thought of how to best illustrate the birds. He knew he wanted to do a field guide book on birds. His challenge was to find the right blend of physical details of the bird, and the impression one has of it when observing from a distance through binoculars. After more than a decade of field work, Sibley began to refine his ideas about what he would include and the format he would use. As a leader of bird watching tours, he had often been frustrated to point out a bird, show it in the field guide, and then have to explain why it looked different from the illustration. So he had determined to show the birds in every possible plumage, as well as at rest and in flight, in his bird guide, but for years he struggled with how to do this in a manageable way. In thinking about how he would achieve his goal, he studied every bird guide he could find, as well as field guides to flowers, trees, and reptiles, analyzing the pros and cons of each. He found that after Roger Tory Peterson's work, there was more innovation in Europe than in North America. He was especially impressed by the two completely different approaches he saw in the Mitchell Beazley *Birdwatcher's Pocket Guide* by Peter Hayman, which is a compact yet detailed technical representation, and the great artistry of Lars Jonsson's paintings in *Birds of Europe*.

Sibley wanted to make sure that all the illustrations in his field guide would be perfectly comparable to all the others. He describes his revelation as follows:

> So when I started working on pages, at one point I put all plumages of Horned Grebes on the left and those of Eared Grebes on the right, and that was my eureka moment! It dawned on me in a few minutes that the whole book could be done that way. It would answer all the questions I'd been struggling with. The format for the entire book was very deliberate: every illustration shows the bird facing right; flying birds at top.[5]

When *The Sibley Guide to Birds* came out in October of 2000, it met with astounding success. It became the fastest-selling bird book of all time. Over a million copies have been sold. There are over 6,600 individual drawings that went into the field guide. The final artwork took Sibley six years to complete. *The New York Times* wrote of it: "Once in a great while, a natural history book changes the way people look at the world."[6]

The companion volume to *The Sibley Guide to Birds*, titled *The Sibley Guide to Bird Life and Behaviour*, was published in the fall of 2001, and was also met with great success. This was followed in 2002 by *Sibley's Birding Basics*, as well as several more bird field guides. David Sibley had become a bestselling author.

In deciding on his next major project, as a naturalist Sibley considered various subjects, but early on decided that the study and identification of trees was a logical choice. Trees, like birds, are visible everywhere, from the heart of cities to the edge of the treeline. As a birdwatcher he had always noticed and been interested in trees. His next work would be to produce a field guide to the trees of North America. He found that existing tree guides were hard to use, relying more on text and keys than on illustrations. This was what bird guides were like one hundred years ago. With all of the advances in modern bird guides, Sibley set himself a goal of creating a more visual guide to trees that would feel familiar to present-day birders.

Seven years in the making, *The Sibley Guide to Trees* was published in 2009. This guide has also met with great acclaim. Similar to his guide to birds, his guide to trees takes a unique approach, choosing to place the trees as families, and emphasizing the shapes and colours of the leaves at various times of year, the appearance and texture of the bark, and the outline of winter trees devoid of foliage. For this book Sibley moved from painting in gouache or opaque watercolour, which he uses for the birds, to using acrylic paint, which works better for the deep greens of leaves.

In his study of trees, Sibley became very aware of the way in which man has altered the landscape. Whereas birds maintain their distinct species' status, man is able to consciously manipulate the types and characteristics of many of the trees he plants, thereby altering the natural world. A few tree species account for most of the human plantings. Often genetically identical clones of trees are planted. In some tree species where fruit is considered a nuisance, only male trees are planted. Many of these man-induced changes in the landscape affect nesting and migrating birds, who rely on standing dead trees for nesting and roosting holes, and the insects attracted by flowers and fruit for food. Sibley has emphasized that the best kinds of trees to plant for the birds are native, not introduced, species.

David Sibley's goal with his field guides is primarily to get people excited about birding and about being outdoors in nature. He wants to convey some of his own interest and the satisfaction he obtains from birding, and also to cause people to become concerned about conserving nature so they can continue to enjoy the birds. The field guides in general serve as a starting point for people to know the birds. This leads them on to want to know more about them, such as their food habits, migration routes, and habitat preferences. This knowledge then results in a better understanding of both birds and their environments, and an interest in the conservation of both.

David Sibley's study and love of nature has motivated him to become an ardent advocate for the welfare of birds and the natural environment. In the Introduction to *Birds of the Arctic National Wildlife Refuge: Arctic Wings*, he writes:

> Nobody knows what drove the Labrador Duck to extinction in the 1800s, and nobody can predict what will happen with increased human activity in the Arctic. Oil exploration could be enough to tip already-threatened birds such as the Steller's Eider and the Buff-breasted Sandpiper into extinction. Helicopters and drilling equipment will disturb nesting birds. Pipeline and road construction will alter the delicate balance of tundra plants and ponds. Garbage that often comes along with modern human settlements could lead to an increased population of scavenging arctic foxes, ravens, and Glaucous Gulls, which will then eat the eggs and young of nesting birds, potentially leading to declines of many species. Whatever the results of development may be, it is certain that migrating birds will make those effects, large or small, visible all around the world.[7]

Notes

CHAPTER ONE: ALEXANDER WILSON

1. David Starr Jordan, "Alexander Wilson, Ornithologist," *Leading American Men of Science* (New York: Henry Holt and Company, 1910), 53.
2. *Ibid.*, 58.
3. *Ibid.*
4. Alexander Wilson, *American Ornithology; or the Natural History of the Birds of the United States, With a Sketch of the Author's Life, by George Ord, in Three Volumes, Vol. 1* (New York: Collins & Co., 1983), lxx–lxxi.
5. Jordan, *Leading American Men of Science*, 61.
6. Wilson, *American Ornithology*, xcv–xcvi.
7. B. and R. Mearns, *Audubon to Xantus: The Lives of Those Commemorated in North American Bird Names* (London: Academic Press, Ltd., 1992), 488.
8. *Ibid.*, 489.
9. C. Hunter, ed., *The Life and Letters of Alexander Wilson* (Philadelphia: 1983), 359.
10. Mearns, *Audubon to Xantus*, 489.
11. *Ibid.*, 493.
12. Jordan, *Leading American Men of Science*, 68.
13. *Ibid.*

CHAPTER TWO: JOHN JAMES AUDUBON

1. Richard Rhodes, *John James Audubon: The Making of an American* (New York: Alfred A. Knopf, 2004), 15.

2.   Ibid., 78-79.

3.   John James Audubon and William MacGillivray, *Ornithological Biography, or An Account of the Habits of the Birds of the United States of America: Accompanied by Descriptions of the Objects Represented in the Work Entitled The Birds of America, and Interspersed with Delineations of American Scenery and Manners* / 4 volumes (Philadelphia, Pennsylvania: E. L. Carey and A. Hart, 1831-1849), xiii-xiv.

4.   Maria R. Audubon and Elliott Coues, *Audubon and His Journals, Volume I* (New York: Charles Scribner's Sons, 1897), 47.

5.   Ibid., 51.

6.   Rhodes, *John James Audubon*, 211.

7.   Lucy Bakewell Audubon, *The Life of John James Audubon, the Naturalist* (New York: G.P. Putnam's Sons, 1890), 102.

8.   Rhodes, *John James Audubon*, 222.

9.   Audubon, *The Life of John James Audubon*, 103.

10. Ibid., 125.

11. Ibid., 128.

12. Rhodes, *John James Audubon*, 351-52.

13. Audubon, *The Life of John James Audubon*, 315-22.

14. John Burroughs, *John James Audubon* (Boston: Small, Maynard & Company, 1902), 123.

15. Ibid., 95.

16. Rhodes, *John James Audubon*, 407.

17. Ibid., 430.

CHAPTER THREE: THOMAS NUTTALL

1.   Thomas Nuttall, *The North American Sylva, or, A Description of the Forest Trees of the United States, Canada and Nova Scotia, Not Described in the work of F. Andrew Michaux* (Philadelphia, Pennsylvania: W. Rutter, 1871), preface.

2.   Francis W. Pennell, "Terms of Agreement, dated April 7, 1810, between Barton and Nuttall," *Bartonia*, Vol. XVIII (1936), 45-46.

3.   Jeannette E. Graustein, *Thomas Nuttall, Naturalist: Explorations in America, 1808-1841* (Cambridge: Harvard University Press, 1967), 51.

4.   Ibid., 52.

5.   Thomas Nuttall, *A Manual of Ornithology of the United States and Canada, I, Land Birds* (Cambridge, Massachusetts: Hilliard & Brown, 1832), 546.

6.   Thomas Nuttall, *A Journal of Travels into the Arkansas Territory During the Rear 1819, with Occasional Observations on the Manners of the Aborigines* (Philadelphia, Pennsylvania: Thomas H. Palmer, 1821), 157-59.

7. Graustein, *Thomas Nuttall*, 152–53.

8. Nuttall, *A Journal of Travels into the Arkansas Territory*, preface.

9. Nuttall, *A Manual of Ornithology, 1, Land Birds*, 312.

10. Thomas Nuttall, *A Manual of Ornithology of the United States and Canada, II, Water Birds* (Cambridge, Massachusetts: Hilliard, Gray & Co., 1834), 216.

11. Maria R. Audubon and Elliott Coues, *Audubon and His Journals, Volume I* (New York: Charles Scribner's Sons, 1897), 445.

12. Richard Henry Dana, *Two Years Before the Mast* (London: T. Nelson and Sons Ltd., 1912), chapter 30.

13. R. Buchanan, *Life and Adventures of John James Audubon, the Naturalist*, 2nd edition (London: Sampson Low, Son & Marston, 1869), 322.

14. John James Audubon and William MacGillivray, *Ornithological Biography, or An Account of the Habits of the Birds of the United States of America: Accompanied by Descriptions of the Objects Represented in the Work Entitled The Birds of America, and Interspersed with Delineations of American Scenery and Manners / 4 volumes* (Philadelphia, Pennsylvania: E.L. Carey and A. Hart, 1831–1849), introduction.

15. Thomas Nuttall, "Descriptions of Plants Collected by William Gambel, M.D., in the Rocky Mountains and Upper California," *Journal of the Academy of Natural Sciences of Philadelphia* (1848), 149–89.

16. Susan Delano McKelvey, *Botanical Exploration of the Trans-Mississippi West, 1790–1850* (Jamaica Plain, Massachusetts: Arnold Arboretum, Harvard University, 1955), xxi.

CHAPTER FOUR: SPENCER FULLERTON BAIRD

1. B. and R. Mearns, *Audubon to Xantus: The Lives of Those Commemorated in North American Bird Names* (London: Academic Press, Ltd., 1992), 45.

2. William Healey Dall, *Spencer Fullerton Baird: A Biography* (Philadelphia: J.B. Lippincott Company, 1915), 38.

3. *Ibid.*, 45.

4. This published paper appeared in *Proceedings of the Academy of Natural Sciences of Philadelphia* in 1843, 283–85.

5. Dall, *Spencer Fullerton Baird*, 57–59.

6. David Starr Jordan, *Leading American Men of Science* (New York: Henry Holt and Company, 1910), 271.

7. Dall, *Spencer Fullerton Baird*, 237–38.

8. *Ibid.*, 390.

9. Jordan, *Leading American Men of Science*, 279.

CHAPTER FIVE: ROBERT KENNICOTT

1. Ronald S. Vasile, "The Early Career of Robert Kennicott, Illinois' Pioneering Naturalist," *Illinois Historical Journal* 87(3),156.
2. *Ibid.*, 159.
3. "The Megatherium Club," America's Smithsonian, *www.150.si.edu/chap3/club.htm.*
4. John Moring, *Early American Naturalists: Exploring the American West, 1804–1900* (New York: Cooper Square Press, 2002), 155.
5. W. Stimpson, "Robert Kennicott," *Transactions of the Academy of Sciences* I (1869), 146–50.
6. Debra Lindsay, ed., *The Modern Beginnings of Subarctic Ornithology: Northern Correspondence with the Smithsonian Institution, 1856–68*, Vol. 10 (Winnipeg, Manitoba: The Manitoba Record Society publications, 1991), 29.
7. *Ibid.*, 44.
8. Stimpson, "Robert Kennicott," 172.
9. Lindsay, *The Modern Beginnings of Subarctic Ornithology*, 112–15.
10. "The Megatherium Club."
11. William Healey Dall, *Spencer Fullerton Baird: A Biography* (Philadelphia: J.B. Lippincott Company, 1915), 335.
12. J.W. Foster, "Robert Kennicott," *Western Monthly Magazine*, Vol. III, No. 15 (March 1870) 165–72.
13. B. and R. Mearns, *Audubon to Xantus: The Lives of Those Commemorated in North American Bird Names* (London: Academic Press, Ltd., 1992), 250.
14. *Ibid.*
15. William Healey Dall, *Alaska and Its Resources* (Boston: Lee and Shepard Publishers, 1897), 358.
16. *Ibid.*, 70.
17. *Ibid.*

CHAPTER SIX: ROBERT RIDGWAY

1. Harry Harris, "Robert Ridgway, With a Bibliography of his Published Writings and Fifty Illustrations," *The Condor*, Volume XXX, Number 1 (January–February 1928), 8.
2. *Ibid.*, 13.
3. *Ibid.*, 25.
4. *Ibid.*, 35.
5. *Ibid.*, 43–44.

6. *Ibid.*, 44.
7. *Ibid.*, 63.

CHAPTER SEVEN: FLORENCE MERRIAM BAILEY

1. Harriet Kofalk, *No Woman Tenderfoot: Florence Merriam Bailey, Pioneer Naturalist* (College Station: Texas A&M University Press, 1989), 11.
2. *Ibid.*, 29.
3. Robin W. Doughty, *Feather Fashions and Bird Preservation* (Berkeley: University of California Press, 1975), 64–65.
4. *Ibid.*, 81–82.
5. Florence Merriam Bailey, "Our Smith College Audubon Society," *Audubon Magazine* 1:1 (1887), 176.
6. Kofalk, *No Woman Tenderfoot*, 43.
7. Florence Merriam Bailey, *Birds Through an Opera Glass* (Boston: Houghton Mifflin and Company, 1890), ix–x.
8. *Ibid*, 187.
9. Florence Merriam Bailey, *A-Birding on a Bronco*, (Boston: Houghton Mifflin and Company, 1896), 103–08.
10. Kofalk, *No Woman Tenderfoot*, 103.
11. Florence Merriam Bailey, *Handbook of Birds of the Western United States* (Boston: Houghton Mifflin and Company, 1902), 471–72.
12. Kofalk, *No Woman Tenderfoot*, 124.
13. Paul H. Oehser, "In Memoriam: Florence Merriam Bailey," *The Auk*, Vol. 69 (January 1952), 23.
14. Kofalk, *No Woman Tenderfoot*, 130.
15. *Ibid.*, 133.
16. *Ibid.*, 181–82.

CHAPTER EIGHT: ALLAN BROOKS

1. Keir B. Sterling, Richard Harmond, George A. Cevasco, and Lorne Hammond, eds., *Biographical Dictionary of American and Canadian Naturalists and Environmentalists* (Greenwood Press, 1997), 117–20.
2. Jean Webber, "Major Allan Brooks of Okanagan Landing," Royal British Columbia Museum "Living Landscapes" project.
3. Marjorie Brooks, "Allan Brooks: A Biography," *The Condor*, Vol. XL (January 1938), 12.

4. *Ibid.*
5. William Leon Dawson, "Allan Brooks: An Appreciation," *The Condor*, Vol. XV (March 1913), 71.
6. *Ibid.*
7. *Ibid.*
8. *Ibid.*, 72.
9. Harry Harris, "An Appreciation of Allan Brooks, Zoological Artist: 1869-1946," *The Condor*, Volume 48, Number 4 (July–August 1946), 151–53.
10. Hamilton M. Laing, "Allan Brooks, 1869-1946," *The Auk*, Vol. 64 (1947) 442–43.
11. Webber "Major Allan Brooks of Okanagan Landing."
12. *Ibid.*
13. Dawson, "Allan Brooks: An Appreciation," 74.
14. "Brooks Allan Cyril (1869-1946)," *www.scricciolo.com/Nuovo_Neornithes/Brooks_Allan_Cyril.htm.*
15. Webber, "Major Allan Brooks of Okanagan Landing."
16. In addition to the primary and secondary feathers, all bird wings have a small cluster of stiff feathers, the alula, attached to the thumb bone. The alula provides a forward slot, increasing lift and manoeuverability. These feathers function in the same way as the slats on an airplane wing, allowing the wing to achieve a higher than normal angle of attack – and thus lift – without resulting in a stall. By manipulating its thumb to create a gap between the alula and the rest of the wing, a bird can avoid stalling when flying at low speeds or landing.
17. Allan Brooks, "The Under-Water Actions of Diving Ducks," *The Auk*, Vol. 62 (October 1945), 517–18 and 521–22.

CHAPTER NINE: CORDELIA STANWOOD

1. Chandler S. Richmond, *Beyond the Spring: Cordelia Stanwood of Birdsacre* (Maine: The Latona Press, 1989), 11.
2. Marcia Myers Bonta, *Women in the Field: America's Pioneering Women Naturalists* (College Station, Texas: Texas A&M University Press, 1991), 213.
3. Cynthia Watkins Richardson, "Picturing Nature: Education, Ornithology and Photography in the Life of Cordelia Stanwood: 1865-1958," thesis (Orono, Maine: The Graduate School, The University of Maine, December 2002), 90.
4. Richmond, *Beyond the Spring*, 41–42.
5. *Ibid.*, 45.

6. *Ibid.*, 54.
7. *Ibid.*, 58.
8. Cordelia Stanwood, "A Series of Nests of the Magnolia Warbler," *The Auk*, Vol. 27 (Winter 1910), 385–86.
9. Richardson, "Picturing Nature," 160.
10. *Ibid*, 167.
11. Bonta, *Women in the Field*, 218.
12. *Ibid.*, 219.
13. Richardson, "Picturing Nature," 118.
14. *Ibid*, 84.
15. Bonta, *Women in the Field*, 221.
16. Richmond, *Beyond the Spring*, 113.
17. Birdsacre, Stanwood Wildlife Sanctuary, *www.birdsacre.com*.

CHAPTER TEN: JACK MINER

1. Jack Miner, *Jack Miner and the Birds and Some Things I Know About Nature* (Chicago: The Reilly & Lee Co., 1925), 2.
2. *Ibid.*, preface.
3. *Ibid.*
4. *Ibid.*, 14–15.
5. *Ibid.*, 42–43.
6. Manly F. Miner, "Migration of Canada Geese From the Jack Miner Sanctuary and Banding Operations," *The Wilson Bulletin* (March 1931), 30.
7. *Ibid.*
8. *Ibid.*, 32.
9. *Ibid.*, 34.
10. Jack Miner, *Jack Miner and the Birds and Some Things I Know About Nature*, 293.
11. *Ibid.*, 117.
12. *Ibid.*, 183.
13. *Ibid.*, 184.
14. *Ibid.*, 210–11.
15. *Ibid.*, 170–71.
16. James Peterson Graham, "Point Pelee National Park of Canada: A Park Is Born," *Where Canada Begins*, Parks Canada, *www.pc.gc.ca/eng/pn-np/on/pelee/natcul/natcul2/3.aspx*.

CHAPTER ELEVEN: JAMES HENRY FLEMING

1. P.A. Taverner, "James Henry Fleming 1872–1940: An Appreciation by P.A. Taverner," *The Canadian Field-Naturalist*, Vol. LV, No. 5 (May 1941), 63.
2. L.L. Snyder, "In Memoriam: James Henry Fleming," *The Auk*, Vol. 58, No. 1 (January 1941), 3.
3. *Ibid.*
4. *Ibid.*, 5.
5. *Ibid.*, 7–8.
6. William E. David, Jr. and Jerome A. Jackson, eds. *Contributions to the History of North American Ornithology*, Memoirs of the Nuttall Ornithological Club, No. 12. (Cambridge, Massachusetts: Nuttall Ornithological Club, 1995), 330–31.
7. J.H. Fleming, "The Great Lakes Orinthological Club," *The Wilson Bulletin*, Vol. 51, No. 1 (March 1939), 42.
8. *Ibid.*, 43.
9. Snyder, "In Memoriam," 10–12.
10. *Ibid.*, 9.
11. Keir B. Sterling, Richard Harmond, George A. Cevasco, and Lorne Hammond, eds., *Biographical Dictionary of American and Canadian Naturalists and Environmentalists* (Greenwood Press, 1997), 272.
12. Taverner, "James Henry Fleming 1872–1940," 64.

CHAPTER TWELVE: PERCY ALGERNON TAVERNER

1. W.L. McAtee, "Percy Algernon Taverner, 1875–1947," *The Auk*, Vol. 65 (January 1948), 94–96.
2. *Ibid.*, 87.
3. *Ibid.*
4. *Ibid.*, 96.
5. *Ibid.*, 89.
6. *Ibid.*, 90.
7. *Ibid.*, 85.
8. *Ibid.*, 86.
9. J. Alexander Burnett, *A Passion for Wildlife: The History of the Canadian Wildlife Service* (Vancouver: UBC Press, 2003), 4.
10. *Ibid.*, 11.
11. P.A. Taverner, "Recommendations for the Creation of Three New National Parks in Canada," Report of the Sixth Annual Meeting of the Commission of Conservation, Ottawa, Appendix 3 (1915).

12. P.A. Taverner, "The Double-Crested Cormorant (*Phalacrocorax auritus*) and its Relation to the Salmon Industries on the Gulf of St. Lawrence," Canada, *Geological Survey Museum Bulletin No. 13* (1915).
13. P.A. Taverner, "The Gannets of Bonaventure Island," *Ottawa Naturalist*, 32:21–26 (1918).
14. Henri Ouellet, "Profile of a Pioneer: P.A. Taverner," *American Birds* (Spring 1987), 23.
15. McAtee, "Percy Algernon Taverner," 98.
16. *Ibid.*, 97.

CHAPTER THIRTEEN: MARGARET MORSE NICE

1. A talisman is a charm that averts evil.
2. Margaret Morse Nice, *Research Is a Passion With Me* (Toronto: Consolidated Amethyst Communications Inc., 1979), foreword.
3. *Ibid.*, 5.
4. *Ibid.*, 20.
5. *Ibid.*, 29.
6. *Ibid.*, 35.
7. *Ibid.*, 93.
8. Milton B. Trautman, "In Memoriam: Margaret Morse Nice," *The Auk*, Vol. 94 (July 1977), 434.
9. Nice, *Research Is a Passion With Me*, 90.
10. *Ibid.*, 106.
11. Many different subspecies of Song Sparrow (*Melospiza melodia*) are recognized by taxonomists.
12. Nice, *Research Is a Passion With Me*, 288.
13. *Ibid.*, 152.
14. The young of precocial birds are born covered with down, and are able to run about when newly hatched.
15. The young of altricial birds are born naked and blind, and are completely dependent on their parents for care.
16. Trautman, "In Memoriam: Margaret Morse Nice," 441.

CHAPTER FOURTEEN: JOSEPH DEWEY SOPER

1. Roland Soper and Tom Beck, "Joseph Dewey Soper, 1893–1982," *Arctic*, Vol. 36, No. 1 (March 1983), 118.

2. *Ibid.*, 119.

3. "Biography of J. Dewey Soper," *J. Dewey Soper Fonds*, University of Alberta Archives, *http://archive1.macs.ualberta.ca/FindingAids/JDSoper/JDSoper.html*.

4. John Moss, ed. "Science as Poetic and Visual Narrative: J. Dewey Soper (1893–1982)," *Echoing Silence: Essays on Arctic Narrative* (Ottawa: University of Ottawa Press, 1997), 61.

5. *Ibid.*, 63.

6. J. Dewey Soper, "Discovery of the Breeding Grounds of the Blue Goose," *The Canadian Field-Naturalist*, Vol. XLIV, No. 1 (January 1930), 3.

7. Moss, *Echoing Silence*, 63.

8. Constance Martin, *Search for the Blue Goose: J. Dewey Soper – The Arctic Adventures of a Canadian Naturalist* (Calgary: Bayeux Arts Incorporated and the Arctic Institute of North America, 1995), 41.

9. *Ibid.*, 42.

10. *Ibid.*, 41.

11. "Biography of J. Dewey Soper," *J. Dewey Soper Fonds*, University of Alberta Archives, *http://archive1.macs.ualberta.ca/FindingAids/JDSoper/JDSoper.html*.

12. J. Dewey Soper, "Explorations in Baffin Island," *The Geographical Journal*, Vol. 75, No. 5 (May 1930), 435.

13. Douglas R. Stenton, "A Soper Record Cairn from Baffin Island, N.W.T.," *Arctic*, Vol. 39, No. 1 (March 1986), 93.

14. *Ibid.*, 93–94.

15. *Ibid.*, 94.

16. Soper and Beck, "Joseph Dewey Soper, 1893–1982," 118.

17. Moss, *Echoing Silence*, 64.

18. Soper, "Discovery of the Breeding Grounds of the Blue Goose," 4–5.

19. *Ibid.*, 6.

20. J. Alexander Burnett, *A Passion for Wildlife: The History of the Canadian Wildlife Service* (Vancouver, B.C.: UBC Press, 2003), 58.

21. J. Dewey Soper, "Interesting Bird Records for Southern Baffin Island," *The Canadian Field-Naturalist*, Vol. XLVIII (March), 44.

22. J. Dewey Soper, "Local Distribution of Eastern Canadian Arctic Birds," *The Auk*, Vol. 57 (January 1940), 13–14.

23. Soper, "Discovery of the Breeding Grounds of the Blue Goose," 11.

24. "Biography of J. Dewey Soper," *J. Dewey Soper Fonds*, University of Alberta Archives, *http://archive1.macs.ualberta.ca/FindingAids/JDSoper/JDSoper.html*.

25. Burnett, *A Passion for Wildlife*, 53.

26. Soper and Beck, "Joseph Dewey Soper, 1893–1982," 119.

CHAPTER FIFTEEN: LOUISE DE KIRILINE LAWRENCE

1. Louise de Kiriline Lawrence, *The Lovely and the Wild* (Toronto: Natural Heritage Inc., 1987), 5.

2. Louise de Kiriline Lawrence, *Another Winter, Another Spring: A Love Remembered* (Toronto: Natural Heritage Inc., 1987).

3. Doug Mackey, "Heritage Perspectives: Remembering the Late, Great Lady, Louise de Kiriline Lawrence," *Community Voices* (May 2002), *www.pastforward. ca/perspectives/may_102002.htm.*.

4. Jon C. Barlow, "Doris Huestis Speirs Award for Contributions to Canadian Ornithology: Louise de Kiriline Lawrence – 1991," *Picoides* (Fall 1991).

5. Louise de Kiriline Lawrence, "A Comparative Life-History Study of Four Species of Woodpeckers," Ornithological Monographs, No. 5, American Ornithologists' Union (1967).

6. Lawrence, *The Lovely and the Wild*, 301.

7. *Ibid.*, 204–05.

8. *Ibid.*, 227.

9. Barlow, "Doris Huestis Speirs Award for Contributions to Canadian Ornithology: Louise de Kiriline Lawrence – 1991," *Picoides* (Fall 1991).

CHAPTER SIXTEEN: DORIS H. SPEIRS AND J. MURRAY SPEIRS

1. Phenology is the science of the relations between climate and periodic biological phenomenon, such as the migrations and breeding of birds.

2. Margaret Morse Nice, *Research Is a Passion With Me* (Toronto: Consolidated Amethyst Communications Inc., 1979), 268.

3. John W. Sabean, "Names in the News: Doris Huestis Speirs," *Pickering Township Histocial Society Pathmaster*, Vol. 1, No. 2 (Winter 1998), 1.

4. J. Bruce Falls, "Doris Huestis Spears 1984–1989," Picoides, Vol 4., No. 1 (April 1990), 3.

5. *Ibid.*

6. "Community Mourns Death of Dr. J. Murray Speirs," *Pickering News Advertiser* (September 5, 2001), A3.

7. J. Murray Speirs, *Birds of Ontario*, (Toronto: Natural Heritage Inc., 1985), introduction.

8. Interview with Doris Huestis Speirs by Charles Hill on October 15, 1973, transcribed by Nina Berkhout on March 31, 2008. Archival Reference: Canadian Painting in the Thirties Exhibition Records, National Gallery of Canada Fonds, National Gallery of Canada Library and Archives.

9. J. Murray Speirs, *Birds of Ontario*, introduction.

10. Natalie Alcoba, "Naturalist, Bird-Lover J. Murray Speirs, 92," *Toronto Star* (September 7, 2001).

11. Doris Huestes Speirs, "Evening Grosbeak (*Coccothruastes vespertinus*)," (1968).

12. J. Murray Speirs, *Birds of Ontario*, introduction.

13. Natalie Alcoba, "Naturalist, Bird-Lover J. Murray Speirs, 92."

14. Rosemary Speirs, "Dr. J. Murray Speirs: Birdwatcher and Conservationist," *www.altonaforest.org/speirs.html*.

CHAPTER SEVENTEEN: ROGER TORY PETERSON

1. Douglas Carlson, *Roger Tory Peterson: A Biography* (Austin: University of Texas Press, 2007), 5.

2. *Ibid.*, 8.

3. Roger Tory Peterson, *Roger Tory Peterson: The Art and Photography of the World's Foremost Birder*, edited by Roger Tory Peterson and Rudy Hoglund (New York: Rizzoli International Publications, Inc., 1994), 18.

4. Carlson, *Roger Tory Peterson*, 7.

5. Peterson, *Roger Tory Peterson*, 195.

6. Roger Tory Peterson, *All Things Reconsidered: My Birding Adventures*, edited by Bill Thompson III (Boston, New York: Houghton Mifflin Company, 2006), 216.

7. *Ibid.*, 320.

8. Carlson, *Roger Tory Peterson*, 23.

9. Peterson, *Roger Tory Peterson*, 23.

10. Carlson, *Roger Tory Peterson*, 34.

11. Roger Tory Peterson, *Birds Over America* (New York: Dodd, Mead & Company, 1948), 16.

12. *Ibid.*, 109–10.

13. Carlson, *Roger Tory Peterson*, 43.

14. Peterson, *Roger Tory Peterson*, 195.

15. Carlson, *Roger Tory Peterson*, 45.

16. Peterson, *Roger Tory Peterson*, 192.

17. *Ibid.*, 38.

18. Carlson, *Roger Tory Peterson*, 152.

19. Peterson, *Birds Over America*, 95–96.

20. *Ibid.*, v.

21. *Ibid.*, 245–46.

22. *Ibid.*, 267–68.

23. Carlson, *Roger Tory Peterson*, 132.

24. Peterson, *All Things Reconsidered*, 166-68.
25. *Ibid*, 280.
26. Peterson, *Roger Tory Peterson*, 198-201.
27. *Ibid.*, 201.
28. *Ibid.*, 50.

CHAPTER EIGHTEEN: HANS ALBERT HOCHBAUM

1. Donna Tonelli, "James Ford Bell & the Delta Marsh," *Adventure Sports Outdoors Magazine* (February 2008), 110-11.
2. *Ibid.*
3. *Ibid.*
4. *Ibid.*
5. "Delta's Research Program," Delta Waterfowl, *www.deltawaterfowl.org/research/*.
6. H. Albert Hochbaum, *The Canvasback on a Prairie Marsh* (Harrisburg, Pennsylvania: The Stackpole Company, 1944), 3.
7. *Ibid.*, 54.
8. H. Albert Hochbaum, "What the Duck Saw," *Ducks Unlimited Magazine* (September/October 1996).
9. Hochbaum, *The Canvasback on a Prairie Marsh*, 149.
10. *Ibid.*, 149.
11. *Ibid.*, 152.
12. H. Albert Hochbaum, *Travels and Traditions of Waterfowl* (Minneapolis: The University of Minnesota Press, 1955), 54.
13. *Ibid.*, 217.
14. *Ibid.*, 246.
15. Jerome R. Serie, "H. Albert Hochbaum: A Man Not Forgotten," *Prairie Naturalist*, 26(4) (December 1994), 315.
16. *Ibid.*, 316.
17. Hochbaum, *The Canvasback on a Prairie Marsh*, 169.

CHAPTER NINETEEN: ROBERT W. NERO

1. Robert W. Nero, *Spring Again and Other Poems* (Toronto: Natural Heritage Inc., 1997), introduction.
2. Robert W. Nero, *Redwings* (Washington, D.C.: Smithsonian Institution Press, 1984), introduction.
3. *Ibid.*

4. *Ibid.*

5. *Ibid.*, 142–43.

6. "Robert Nero (employed July 1955–late 1961)," *Museum History: Museum Staff*, Royal Saskatchewan Museum, *www.royalsaskmuseum.ca/about/museum_history_staff.shtml#nero.*

7. Robert W. Nero, *The Site: A Personal Odyssey* (Toronto: Natural Heritage Inc., 2001), 33.

8. *Ibid.*, 37.

9. "Robert Nero (employed July 1955–late 1961)," *Museum History: Museum Staff*, Royal Saskatchewan Museum, *www.royalsaskmuseum.ca/about/museum_history_staff.shtml#nero.*

10. Nero, *The Site*, 38.

11. *Ibid.*, 39.

12. *Ibid.*

13. Nero, *Spring Again and Other Poems*, introduction.

14. Joanne Hutlet, "The Cougar in Manitoba," thesis (Winnipeg, Manitoba: Natural Resources Institute, University of Manitoba, June 29, 2005).

15. Robert W. Nero, *The Great Gray Owl: Phantom of the Northern Forest* (Washington, D.C.: Smithsonian Institution Press, 1980), 28.

16. *Ibid.*, 111–12.

17. Robert W. Nero, *Lady Grayl: Owl with a Mission* (Toronto: Natural Heritage Inc., 1994), 29–30.

18. *Ibid.*, 27.

19. *Ibid.*, 31.

20. *Ibid.*, 11–12.

21. Nero, *The Site*, 31–33.

22. Nero, *The Great Gray Owl*, 155.

23. "Manitoba's Provincial Bird Emblem, The Great Gray Owl," NatureNorth. com, *www.naturenorth.com/Gray_Owl/Gray_Owl.html.*

CHAPTER TWENTY: ROBERT BATEMAN

1. Robert Bateman with Kathryn Dean, *Birds* (Toronto: Madison Press Books, 2002), 86.

2. Rick Archbold, *Robert Bateman: An Artist in Nature* (Toronto: Madison Press Books, 1996), 24.

3. J. Bristol Foster, "The Evolution of Mammals on Islands," *Nature*, 202 (1964), 234–35.

4. Bateman, *Birds*, 36.

5. Ramsay Derry, *The World of Robert Bateman* (Toronto: Madison Press Books, 1985), 41.
6. From a telephone conversation between the author and Robert Bateman on March 11, 2011.
7. Derry, *The World of Robert Bateman*, 18.
8. In Cubist art works, objects are broken up, analyzed, and re-assembled in an abstracted form.
9. Archbold, *Robert Bateman: An Artist in Nature*, 41.
10. Robert Bateman Centre at Royal Roads University, *www.batemancentre.ca.*
11. From a telephone conversation between the author and Robert Bateman on March 11, 2011.
12. Bateman, *Birds*, 60.
13. "Last Mountain Lake Bird Sanctuary," Saskatchewan's Environmental Champions, *www.econet.sk.ca/sk_enviro_champions/last_mountain_lake.html.*
14. Rick Archbold, *Robert Bateman: Natural Worlds* (Toronto: Madison Press Books, 1990), 60.
15. "Environmental Paintings," Robert Bateman, *www.robertbateman.ca/art/environmental/environmental2.html.*
16. "Biography," Robert Bateman, *www.robertbateman.ca/biography.html.*
17. From a telephone conversation between the author and Robert Bateman on March 11, 2011.

CHAPTER TWENTY-ONE: KENN KAUFMAN

1. Kenn Kaufman, *Kingbird Highway: The Story of a Natural Obsession That Got a Little Out of Hand* (Boston, New York: Houghton Mifflin Harcourt, 1997), 4.
2. *Ibid.*, 13.
3. *Ibid.*, 316.
4. Kenn Kaufman, *Peterson Field Guide to Advanced Birding* (Boston, New York: Houghton Mifflin Harcourt, 1990), editor's note.
5. "Kenn Kaufman, Birding Guru, Answers Questions," Grist, *www.grist.org/article/kaufman1/.*
6. "Kenn Kaufman," Birds and Beans, *www.birdsandbeans.com/voices.html.*
7. Kenn Kaufman, "Magee: Anatomy of a Migrant Hotspot," *Birding* (January 2010), 43.
8. Kenn Kaufman, "After the Spark: Too Many Birders?" *Bird Watcher's Digest* (May/June 2010), 21.

CHAPTER TWENTY-TWO: DAVID ALLEN SIBLEY

1. Fred C. Sibley, "The Life History, Ecology and Management of the California Condor (*Gymnogyps californianus*)," Annual Progress Report, Project No. B-22. U.S. Bureau of Sport Fisheries and Wildlife, Patuxent Wildlife Research Center (1968), 34.

2. Fred Bouchard, "Interview with David Sibley," Virtual Birder, *www.virtualbirder.com/vbirder/shelf/guides/sibley/interview.html*.

3. David Allen Sibley, *Hawks in Flight: The Flight Identification of North American Migrant Raptors* (Boston, New York: Houghton Mifflin Company, 1989), foreword.

4. Noah K. Strycker, "A Birding Interview with David A. Sibley," *Birding* (May/June 2007), 19.

5. Fred Bouchard, "Interview with David Sibley," Virtual Birder, *www.virtualbirder.com/vbirder/shelf/guides/sibley/interview.html*.

6. "The Nature Conservancy Co-Sponsors David Sibley Presentation: The Life, Art and Birding of David Sibley," Exhibit at the Ned Smith Center for Nature and Art in Harrisburg, Pennsylvania, *www.nature.org/wherewework/northamerica/states/pennsylvania/press/press2687.html*.

7. Stephen Brown, ed., *Birds of the Arctic National Wildlife Refuge: Arctic Wings* (Seattle: The Mountaineers Books, 2006), 15.

Bibliography

BOOKS

Archbold, Rick. *Robert Bateman: An Artist in Nature*. Toronto: Madison Press Books, 1990.

_____. *Robert Bateman: Natural Worlds*. Toronto: Penguin/Madison Press Books, 1996.

Audubon, John James. *Delineations of American Scenery and Character*. New York: G.A. Baker & Company, 1926.

Audubon, John James and William MacGillivray. *Ornithological Biography, or An Account of the Habits of the Birds of the United States of America: Accompanied by Descriptions of the Objects Represented in the Work Entitled The Birds of America, and Interspersed with Delineations of American Scenery and Manners / 4 volumes*. Philadelphia, Pennsylvania: E. L. Carey and A. Hart, 1831–1849.

Audubon, Lucy Bakewell. *The Life of John James Audubon, the Naturalist*. New York: G.P. Putnam's Sons, 1890.

Audubon, Maria R. and Elliott Coues. *Audubon and His Journals, Volume I*. New York: Charles Scribner's Sons, 1897.

Bailey, Florence Merriam, *A-Birding on a Bronco*. Boston: Houghton Mifflin and Company, 1896.

_____. *Birds of New Mexico*. Santa Fe, New Mexico: New Mexico Department of Game and Fish, 1928.

_____. *Birds of Village and Field*. Boston: Houghton Mifflin and Company, 1898.

_____. *Birds Through an Opera Glass*. Boston: Houghton Mifflin and Company, 1890.

_____. *Handbook of Birds of the Western United States*. Boston: Houghton Mifflin and Company, 1902.

Bateman, Robert with Kathryn Dean. *Birds*. Toronto: Madison Press Books, 2002.

Bonta, Marcia Myers. *Women in the Field: America's Pioneering Women Naturalists*. College Station, Texas: Texas A&M University Press, 1991.

Brown, Stephen, ed. *Birds of the Arctic National Wildlife Refuge: Arctic Wings*. Seattle: The Mountaineers Books, 2006.

Buchanan, R. *Life and Adventures of John James Audubon, the Naturalist, 2nd edition*. London: Sampson Low, Son & Marston, 1869.

Burnett, J. Alexander. *A Passion for Wildlife: The History of the Canadian Wildlife Service*. Vancouver, B.C.: UBC Press, 2003.

Burroughs, John. *John James Audubon*. Boston: Small, Maynard & Company, 1902.

Cantwell, Robert. *Alexander Wilson: Naturalist and Pioneer*. Philadelphia: J. B. Lippincott Company, 1961.

Carlson, Douglas. *Roger Tory Peterson: A Biography*. Austin: University of Texas Press, 2007.

Dall, William Healey. *Alaska and Its Resources*. Boston: Lee and Shepard Publishers, 1897.

_____. *Spencer Fullerton Baird: A Biography*. Philadelphia: J.B. Lippincott Company, 1915.

Dana, Richard Henry. *Two Years Before the Mast*. London: T. Nelson and Sons Ltd., 1912.

David, William E. Jr. and Jerome A. Jackson, ed. *Contributions to the History of North American Ornithology*. Memoirs of the Nuttall Ornithological Club, No. 12. Cambridge, Massachusetts: Nuttall Ornithological Club, 1995.

Derry, Ramsay. *The Art of Robert Bateman*. Toronto: Madison Press Books, 1981.

_____. *The World of Robert Bateman*. Toronto: Madison Press Books, 1985.

Doughty, Robin W. *Feather Fashions and Bird Preservation*. Berkeley: University of California Press, 1975.

Graham, A. *Six Little Chickadees: A Scientist and her Work with Birds*. New York: Four Winds Press, 1982.

Graustein, Jeannette E. *Thomas Nuttall, Naturalist: Explorations in America, 1808–1841*. Cambridge: Harvard University Press, 1967.

Hochbaum, H. Albert. *The Canvasback on a Prairie Marsh*. Harrisburg, Pennsylvania: The Stackpole Company, 1944.

_____. *To Ride the Wind*. Winnipeg: Richard Bonnycastle Books, 1973.

_____. *Travels and Traditions of Waterfowl*. Minneapolis: The University of Minnesota Press, 1955.

_____. *Wings Over the Prairie*. Compiled and edited by George Hochbaum. Winnipeg: Tamos Books Inc., 1994.

Hunter, C., ed. *The Life and Letters of Alexander Wilson*. Memoirs of the American Philosophical Society, Vol. 154. Philadelphia, 1983.

Hutlet, Joanne. "The Cougar in Manitoba." Thesis. Winnipeg, Manitoba: Natural Resources Institute, University of Manitoba, June 29, 2005.

Jeremy, David J., ed. *Henry Wansey and His American Journal, 1794*. Philadelphia: American Philosophical Society, 1970.

Jordan, David Starr, ed. *Leading American Men of Science*. New York: Henry Holt and Company, 1910.

Kaufman, Kenn. *Birds of North America*. Boston, New York: Houghton Mifflin Harcourt, 2001.

_____. *Flights Against the Sunset: Stories that Reunited a Mother and Son*. Boston, New York: Houghton Mifflin Harcourt, 2008.

_____. *Guia de Campo Kaufman: a las Aves Norteamericanas*. Boston, New York: Houghton Mifflin Harcourt, 2005.

_____. *Kaufman Field Guide to Advanced Birding*. Boston, New York: Houghton Mifflin Harcourt, 2011.

_____. *Kingbird Highway: The Story of a Natural Obsession That Got a Little Out of Hand*. Boston, New York: Houghton Mifflin Harcourt, 1997.

_____. *Lives of North American Birds*. Boston, New York: Houghton Mifflin Harcourt, 1996.

_____. *Peterson Field Guide to Advanced Birding*. Boston, New York: Houghton Mifflin Harcourt, 1990.

Kaufman, Kenn and Eric R. Eaton. *Insects of North America*. Boston, New York: Houghton Mifflin Harcourt, 2007.

Kaufman, Kenn and Jim P. Brock. *Butterflies of North America*. Boston, New York: Houghton Mifflin Harcourt, 2003.

Kaufman, Kenn and Nora and Rick Bowers. *Mammals of North America*. Boston, New York: Houghton Mifflin Harcourt, 2004.

Kofalk, Harriet. *No Woman Tenderfoot: Florence Merriam Bailey, Pioneer Naturalist*. College Station: Texas A&M University Press, 1989.

Lawrence, Louise de Kiriline. *Another Winter, Another Spring: A Love Remembered*. Toronto: Natural Heritage Inc., 1987.

_____. *A Comparative Life History Study of Four Species of Woodpeckers*. American Ornithologists' Union, Ornithological Mongraphs No. 5, 1967.

_____. *The Loghouse Nest*. Natural Heritage Inc., 1988.

_____. *The Lovely and the Wild*. Toronto: Natural Heritage Inc., 1987.

_____. *Mar: A Glimpse Into the Natural Life of a Bird*. Toronto: Natural Heritage Inc., 1986.

_____. *To Whom the Wilderness Speaks*. Toronto: Natural Heritage Inc., 1989.

Lindsay, Debra, ed. *The Modern Beginnings of Subarctic Ornithology: Northern Correspondence with the Smithsonian Institution, 1856–68*. Vol. 10. Winnipeg, Manitoba: The Manitoba Record Society publications, 1991.

Martin, Constance. *Search for the Blue Goose: J. Dewey Soper – The Arctic Adventures of a Canadian Naturalist*. Calgary: Bayeux Arts Incorporated and the Arctic Institute of North America, 1995.

McKelvey, Susan Delano. *Botanical Exploration of the Trans-Mississippi West, 1790–1850*. Jamaica Plain, Massachusetts: Arnold Arboretum, Harvard University, 1955.

Mearns, B. and R. Mearns. *Audubon to Xantus: The Lives of Those Commemorated in North American Bird Names*. London: Academic Press, Ltd., 1992.

Merriam, Florence A. *Birds of Village and Field: A Bird Book for Beginners*. Cambridge, Massachusetts: The Riverside Press, 1898.

Miner, Jack. *Jack Miner and the Birds and Some Things I Know About Nature*. Chicago: The Reilly & Lee Co., Fifth Printing Memorial Edition, 1925.

Moring, John. *Early American Naturalists: Exploring the American West, 1804–1900*. New York: Cooper Square Press, 2002.

Moss, John, ed. *Echoing Silence: Essays on Arctic Narrative*. Ottawa: University of Ottawa Press, 1997.

Nero, Robert W., *The Great Gray Owl: Phantom of the Northern Forest*. Washington, D.C.: Smithsonian Institution Press, 1980.

_____. *Growing Old Together and Other Poems*. Toronto: Natural Heritage Inc., 2005.

_____. *Lady by the Shore and Other Poems: A Tribute to Louise de Kiriline Lawrence*. Toronto: Natural Heritage Inc., 1990.

_____. *Lady Grayl: Owl with a Mission*. Toronto: Natural Heritage Inc., 1994.

_____. *The Mulch Pile and Other Poems*. Toronto: Natural Heritage Inc., 1993.

_____. *Out with the Dog: Poems for Dog-Lovers*. Self-published, 2010.

_____. *Redwings*. Washington, D.C.: Smithsonian Institution Press, 1984.

_____. *The Site: A Personal Odyssey*. Toronto: Natural Heritage Inc., 2001.

_____. *Spring Again and Other Poems*. Toronto: Natural Heritage Inc., 1997.

Nero, Robert W., Aleta Karstad, and Frederick W. Schueler. *Owls in North America: Nature Stories for Children*. Canadian Album Series. Winnipeg: Hyperion Press, 1987.

Nice, Margaret Morse. *Research Is a Passion With Me*. Toronto: Consolidated Amethyst Communications Inc., 1979.

Nuttall, Thomas, *The Genera of North American Plants, and a Catalogue of the Species, to the Year 1817*. Philadelphia, Pennsylvania: Printed for the Author by D. Heart, 181.

_____. *An Introduction to Systematic and Physiological Botany*. Cambridge, Massachusetts: Hilliard and Brown, 1827.

_____. *A Journal of Travels into the Arkansas Territory During the Rear 1819, with Occasional Observations on the Manners of the Aborigines*. Philadelphia, Pennsylvania: Thomas H. Palmer, 1821.

_____. *A Manual of the Ornithology of the United States and Canada, I, Land Birds.* Cambridge, Massachusetts: Hilliard & Brown, 1832.

_____. *A Manual of the Ornithology of the United States and Canada, II, Water Birds.* Cambridge, Massachusetts: Hilliard, Gray & Co., 1834.

_____. *The North American Sylva, or, A Description of the Forest Trees of the United States, Canada and Nova Scotia, Not Described in the work of F. Andrew Michaux.* Philadelphia, Pennsylvania: W. Rutter, 1871.

Peterson, Roger Tory. *All Things Reconsidered: My Birding Adventures.* Edited by Bill Thompson III. Boston, New York: Houghton Mifflin Company, 2006.

_____. *Birds Over America.* New York: Dodd, Mead & Company, 1948.

_____. *Roger Tory Peterson: The Art and Photography of the World's Foremost Birder.* Edited by Roger Tory Peterson and Rudy Hoglund. New York: Rizzoli International Publications, Inc., 1994.

Rhodes, Richard. *John James Audubon: The Making of an American.* New York: Alfred A. Knopf, 2004.

Richardson, Cynthia Watkins. "Picturing Nature: Education, Ornithology and Photography in the Life of Cordelia Stanwood: 1865-1958." Thesis. Orono, Maine: The Graduate School, The University of Maine, December 2002.

Richmond, Chandler S., *Beyond the Spring: Cordelia Stanwood of Birdsacre.* Maine: The Latona Press, 1989.

Ridgway, Robert. *A Manual of North American Birds, 2nd Edition.* Philadelphia: J.B. Lippincott Company, 1896.

_____. *A Nomenclature of Colors for Naturalists and Compendium of Useful Knowledge for Ornithologists.* Boston: Little, Brown and Company, 1886.

_____. *Color Standards and Color Nomenclature, With Fifty-Three Colored Plates and Eleven Hundred and Fifteen Named Colors.* Washington, D.C.: self-published, 1912.

Sibley, David Allen. *Hawks in Flight: The Flight Identification of North American Migrant Raptors.* Boston, New York: Houghton Mifflin Company, 1989.

_____. *Sibley's Birding Basics.* New York: Alfred A. Knopf, 2002.

_____. *Sibley Field Guide to the Birds of Western North America.* New York: Alfred A. Knopf, 2003.

_____. *The Sibley Field Guide to Birds of Eastern North America.* New York: Alfred A. Knopf, 2003.

_____. *The Sibley Guide to Bird Life and Behavior.* New York: Alfred A. Knopf, 2001.

_____. *The Sibley Guide to Birds.* New York: Alfred A. Knopf, 2000.

_____. *The Sibley Guide to Trees.* New York: Alfred A. Knopf, 2009.

Soper, J. Dewey. *Life History of the Blue Goose.* Proceedings of the Boston Society of Natural History, Volume 42, Number 2, pages 121-225, plates 15-26. Boston, Massachusetts: Printed for the Boston Society of Natural History, 1942.

Speirs, J. Murray. *Birds of Ontario.* 2 volumes. Toronto: Natural Heritage Inc., 1985.

Sterling, Keir B., Richard Harmond, George A. Cevasco, and Lorne Hammond, eds. *Biographical Dictionary of American and Canadian Naturalists and Environmentalists.* Westport, Connecticut: Greenwood Press, 1997.

Taverner, Percy Algernon. *Birds of Canada.* Ottawa: National Museum of Canada, Bulletin No. 72, 1934.

_____. *Birds of Eastern Canada.* Ottawa: Geological Survey of Canada, Memoir No. 104, 1919.

_____. *Birds of Western Canada.* Ottawa: National Museum of Canada, Bulletin No. 41, 1926.

Wilson, Alexander. *American Ornithology; or the Natural History of the Birds of the United States, With a Sketch of the Author's Life, by George Ord, in Three Volumes, Vol. 1.* New York: Collins & Co., 1983.

Wrigley, R. E. and Robert W. Nero. *Manitoba's Big Cat: The Story of the Cougar in Manitoba.* Winnipeg, Manitoba: Manitoba Museum of Man and Nature, 1982.

ARTICLES

Ainley, Marianne Gosztonyi. "In Memoriam: Louise de Kiriline Lawrence, 1894–1992." *The Auk* 109, No. 4, 1992; 909–10.

Bailey, Florence Merriam. "Our Smith College Audubon Society." *Audubon Magazine* 1:1, 1887; 175–78.

Barlow, Jon C. "Doris Huestis Speirs Award for Contributions to Canadian Ornithology: Louise de Kiriline Lawrence – 1991." *Picoides*, Fall 1991.

Brooks, Allan. "The Under-Water Actions of Diving Ducks." *The Auk*, Vol. 62, October 1945; 517–23.

Brooks, Marjorie. "Allan Brooks: A Biography." *The Condor*, Vol. XL, January 1938; 12–17.

Christy, Bayard Henderson. "Pileated Woodpecker (*Dryocopus pileatus*)." Washington, D.C.: *Smithsonian Institution United States National Museum Bulletin 174*, 1939; 171–89.

Cranmer-Byng. "P.A. Taverner: Dominion Ornithologist, 1911–1942." *Picoides*, Vol. 2, No. 1, April 1988; 6–8.

Dawson, William Leon. "Allan Brooks: An Appreciation." *The Condor*, Vol. XV, March 1913; 69–76.

Deane, Ruthven. "Audubon's Labrador Trip of 1833." *The Auk*, Vol. 27, No. 1, January 1910; 42–52.

Egerton, F.N. "History of the Ecological Sciences, Part 33: Naturalists Explore North America, mid-1780s–mid-1820s." *Ecological Society of America Bulletin* 90, 2009; 434–87.

Falls, J. Bruce. "Doris Huestis Speirs 1894-1989." *Picoides*, Vol. 4, No. 1, April 1990; 3-4.

Fleming, J. H. "The Great Lakes Ornithological Club." *The Wilson Bulletin*, Vol. 51, No. 1, March 1939; 42-43.

Foster, J. Bristol. "The Evolution of Mammals on Islands." *Nature*, 202, 1964; 234-35.

_____. "The Evolution of the Mammals of the Queen Charlotte Islands, British Columbia." Occasional papers of the British Columbia Provincial Museum, 14; 1-130.

Foster, J.W. "Robert Kennicott." *Western Monthly Magazine*, Vol. III, No. 15, March 1870; 165-72.

Harris, Harry. "An Appreciation of Allan Brooks, Zoological Artist: 1869-1946." *The Condor*, Vol. 48, No. 4, July-August 1946; 145-53.

_____. "Robert Ridgway, With a Bibliography of his Published Writings and Fifty Illustrations." *The Condor*, Vol. XXX, No. 1, January-February 1928; 5-118.

Hochbaum, H. Albert. "What the Duck Saw." *Ducks Unlimited Magazine*, September/October 1996.

Hodgson, Marguerite. "Major Allan Brooks at Okanagan Landing." MS, Okanagan Historical Society, 1977.

Houston, C. Stuart. "In Memoriam: Hans Albert Hochbaum." *The Auk*, Vol. 105, October 1988; 769-72.

Kaufman, Kenn. "After the Spark: Too Many Birders?" *Bird Watcher's Digest*, May/June 2010.

_____. "Magee: Anatomy of a Migrant Hotspot." *Birding*, January 2010.

Kennicott, Robert. "The Quadrupeds of Illinois, Injurious and Beneficial to the Farmer." Washington, D.C.: U.S. Patent Office, Report of the Commissioner of Patents for the Year, 1856, 52-110; 1857, 72-107; 1858, 241-56.

Laing, Hamilton M. "Allan Brooks, 1869-1946." *The Auk*, Vol. 64, 1947; 430-44.

Lawrence, Louise de Kiriline. "A Comparative Life-History Study of Four Species of Woodpeckers." Ornithological Monographs, No. 5, American Ornithologists' Union, 1967; 1-156.

_____. "Notes on the Nesting Behavior of the Blackburnian Warbler." *The Wilson Bulletin*, Vol. 65, No. 3, September 1953; 135-44.

_____. "Why Did You Come to Canada?" *Chatelaine*, October, 1937; 21, 53.

Mackey, Doug. "Heritage Perspectives: Remembering the Late, Great Lady, Louise de Kiriline Lawrence." *Community Voices*, May 2002. www.pastforward. ca/perspectives/may_102002.htm.

McAtee, W.L. "Percy Algernon Taverner, 1875-1947." *The Auk*, Vol. 65, January 1948; 85-106.

Miner, Manly F. "Migration of Canada Geese From the Jack Miner Sanctuary and Banding Operations." *The Wilson Bulletin*, March 1931; 29–34.

Nuttall, Thomas. "Descriptions of Plants Collected by William Gambel, M.D., in the Rocky Mountains and Upper California." *Journal of the Academy of Natural Sciences of Philadelphia*, 1848; 149–89.

Oehser, Paul H. "In Memoriam: Florence Merriam Bailey." *The Auk*, Vol. 69, January 1952; 19–26.

Ouellet, Henri. "Profile of a Pioneer: P.A. Taverner." *American Birds*, Spring 1987; 20–26.

Pennell, Francis W. "Travels and Scientific Collections of Thomas Nuttall." *Bartonia*, Vol. XVIII, 1936; 1–51.

Ridgway, Robert. "The Hummingbirds." Washington: Government Printing Office, 1892. From the Report of the National Museum for 1890; 253–383 (with plates I–XLVI).

Sabean, John W. "Names in the News: Doris Huestis Speirs." *Pickering Township Historical Society Pathmaster*, Vol. 1, No. 2, Winter 1998; 1, 14.

Serie, Jerome R. "H. Albert Hochbaum: A Man Not Forgotten." *Prairie Naturalist* 26(4), December 1994.

Snyder, L.L. "In Memoriam: James Henry Fleming." *The Auk*, Vol. 58, No. 1, January 1941; 1–12.

Soper, J. Dewey. *Canadian Wildlife Service Management Bulletin Series I*, Numbers 3, 5, and 7; Series 2, Numbers 2,3,4, and 6. Ottawa, Ontario: Canadian Wildlife Service, 1952, 1953.

_____. "Discovery of the Breeding Grounds of the Blue Goose." *The Canadian Field-Naturalist*, Vol. XLIV, No. 1, January 1930; 1–11.

_____. "Explorations in Baffin Island." *The Geographical Journal*, Vol. 75, No. 5, May 1930; 435–43.

_____. "In Memoriam: Rudolph Martin Anderson, 1876–1961." *The Canadian Field-Naturalist*, Volume 76, Number 3, July–September, 1962; 127–33.

_____. "Interesting Bird Records for Southern Baffin Island." *The Canadian Field-Naturalist*, Vol. XLVIII, March, April, May, 1934.

_____. "Local Distribution of Eastern Canadian Arctic Birds." *The Auk*, Vol. 57, January 1940; 13–21.

Soper, Roland and Tom Beck. "Joseph Dewey Soper, 1893–1982." *Arctic*, Vol. 36, No. 1, March 1983; 118–19.

Speirs, Doris Huestis. "Evening Grosbeak (*Coccothraustes vespertinus*)." 1968. In O.L. Austin, ed., *Life Histories of North American Cardinals, Grosbeaks, Buntings, Towhees, Finches, Sparrows and Allies, Part 1, U.S. National Museum Bulletin* 237, 206–36.

Stanwood, Cordelia. "A Series of Nests of the Magnolia Warbler." *The Auk*, Vol. 27, Winter 1910; 384–89.

Stenton, Douglas R. "A Soper Record Cairn from Baffin Island, N.W.T." *Arctic*, Vol. 39, No. 1, March 1986; 92-94.

Stevens, W. E. and George W. Scotter. "Joseph Dewey Soper, 1893-1982." *The Canadian Field-Naturalist*, Vol. 97, 1983; 350-55.

Stimpson, W. "Robert Kennicott." *Transactions of the Academy of Sciences* I, 1869; 133-226.

Strycker, Noah K. "A Birding Interview with David A. Sibley." *Birding*, May/June 2007; 18-21.

Taverner, P.A., "The Double-Crested Cormorant (*Phalacrocorax auritus*) and its Relation to the Salmon Industries on the Gulf of St. Lawrence." Canada, *Geological Survey Museum Bulletin No. 13*, 1915.

_____. "The Gannets of Bonaventure Island", *Ottawa Naturalist* 32:21-26, 1918.

_____. "James Henry Fleming 1872-1940: An Appreciation by P. A. Taverner." *The Canadian Field-Naturalist*, Vol. LV, No. 5, May 1941; 63-64.

_____. "Recommendations for the Creation of Three New National Parks in Canada." Report of the Sixth Annual Meeting of the Commission of Conservation, Ottawa, Appendix 3, 1915.

Tonelli, Donna. "James Ford Bell & the Delta Marsh." *Adventure Sports Outdoors Magazine*, February 2008; 110-11.

Trautman, Milton B. "In Memoriam: Margaret Morse Nice." *The Auk*, Vol. 94, July 1977; 430-41.

Vasile, Ronald S. "The Early Career of Robert Kennicott, Illinois' Pioneering Naturalist." *Illinois Historical Journal* 87(3); 150-70.

Webber, Jean. "Major Allan Brooks of Okanagan Landing." Royal British Columbia Museum "Living Landscapes" project.

Wetmore, Alexander. "Robert Ridgway, 1850-1929." *National Academy Biographical Memoirs*, Vol. XV, 1931; 57-101.

Index